Toward A Sustainable Society

Toward A Sustainable Society

An Economic, Social and
Environmental Agenda
for Our Children's Future

James Garbarino

The Noble Press, Inc.
CHICAGO

Printed in the United States of America

Library of Congress Cataloging-in-Publication Data:

Garbarino, James.
    [Future as if it really mattered]
    Toward a sustainable society : an economic, social, and environmental agenda for our children's future / James   Garbarino.
        p.   cm.
    Originally published: The Future as if it really mattered. Longmont, Calif. : Bookmakers Guild, 1988.
    Includes bibliographical references and index.
    ISBN 1-879360-15-2 : $19.95
    1. Economic development—Environmental aspects. 2. Social policy. 3. Family policy. 4. Human ecology. 5. Social problems.   I. Title.
    HD75.6.G37 1992
    361.6'1—dc20   92-7359
                        CIP

10 9 8 7 6 5 4 3 2 1

Grateful acknowledgment is made to William Morrow and Co., Inc. for permission to reprint excerpt, on pages 36 to 38, from *Voluntary Simplicity: Toward A Way of Life That is Outwardly Simple, Inwardly Rich,* by Duane Elgin, copyright 1981.

Originally published under the title *The Future as if it Really Mattered,* Bookmakers Guild, 1988.

The Noble Press

For
Josh and Joanna
Ben and Noah
and Ashley

Contents

Preface

This book began in 1979, in a taxicab. Having landed in Houston to attend the Woodlands Conference on Sustainable Societies, I found myself sharing a cab downtown with Don Lesh, who, at that time, was executive director of the Global 2000 Coalition. I was in Texas to receive a Mitchell Prize for my essay "The Issue is Human Quality: In Praise of Children." Hearing of Don's affiliation, I expressed an interest in learning more about sustainable societies that are economically, environmentally, demographically, and ethically sane.

Don directed me to the book *The Human Quality* by Aurelio Peccei, who was the founder of the Club of Rome, an international group of futurists. I read the book and went on to other Club of Rome publications, including the ground-breaking *The Limits to Growth*. Before long I was a member of the U.S. Association for the Club of Rome and was being exposed to a wealth of ideas and information about the prospects for a sustainable society. As I listened and read, I found myself wondering what all this implied for families. I recalled an article my wife Nan and I had written together some years earlier entitled "Where Are the Children in Utopia?" This book is the result of asking that question, and thus it owes its origins to my serendipitous conversation with Don Lesh. And as I approached it, I realized that writing a book that would address this question of families would give me an opportunity to put together what I had been reading with what I was seeing in my travels across the United States (thirty-nine states) and Canada (six provinces) and around the world (four continents). Looking at the future in the faces of children I met, I felt something growing in my mind and my heart. This book is that something, something both personal and professional.

This effort to bring together personal and professional concerns is natural for me in part, I believe, because of who I am and where I come from—the merging of an Italian and Anglo-Saxon ethnic heritage. I have always been aware of my strong family orientation, but I have never understood it so well as when I saw it expressed in a 1983 *New York Times Sunday Magazine* article by Stephen Hall, "Italian-Americans Coming into Their Own." Hall asks: "Is there a single thread that runs through these people?" and answers: "If anything, it is the unusual propensity to merge, rather than separate the professional and the personal." Family is at the heart of my personal and professional identity, and this book is testimony to that. I look at my children and see my grandchildren to be. But I also see the grandchildren to be in the children I have met in cities, towns, and villages in South America, Asia, Europe and Africa. And I see a thread connecting all the people who have helped me in this task.

Pediatrician Robert Aldrich played a big role. He took me under his wing and arranged for me to travel to Japan in 1981 to participate in an international Symposium on "The Child in the City." Visiting Japan was a decisive experience. Aurelio Peccei helped me in our brief face-to-face conversation in Washington, D.C., in 1982. Nicholas Georgescu-Roegen helped me in one short letter of encouragement.

The Kellogg Foundation played a facilitating role by supporting me as a Kellogg National Fellow from 1981 to 1984. I used my Fellowship resources to read and travel as I sought out ideas and experiences to help me answer my questions about the place of children and families within the sustainable society. The Kellogg Fellowship took me to Brazil, China, and Hawaii. All three trips helped me see things more clearly, and they have found a place in the book.

The Kellogg Fellowship allowed me to seek the help and advice of many individuals much more knowledgeable than I about the economics, demographics, physics, biology, and politics of the sustainable society and the interrelated issues we call the "world problematique." This process has reinforced and strengthened my belief in the collective nature of the struggle to understand and nurture the world and its living beings. I am grateful for all the help I have received from the Foundation.

Foster Parents Plan International helped by hosting my trip to the Sudan in 1985. In the midst of political turmoil (President Nemerye had just been overthrown) and devastating drought and economic dislocation, I saw a demonstration of hope and a concrete statement of what "meeting basic human needs" really means. I was helped in the field by PLAN's staff of genuine do-gooders, really doing good.

A special group commented upon the first version of this book, and I want to acknowledge its help: Rob Abramowitz, Umberto Colombo, Bob Cory, Duane Elgin, Liz Dodson-Gray, Jay Forrester, Bob Garretson, Nicholas Georgescu-Roegen, Ann Heider, William Henry, John Hershberger, Gary Hirshberg, Michael Hoffman, George Mitchell, John Ogbu, Dana Raphael, John Scanzoni, Townsend Scudder, Bob Stecker, Jess Stein, Joan Vondra, Page Wilson, and my favorite in-house critic Nan Garbarino. Others have helped through chats on buses driving the backroads of Brazil, around the dinner table in China, in land rovers in the Sudan, in the classroom, and anywhere else I could learn something I needed to know.

The secretarial support of Erikson Institute for Advanced Study in Child Development—where I make my professional home—has proved invaluable. Thanks to Norma Richman, Denise Robinson and Sharon Dudley.

Special thanks to The Noble Press for publishing *Toward a Sustainable Society*.

> Jim Garbarino
> Chicago

ONE

An Introduction to Limits: Have We Sold Out Our Children's Future?

November 1979. Houston, Texas. Houston claims to be the oil capital of the world—a dubious honor, it seems to me. I am at The Woodlands, a pleasant residential and commercial enclave of affluence developed near Houston by my host, George Mitchell, whose commercial activities involve oil exploration and real estate development. Both are primary forces shaping life in the modern era, and therein lies both the promise and the problem. I am here as winner of one of eight Mitchell Prizes awarded for essays on the theme "Building a Sustainable Society." Paul Ehrlich, author of The Population Bomb, *has won first prize for a piece on diversity and its value to society. My essay is entitled "The Issue Is Human Quality: In Praise of Children." All the winning essays emphasize conservation and doing more and doing better with less. The conference's keynote address, delivered by U.S. Senator Lloyd Bentsen, does little to alter my stereotyped view of Texas as a metaphor for America: "More growth! More Oil! More production! More land development! More! More! More!" His speech, which the prizewinners consider publicly disavowing, reminds me of a joke I heard long ago, in a very different context:*

> Patient: *Doctor, I have a problem. I feel anxious, worried, overburdened, and generally miserable.*
> Doctor: *Why is that?*

1

Patient: *I don't know exactly.*
Doctor: *Well, tell me about your life.*
Patient: *I live in a nice neighborhood in a big house full of expensive furniture. We have two cars, a station wagon and a sports car. The kids have all the toys they could ever want. My wife dresses in the newest fashions, and so do I. We belong to the country club and have a condominium at a ski resort.*
Doctor: *That all sounds wonderful. So what's your problem?*
Patient: *Well, Doctor, I only make $100 a week.*

Listening to Senator Bentsen's speech, I see America playing the role of the patient and the Senator the role of the doctor. And he doesn't get the joke. (Looking back on this thirteen years later, with the oil boom having gone bust for the moment at least, and with Texas in the midst of a severe recession, I wonder if he gets it now.)

The meaning of social welfare

The term "social welfare" refers to a society's ability and willingness to protect and care for its members, particularly its more dependent members—children, the frail elderly, the physically and mentally disabled, and anyone else who needs special assistance in meeting basic needs. Even healthy adults may need the support of social welfare systems when faced with special crises, such as when a single mother who, on her own, must care for her young children. These systems offer greatly needed assistance to many, including workers who lose their jobs and are thus deprived of their regular income, or sick parents who are unable to meet their child care responsibilities. Such social welfare systems may be formal (government food stamp programs, for example) or informal (neighbors or church members stepping in to help a family in need). We know that state assistance programs, church outreach, and philanthropic organizations are critical pillars of social welfare in modern societies; and we also recognize the multitude of less formal social support networks formed by kinship, friendship, self-help groups, clubs, neighborhood associations, and churches.

The adequacy of social welfare systems depends upon several things. One is the nature and quality of the economy. Does it allow individuals to meet their basic need for food, shelter, and clothing? How much wealth does it generate? How is wealth distributed? What is the society's class structure? Of course, once we move beyond the level of basic subsistence (and even before we do), wealth is quite a relative term. This comes sharply into focus when we recognize that a family of modest means in the United States enjoys a luxurious standard of living by Third World standards, as anyone will attest who has traveled to the refugee camps of Ethiopia and the Sudan or to the slums of Brazil or Ecuador. A modern society should always be skeptical, even suspicious, when it is told that it "can't afford" to support social welfare systems. We have the wealth; it's just a matter of priorities.

Thus, the second factor in shaping social welfare systems is politics. Does the political system serve the interests of a small ruling class at the expense of the larger population? Is social justice a political priority? Is there a commitment to meeting the basic human needs of dependent individuals and their families? A third factor is knowledge. Do the society's institutional leaders possess a valid understanding of how society works and changes, of what children and adults need in order to advance developmentally? Do they use that knowledge? Do they understand the relationship between economic and political forces in maintaining social welfare systems? Do they understand the long-term implications of short-term decisions?

The history of social welfare systems reflects the interplay of three factors—economics, politics, and knowledge. For the most part, formal social welfare systems are a modern creation. They depend upon an economy capable of producing enough wealth to assist those in need, and to support an organizational structure whose job it is to redistribute that wealth. Further, social welfare systems need a political system that is capable of establishing and maintaining them. Finally, they require a knowledge base for policy and program development. All three preconditions are primarily modern creations (Rostow, 1972). Like the complex, high-powered societies they represent, social welfare systems are in their infancy when contrasted with the long span of human history behind and before us.

Against the backdrop of human existence on Earth, the modern period is but a blink of an eye. Only in the last few moments of human history have the powerful economies, the complex governments, and the sophisticated databases we take for granted appeared. Economic, political, and intellectual growth has accelerated astronomically in the centuries since Christopher Columbus crossed the Atlantic, the decades since the Wright brothers flew at Kitty Hawk, and the years since Neil Armstrong stepped out onto the moon. But what does this acceleration mean for families? What does the future hold for social welfare systems if current trends continue? What are the Earth's own limiting factors that will shape this process of change? How will families fare in the future? These are the questions before us. We begin with a look at the hypothesis that our current foundations for social welfare are fraught with danger.

Giants walk the earth

"Limits to Growth," "Small Is Beautiful," "Doing More with Less," "Voluntary Simplicity," "Beyond the Age of Waste," "A Sustainable Society." The ideas behind these slogans represent various responses to the challenge of adapting modern civilization to the startling success it has had in transforming the planetary relationship between the naturally occurring and the humanly built environment. The slogans presuppose that we have failed to develop a physically and morally sustainable relationship with the Earth—a failure that undermines the economic and environmental foundations of social welfare and, ultimately, of family well-being. Commentator after commentator has remarked on the astounding success humans have had in applying ingenuity, industriousness, and brute force in wresting out for themselves a dominant place on the Earth. Until recently, most Western or Western-oriented observers watched with awe and pride as this process literally conquered the world. This attitude approaches reverence in *The Ascent of Man*, in which Jacob Bronowski glorifies the scientific and technocratic genius of the human species. He rightly sees that humans stand in unique relationship to the Earth because of their intellectual capacity.

> Man[1] is a singular creature. He has a set of gifts which make him unique among the animals, so that, unlike them, he is not a figure in the landscape—he is a shaper of the landscape. (p. 19)

Bronowski sees human cultural evolution as a series of technological breakthroughs that have brought humanity into a position of dominance over all creatures great and small. In his eloquent essay, he examines the evolution of the human mind through its long childhood, in its interplay with the physical and social environment. His voice is one of praise for human accomplishment, of exhortation to mankind to go beyond the present and challenge the future. It is the modern voice speaking for mankind as the cultural giant, as Lord of the Earth and the skies and all that is. Though more eloquent than most, Bronowski speaks in a voice familiar to us. But it is not the only voice.

Another voice expresses a wariness of giants. Psychologist Carol Gilligan hears it in Anton Chekov's *The Cherry Orchard*, in which:

> Lopalin, a young merchant, describes his life of hard work and success. . . . he reveals the image of man that underlies and supports his activity: "At times when I can't go to sleep, I think: Lord, thou gavest us immense forests, unbounded fields and the widest horizons, and living in the midst of them we should indeed be giants"—at which point Madame Ranevskaya interrupts him saying, "you feel the need for giants—they are good only in fairy tales, anywhere else they only frighten us." (Gilligan, 1982, p. 5)

There has long been a second voice, crying out *for* the wilderness, questioning the process by which mankind has dominated the Earth—indeed, seeing the assertion of human power as a threat to the social fabric into which children and adults are woven through the day-to-day business of family life. This voice has come from those in a more harmonious relationship with the land (e.g., the Sino-Confucian "conservative" philosophers). In the past decade, the first voice has continued its cheerleading for "more! more! more!" But as increasingly sophisticated documentation and analysis has made the degradation and destruction of the physical environment more evident, the second voice has spoken with renewed persuasiveness for "living lightly upon the Earth." It argues that the energy intensive, environmentally degrading, and socially imperious "modern industrial order" will lead to cataclysmic global consequences which will erode environmental and economic foundations of social well-being. The futurist Aurelio Peccei (1976) calls this growing crisis in the relationship between human civilization and the Earth's resources "the world problematique."

The world problematique

The harmonious use of human power would create a sustainable society, one that establishes justice and holds the material world steady and constant so that creative, spiritual, intellectual, and interpersonal worlds may flourish. Movement toward a sustainable society would strengthen the foundations of social welfare so that families could proceed with the important business of transforming human organisms into human beings. Technologically and economically advanced societies must shed their roles as environmental brutes and become instead the world's nurturers, while the less industrialized must avoid becoming brutish in the first place. Perhaps the garden provides an apt metaphor of this better society.

Having cut back the underbrush, plowed the fields, and planted our seeds and watched them grow, we must tend and care for our plantings in a way that harmonizes our immediate needs with the future well-being of the garden itself. This task requires a special blend of far-seeing idealism and concrete planning and analysis. It requires a hard-nosed but warmhearted look at our place in the world—a kind of visionary pragmatism. It requires not that we blindly turn away from modern technology but rather that we harmonize its ends and means. An important aspect of this challenge lies in the recognition that families are the headquarters for human development, the lifeboats[2] for the human species in the modern era.

If its adherents are to bring their plans to fruition, every social, economic, and political perspective must make its peace with the family—or otherwise make war upon it. For some, the durability of the family as a social and biological unit is a source of hope and confidence: The family will survive and see us through. Others, who would restructure society to liberate individual children and adults—and perhaps realign them into new social entities—find the family a frustrating roadblock to progress. I, however, am with those who see hope in the family; I believe that the family, which is an enduring set of relationships among biologically or legally connected adults caring for dependent generations younger or older, can fulfill a holding function while other socioeconomic relationships are being reformed to meet the needs of a sustainable society. Families echo the past, inspire the present, and portend the future. They are our most direct connection with historical times and the focal point for motivating the changes needed to bring about a sustainable society.

The need for a new economic perspective

Recent history provides a flawed model of economic civilization, one we cannot continue to follow if we are concerned about treating our fellow man in a humane manner. Future generations will require an expansion and transformation of the kind of economic thinking that provided the foundation for the Industrial Revolution in the seventeenth, eighteenth, and nineteenth centuries. "Old" economic thinking may have been adequate to create the banking and accounting systems that transformed agrarian barter economies into industrialized cash economies, but the old model focuses exclusively on "monetarized" aspects of the environment. Anything with a cash price attached to it becomes a factor in calculating cost; anything without a cash price is "free." Thus, for example, dumping the waste product from your factory in the river is "free," while hiring someone to cart it away is a cost. Activities that do not generate cash income are economically invisible. But if a way can be found to attach a cash price to them and cause people to pay their cash price, then these activities enter the monetarized economy.

The monetarized model provided a gross approximation of the actual costs of production for the period it served as a model, particularly the years between 1750 and 1950. Those times were characterized by "free" raw materials, including petro-energy and "free" waste disposal, as well as an enormous reservoir of "free" social resources to absorb the psychological and interpersonal side effects of industrialization. When these "free" factors were added to the actual cost of production, the net result was improved social welfare. The addition of these "free" factors resulted in lower monetarized production costs per unit produced, in more monetarized wealth for societies that succeeded in industrializing, and in population growth. This last point is an important one. After thousands of years with only a tenuous hold on the planet, the human species established itself in a supreme position. But that very success and the means used to establish it now threaten to overwhelm and destroy civilization, rather than sustain it.

As the magnitude of Western industrialization and cash economy has increased since 1950, several of its critical assumptions have begun to crumble in technocratically-developed nations and have shown signs of being untenable in the preindustrial Third World. In many cases we have reached and even exceeded the point of diminishing returns. The costs associated with increased monetarized wealth are being offset in both the already monetarized and the as yet nonmonetarized domains of human existence. This has imposed a socioeconomic injunction on modern industrial development. Raw materials are no longer "free." Waste disposal is an ever increasing cost, and—in the case of nuclear wastes—a problem with no good solution at any cost. The concepts of cost and value that served us well for nearly two centuries have become increasingly inaccurate, even obsolete, because changing conditions have exposed their long-term invalidity. The conventional short-term economic view is now neither life-giving nor a valid picture of reality but instead a demonic force. If we cannot change our thinking, we will face a future ever more brutal as the "haves" seek even more ruthlessly to maintain the status quo, and the "have-nots" try more desperately to grab more for themselves. The social consequences for families include alienation, disorganization, dissatisfaction, and disruption, as the foundations for social welfare systems crumble and erode. This is hardly the basis for a kinder and gentler society.

Shifting our economic thinking requires altering our basic assumptions about the nature and function of human institutions in relation to human enterprise. It requires that we make decisions and policies based on their total contribution to our store of physical and social resources, rather than on what they appear to cost in dollars. We must examine both aspects of the economy, those with a cash price tag and those yet outside the realm of monetarized accounting (such as housework and child care provided by a family member). Economist Orio Giarini (1981) calls this total worth our "dowry and patrimony," and it is one foundation for social welfare (the others being political will and knowledge of how social systems work). It underlies the wealth of families. To develop a sustainable society, domestically and internationally, we must evaluate human activities by the criterion of their net contribution to total wealth and ultimately to social welfare, rather than by the increasingly unrealistic criterion of monetarized value. We seem to be in a pivotal period in human history.

The role of great leaders and great books in history

Much has been written about the role of "great men" in historical transformations, but great *ideas* are just as important. Consider John Evelyn's *Sylva: A Discourse of Forest Trees and the Propagation of Timber*, published in London in 1664.[3] As Evelyn wrote, deforestation was proceeding at an alarming rate in seventeenth-century England, and he sought to demonstrate the need to reverse this trend. His book stimulated widespread planting of trees; even King Charles II took notice and ordered that the royal forests be replenished. Evelyn's book was so successful in its aim that one historian, Robert Southey, has observed that it stands as "one of the few books in the world which completely affected what it was designed to do." As we face the immensely complicated crisis of the world problematique, one book in our time occupies a similar position of historical significance. In *The Limits to Growth*, published in 1972, Dennis and Donella Meadows and a team of allied investigators presented a gross empirical analysis of the recent past and the projected future course of human civilizations, taking into account population and resources. It throws down the gauntlet to the modern industrial order: reform or destroy, redirect or self-destruct.

> Man possesses, for a small moment in his history, the most powerful combination of knowledge, tools, and resources the world has ever known. He has all that is physically necessary to create a totally new form of human society—one that would be built to last for generations.[4]

The Limits to Growth reached millions of people, but it remains a secret to most people in most places. And it appeared in a historical moment of the greatest importance. As we look at the world two decades after its publication, we still see a mixed picture. The causes for hope and despair are, as ever, abundant and in dynamic tension. A colleague of mine was fond of telling his students that to deal with the twentieth century one needs to be an ambulatory schizophrenic. That is to say, one needs to acknowledge the craziness but continue trying to lead a sensible life.

Finding a sensible path in a crazy world

The threat of nuclear weapons has abated somewhat with the end of the Cold War, although proliferation of nuclear weapons seems to increase the risk of their "independent" use. Even after the Superpower thaw, the world's nuclear arsenals threaten to do unholy violence to human life, and indeed to the very life of the planet. Many scientists now believe that even a "limited" nuclear war could generate a global environmental disaster. Clouds of dust would blanket the planet, leading to a cold and dark "Nuclear Winter," resulting in massive famine and an end to human civilization as we know it. Recent hypothetical analyses also suggest that a "limited" nuclear war would disrupt society to such a degree as to neutralize or incapacitate it. If we add to the prospect of nuclear horror the less dramatic but nonetheless terrible toll modern civilization takes on the environment, it becomes clear that the psychological basis for pessimism and despair is in place, and in more than adequate supply.

What stands against these negative forces within and around us? Hope. Imagination. A human will to survive. The very human genius that has brought on the crisis can provide the resources to solve the problems before us. We must neither despair nor believe that we can somehow muddle through by doing business as usual. Neither "doom and gloom" nor "boom and bloom" will do the trick. The solutions we need must arise from the application of intelligence, imagination, love, work, and the will to survive.

Families provide an anchoring point for our efforts. They are organized around basic and enduring human dynamics. Meeting the needs of families will take us a long way toward creating a sound foundation for a sustainable society. If we fail them, our other efforts at social engineering will crumble or be torn down. Families, as lifeboats for the human species, are at the center of our analysis of the economic and environmental foundations of social welfare systems. This focus on their needs and their wealth provides us with a perspective with which to understand both the present and the various alternative futures open to us.

Social welfare as the foundation for a sustainable future

We need a new paradigm that incorporates two concepts. The first is an ethic of accountability. Individuals, corporations, and governments must assume full social and ecological responsibility for their actions. Is this possible without an elaborate and intrusive governmental bureaucracy? In his comparative analysis of societal blueprints for the future, Bohdan Hawrylshyn (1979) concludes that it is possible—but only if we work for values and institutions that encourage cooperation and pluralism. And, I would add, the family is central to these values and institutions. It is a culturally invigorating challenge, a new frontier that can call into action all the resources of human hearts and minds.

In addition to accountability, we need a community-oriented perspective on social welfare systems. This requires that major institutions within communities act in concert to develop plans consistent with local resources, both material and human. In *Cities and the Wealth of Nations* (1984), Jane Jacobs presents the view that primary economic transactions occur between cities and the regions that coalesce around them. Cities and their regions—not societies—are the actual and appropriate units for economic analysis. This focus on community makes some sense from the perspective of understanding and sustaining social welfare systems. Whether it be child protective services, education, or material support, what matters is the ability and willingness of local systems to implement social welfare policy.

A sane planetary strategy for human survival and quality of life implies national and international planning, of course. But just as one recognizes the virtue of individual initiative in regulating day-to-day enterprise, one also sees that community-based effort is necessary for a safe and sane world order. Trade is essential, but it must be trade among cooperating and independently sustainable communities. The idea of a sustainable society is not a chimera; it is feasible. Even cold-weather climates permit self-reliance when cooperation and innovative thinking are the norm. In *Helping Ourselves* (1981), Bruce Stokes discusses "local solutions for global problems," such as computer links between urban industrial plants that would help them recycle waste. Third World countries may have a more natural basis for trade among themselves than with more industrialized nations. Small-scale family and neighborhood projects involving recycling, food production, and child care can be productive and sustainable. Herein lies the wealth of families.

As the mother and father are parents to the child, so too is the community a parent to the family. A family-oriented society built upon collective accountability is the necessary successor to Adam Smith's invisible guiding hand in transforming the social savage into the noble caretaker who will tend our planetary garden. If we realize this concept in an ecologically sound fashion, the sustainable society will come to pass. If not, modern civilization will degenerate into a new, more pernicious form of barbarism.

The concepts of limits to growth:
Coping with the finite in human affairs

The limits-to-growth thesis seems elegantly simple and undeniable[5] in principle: the material Earth is finite. One wonders how anyone could disagree. But how relevant are the limits to growth on a day-to-day, year-to-year, and decade-to-decade basis? There's the rub. Generally we accept the counterproposition of "the inexhaustible supply of solar energy." The difference between the limited material Earth and the limitless sun lies, of course, in order of magnitude. Both are limited—everything is limited from nearly any theological or teleological perspective. (Perhaps only in regards to the concept of God do we really speak of the infinite, now that astronomers tell us that even the universe is finite.) For almost any practical purpose we can disregard the sun's limits (it will last five billion years at current levels of solar activity), but we must take into account the Earth's limits—perhaps in year-to-year, probably in decade-to-decade, and certainly in century-to-century calculations and operations. The issue, then, is the nature of the limits to the material Earth.

It is ironic that it is the Earth's limits and not the sun's with which we must be concerned. As a "system," it is the sun, not the Earth, that seems less promising (in principle). The sun is a system so enormous in relation to astronomical bodies near it that it has virtually nothing to gain from them. With respect to outside input, it is essentially a "closed system." On the other hand, with respect to what it provides its neighbors, the sun is a benevolently open system. It radiates the energy upon which all the other systems depend. (The third planet, Earth, is the most graceful recipient, according to our astronomers.) And its enormous mass establishes a gravitational locus for the dependent entities that cluster around it, and in doing so, form the solar system.

As one of those entities, the Earth is a system very open to input. Economist Nicholas Georgescu-Roegen (1976) tells us solar energy is enormous in its direct impact: the Earth reflects back half of this energy but "accepts" roughly 2,650 Q of energy (a Q is about 10^{18} BTU; yearly energy use on Earth is about .2 Q). This solar energy reverberates through the Earth's systems in many ways, primarily through wind, waves, and wood. In addition, the Earth could theoretically be open to input from other entities in its near environment, such as from minerals from the moon or other planets and additional direct solar radiation captured by orbiting space stations.

In principle, it seems we should be concerned with the sun when we discuss limits. The sun seems so very finite, with its massive consumption of matter and production of outgoing energy, while the Earth is open to alternative solutions to its energy and materials problem. In practice the tables are turned. Limits to growth is so much an earthly concern that the most apt and widely used metaphor for the planet is "Spaceship Earth."[6] The planet is a self-contained habitat. We, as crew, must husband our provisions and expect little help from the void out-side, except whatever solar energy we can capture using the ship's inge-nious equipment and whatever else we can create using the materials at hand.

The limits-to-growth thesis rests ultimately on the principle of "en-tropy," one of the key principles of thermodynamics. Georgescu-Roegen (1976) has pointed out its critical importance in relation to sus-tainable societies. Entropy refers to the fact that energy exists in two states. One is "available" or "free" energy, which we can use to accom-plish work. The second is "unavailable" or "bound" energy, which we cannot use. The chemical energy in a piece of wood, for example, is available to us: we can burn the wood to produce heat, which we can then use. The energy needed to light the fire is small compared to the energy it releases. But the heat from the fire disperses, and once dis-persed it is no longer free. That is, greater energy is required to recap-ture it than we will have available once we do so. Free energy is orga-nized and concentrated; bound energy is chaotic and dissipated. Put simply, the law of entropy tells us that energy within systems moves from free to bound, from available to unavailable, from order to disor-der. This phenomenon may become more and more relevant to daily life as wood to burn becomes less readily available and large amounts of energy are required to find, obtain, transport, and ultimately burn it for heat. In some parts of the world women may spend most of their time (and energy) gathering firewood.

The implications of entropy for social welfare

In principle, one must understand entropy if one is to understand the past, analyze the present, and predict the future of systems. Relative to other systems, human beings are energy eaters. We live off available en-ergy and leave waste (bound energy) in its place. This is human life in its least flattering, most prosaic sense. Procreation is miraculous, but it sets in motion what is essentially a parasitic process, which the institu-tions we call social welfare systems are designed to facilitate. The fetus lives off available energy from the mother, who serves as host. The mother lives off the energy of other biological systems, such as plant and animal food, and nonbiologic sources such as minerals in her diet. Social welfare systems are designed to help her serve this function. In-deed, many of the most persuasive arguments in favor of social welfare systems demonstrate the positive cost-benefit ratio of the community's investment in support of pregnant and lactating women. Prenatal investment is a demonstrably elegant and cost-effective strategy for enhancing human development. In conventional economic terms, every dollar invested in supportive early care saves four dollars in later rehabilitative and compensatory care.

Once weaned, the child becomes a direct user of free energy and again requires social welfare systems to protect his energy supplies. And so the life cycle continues. In death, the body may return its residuals to the Earth (cultural practices permitting), but most likely it will consume one last portion of free energy to avoid even this payback, by cremation (transforming the body into bound energy) or casket burial (making the dead body a closed system by using a barrier against the Earth's biologic systems). No matter how you look at it, it costs the Earth plenty to support the human race[7]—not even considering the vast differences in such cost between the haves and the have-nots of the world.

Of course, the dynamics of entropy are exceedingly complex and open to disagreement even among experts. The mechanics of calculating free and bound energy within systems, the flows across systems, and the process of energy degradation on any large scale are staggering. When population was small and human tools rudimentary (that is to say up until about 300 years ago), we were a negligible influence upon the planet. Crises in energy production, the availability of materials, and population were few and localized: a clan might deforest a small area; a town might pollute a small body of water. But the effects were confined to a small space and were short-lived, because the massive supply of free energy permitted the Earth's systems to respond effectively. Limits were present, but they consisted mainly of the constraints imposed by the minimal size and power of the human race, individually and collectively. Discussions of social welfare systems could proceed without taking entropy into account, because the world was so big and human communities relatively small.

Now, however, entropy is a real factor, and limits are a matter of acute concern in social policy. As Georgescu-Roegen makes clear, even if we are able to achieve a "steady-state" socioeconomic order, we must still acknowledge entropy as a historical threat. That is, while the sun's projected five-billion-year future makes it "permanent" by any human standard, the enormous energy flow from free to bound forms generated by modern urban-industrial societies brings the end of civilization, even existence itself, within historical view. Unless we accept entropy's relevance, we face the prospect of a world bereft of the means for releasing and using free energy form sources, such as coal and even "renewable" sources such as the sun.

The human race has no ultimate control over the sun. But by most ethical standards, undeniable moral superiority is inherent in a society that sustains human enterprise for hundreds of thousands of years rather than devouring the world in hundreds.

How long is the future?

In his science fiction novel *Galaxies Like Grains of Sand* (1973), Brian Aldis puts the law of entropy into unusual historical perspective. His story chronicles the decline of our galaxy; he takes us to a point in the future after it has worn down and run out, an illustration of entropy at its grandest. In a clever twist, the book ends with a postscript from a succeeding species paying its respects to the newly defunct, formerly "new" superbeings who had succumbed to relentless entropy. Human history may be less than a blink of an eye in the span of the galaxies, only a moment in geologic time, but our time is ours. How we live on the Earth will go a long way toward determining how long we continue to exist.

While some people are willing to think about the fate of the Earth and of human societies in general, most are not prepared to do so. Their concerns are limited by kinships, friendships, and self-interests. For most people, the family is the best subject with which to open up a dialogue on the future. While many of us may be willing to turn away from the extinction or impoverishment of others, particularly those removed in time or space, few of us are indifferent to the destruction of our posterity—our children, their children, and their children's children. Family can be the *motivator*, and social welfare systems can be the *vehicle* for understanding and improving the way we are living. If we understand how we live upon the Earth, we will then be in a position to project how well our families will live in the future.

How *are* we living in the material Earth? This question sustains the debate about "limits to growth." The debate begins once we move beyond the necessary recognition that entropy imposes inevitable limits. The imminence of these limits is debatable, but the accumulating evidence makes clear that we are living off capital at an ever-increasing rate because of the growing population's increased demand for important materials. And we cannot be confident that some magical technological fix lies waiting just over the horizon to deliver us from our earthly limits. Apologists for the modern order such as Herman Kahn (1982) and Julius Simon (1983) would have us believe that entropy and limits to growth are irrelevant, that the current order has a long and indefinite future. Critics of the modern order reject these claims. Our task is to understand the basis for acknowledging the limits to growth and the need for the transition to a sustainable society.

Origins of the limits-to-growth thesis

Since the nineteenth century, scientists, artists, and others have seen that modern industrial civilization has become untenable, that population growth, pollution, and material consumption were propelling us toward catastrophe. Some of these precursors of the limits-to-growth hypothesis based their judgments on an intuitive distaste for the modern industrial order. Some observed the transformation of a particular community; others took a broader perspective and extrapolated it to encompass larger units, even the entire world. Some were elitists concerned about threats to their class' dominant position. Some were social democrats concerned about threats to their dominant position. Some were social democrats concerned about mass social welfare systems.

English essayists John Stuart Mill and John Ruskin explored the mistaken concepts of wealth that permeated their society and institutions in the nineteenth century, when England dominated the agenda and mechanisms of the modern world. Gerald Smith (1980) has concluded that these nineteenth-century thinkers were on the mark in their efforts to project a wise course of economic development. Ruskin, for example, urged his countrymen to work toward "true wealth," in which he saw a basis for human betterment and justice. Moderation, generosity, and satisfaction are the hallmarks of true wealth, as he saw it. In the United States, patrician historian Henry Adams (1914) found cause for alarm when he considered the industrialization and urbanization of America at the turn of the twentieth century. He wrote of this age:

> Power seemed to have outgrown its servitude and to have asserted its freedom. The cylinder has exploded, and thrown great masses of stone

and steam against the sky. The city has the air and movement of hysteria, and the citizens were crying, in every accent of anger and alarm, that the new forces must at any cost be brought under control. Prosperity never before imagined, power never yet wielded by man, speed never reached by anything but a meteor, had made the world irritable, nervous, querulous, unreasonable and afraid. (p. 499)

In *Theory of the Leisure Class* (1912), economist Thorsten Veblen introduced the concept of "conspicuous consumption." Veblen and others saw the cultural dangers and the essential falsity of aggressive Western materialism, which reached full bloom with the mass consumption of the twentieth century. The Versailles court of King Louis XIII was lavish and exploitive, but it was trivial compared with the diversion of major rivers and the moving of whole mountains required to sustain today's urban centers, suburban developments, and agribusiness enterprises.

Artists such as D.H. Lawrence, who were aware of the threats to culture posed by the modern industrial order, could evoke an image of change, but few could foresee the physical threats as well. And not many people have the tools to document their criticisms. Ruskin was, after all, something of a romantic crackpot. Lawrence could write the following passage, but he was neither equipped nor inclined to document his analysis scientifically:

This is history. One England blots out another. The mines had made the halls wealthy. Now they were blotting them out, as they had already blotted out the cottages. The industrial England blots out the agricultural England. One meaning blots out another. The new England blots out the old England. And the continuity is not organic, but mechanical. (*Lady Chatterley's Lover*, 1928, p. 146)

One of the biggest problems facing such analyses is that throughout history, dire predictions of catastrophe have proved incorrect because a technological breakthrough altered the course of social and economic development, thus invalidating a projection of the future that was based on previous trends. This is the principal rationale used to dispute the relevance of the limits-to-growth thesis.

Those in privileged positions have always tended to see social change as social catastrophe. This observation may be justly applied to those named earlier, with the patrician Henry Adams as a prime example. Rejoinders to such critics have sometimes rightly been able to portray them as the boy who cried wolf or as Chicken Little, mistakenly thinking that the sky is falling. Contemporary debates are often cast in this light. But what if the wolf really is coming? Or, as a bit of bathroom graffiti put it, what if Chicken Little was right?

In 1962, Rachel Carson published *Silent Spring*, a landmark analysis of the concrete effects of powerful modern technology on the biological environment. The pesticide DDT served as an excellent symbol of the modern era. It exemplified the clearly benevolent intent of modern technology in its early stage (killing insects that harm crops), its ambiguity in the middle stage, when it becomes apparent that it involves costs as well as benefits, and finally, its demonic character (destroying what it is supposed to serve, protect, and enhance). Things were getting out of control.

It was not until the late 1960s that systematic efforts were begun to develop an empirical, comprehensive methodology for projecting the future of the modern industrial order. Aurelio Peccei and a group of futurists founded the Club of Rome to generate, coordinate, and disseminate their understanding of the global prognosis. They started with four powerful, intertwined forces of the modern order—population growth, use of resources, energy consumption, and pollution. These, they said, were part of a broad syndrome, global in its origins and consequences, which they called "the world problematique." The result of an interdisciplinary effort, called the "Project on the Predicament of Mankind," was the historically significant report to the Club of Rome entitled *The Limits to Growth*.

Inspired by pioneering systems analyst Jay Forrester and under the direction of Dennis Meadows, the researchers developed a complex set of equations to relate five global trends: accelerating industrialization, rapid population growth, widespread malnutrition, depletion of nonrenewable resources, and a deteriorating environment. A computer analyzed the available data and projected what would happen in the event of various contingencies. They hoped in this way to predict the future of the economic and environmental foundations of social welfare.

A key feature of the model was its recognition that some variables change at a percentage rate rather than by the addition of the same fixed sum, as, for example, when bank interest is compounded and one receives interest on the interest. This exponential growth can boggle the mind. Consider this classic example: if a man is paid a penny on the first day of the month and his wages are doubled every day, he will receive $5,368,708.80 on the twenty-ninth day of the month and $10,737,417 on the thirtieth! Half the total growth occurs near the very end of the process. Percentage growth rates produce massive increases in the amount of change. This is a key element in the concept of limits to growth and one reason people find it so difficult to grasp.

Lester Brown (1980) offers several helpful metaphors to illustrate this. One invokes the image of lily pads in a pond, starting with one and doubling each day; the pond is half covered on the twenty-ninth day and completely covered on the thirtieth. The point is that crisis can arise precipitously out of seemingly low-grade chronic problems. On the basis of such a model, *The Limits to Growth* concluded:

- Exponential growth in population and material production is a dominant force in socioeconomic change in most contemporary societies.
- Current rates of population growth and material output cannot be sustained indefinitely. Probably, growth will overreach important physical limits if continued in accordance with present patterns for another 50 to 100 years.
- Growth may end either through orderly accommodation to global physical limits (a transition to equilibrium) or by overshooting those limits and collapsing, producing a major world catastrophe.
- Because of the many delays in complex systems governing material output and population, the most probable result of current global trends is the overshooting of limits and eventual collapse.
- Technological solutions designed to reduce pressures caused by growth (starvation, pollution, rising costs of food production and research, etc.) may only postpone the collapse unless accompanied by changes in the social, economic, and political factors stimulating growth.
- It seems possible to identify alternative stages of global equilibrium in which population and material output remain essentially constant and are in balance with our finite resources. They would satisfy man's most fundamental needs, permit cultural progress, and sustain societies indefinitely.
- There is no unique, optimal, long-term population level. Rather, there are many trade-offs involving personal freedom, material and social standards of living, and population level. Given our finite and diminishing resources, we must recognize that, inevi-

tably, a larger population implies a lower material standard of living.

• Delays of 50 to 100 years are involved in negotiating an orderly transition to a state of equilibrium, however defined. Thus, nations must begin now to recognize that progress cannot eternally be equated with growth, and they must stop the implicit and explicit encouragement of population increase and material expansion. Each year of delay decreases man's long-term options and lessens the likelihood of an orderly transition to equilibrium. (Lesh, 1978)

The fate of the limits-to-growth thesis

The years since publication of *The Limits to Growth* have been characterized by intense debate in some quarters and oblivious silence in others. Subsequent reports to the Club of Rome have sought to clarify issues and rectify technical and conceptual weaknesses in the original. For example, *Mankind at the Turning Point* (1974) examined implications of global trends in various regions of the world. The authors, Mihajlo Mesarovic and Edward Pestel, concluded that industrial history, resources, and demographic character produce different projected paths, in different regions—but paths that will eventually converge in disaster, in the collapse of social welfare systems, and in a retreat into barbarism. In the meantime, the prognosis is for an increasingly unjust world order in which the haves struggle mightily to preserve their privileged position in relation to the have-nots. Both reports must be understood as projections of what will happen if fundamental policies and trends continue. Of course, both are calls to change these policies and trends; here, science and propaganda are comrades in arms. Subsequent reports to the Club of Rome are testimony to this (e.g., *Reshaping the International Order*, 1976; *Goals for Mankind*, 1977; *No Limits to Learning*, 1979).

In March 1982, the Smithsonian Institution in Washington, D.C., recognized and celebrated the tenth anniversary of the publication of *The Limits to Growth*. At the meeting many leaders of the movement heard Dennis and Donella Meadows and their colleagues say that events of that decade had reinforced their belief in the validity of their thesis and in the need for global action to avert catastrophe. They reported the results of a 1982 conference on efforts around the world to develop global and regional models. Despite differences in focus and technique, these groups all affirmed that current trends (particularly the population-industrialization-urbanization complex of forces) portend collapse of the global socioeconomic order and social welfare systems sometime within the twenty-first century. In addition, they reaffirmed the conclusion that social changes, not technological fixes, are the primary vehicle for averting disaster and placing humanity on sustainable ecological and socioeconomic footing (Meadows, Richardson, and Bruckman, 1982).

Social welfare ultimately depends upon how well underlying economic, political, and intellectual models correspond with the realities of the environment. The law of entropy tells us that the physical environment imposes limits on these models. Figure 1.1 describes two scenarios. The first assumes that limit-setting takes place within the boundaries of environmental tolerance, both now and in the next hundred years. The second assumes that we are close to environmental boundaries, that we may actually be meeting them at some places already, and that we will overrun them in the twenty-first century. The first model divorces social welfare systems from environmental systems (at least in principle and in general). The second indicates that these two areas will become even more inextricably linked, as physical and political resources are consumed in the struggle to maintain a social life that is increasingly brutish, nasty, and short.

Opponents of the limits-to-growth thesis

Two other views dispute the validity of the limits-to-growth thesis: one that argues for business as usual and one that proposes a popular revolution to free us of limits. Both groups argue for more rather than less population and industrial development, for more consumers and more consumption. Both say that current models of economic life promise to enhance, not undermine, foundations for social welfare systems.

Those boosting "business as usual" maintain that, under the current world order, things are getting better for everyone. They cite worldwide increases in per-capita income, improved health, and progress in telecommunications, transportation, electronics, robotics, agricultural techniques, and petroplastics as harbingers of an even grander future for Earth and its people. They are confident that human ingenuity will produce technological fixes as needed: new substitutes for exhausted

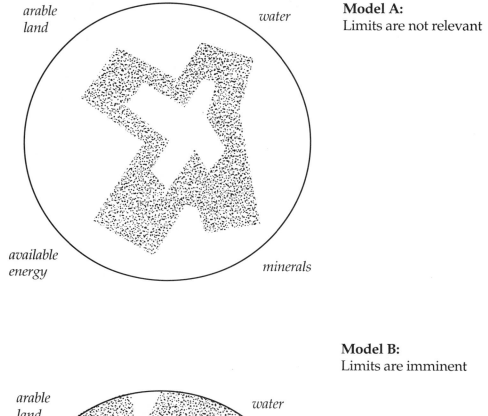

Model A:
Limits are not relevant

Model B:
Limits are imminent

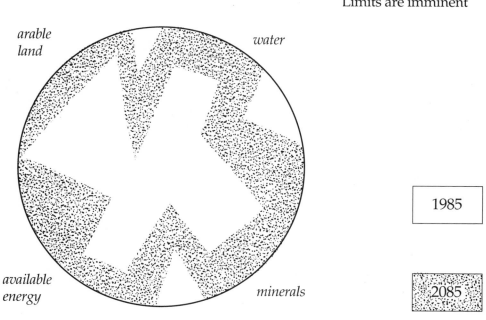

1985

2085

Figure 1-1: Two Alternative Models of "Limits to Growth"

mineral supplies, new energy sources such as nuclear fusion to replace conventional agriculture, space colonies to relieve earthly overcrowding. Herman Kahn titles his "booster" book *The Coming Boom* (1982); Julius Simon calls his *The Ultimate Resource* (1983). Both seek to reassure us that the present path of growth is sustainable and wise. Both have been criticized and repudiated by those who recognize the limits to growth; one review of Kahn's thesis calls it "prayerful economics," because it seems to be based upon a "miraculous" deliverance from the natural process of the world.

These boosters from the Right have counterparts on the Left who argue that the limits-to-growth thesis is a conservative ploy to keep down the masses, that it simply rationalizes an unjust status quo. In its most extreme form, this argument says limits to growth translates to genocide and oppression, that it proposes a political revolution to replace the current world order with a radical socialist society in which environmental and economic issues—like the state in the classic Marxist conception—will wither away. Donella Meadows summarizes (but does not endorse) this socialist perspective with the statement, "Since each new mouth comes equipped with two hands, overpopulation is unthinkable" (p. 21). One might characterize Simon's view as, "Since each mouth comes equipped with a head that has a brain, technological inadequacy becomes unthinkable." Rejections of limits to growth from either political extreme are fatally flawed, however, for both sides fail to recognize that neither labor (the Left's solution) nor technology (the Right's solution) is an unlimited substitute for the physical systems of the Earth. We cannot stop entropy. It always costs something to conduct an economic activity. There really is no such thing as a free lunch. We cannot indefinitely use cheap "available" energy. Running power plants, factories, or households requires ever more costly efforts to use available energy. The more sophisticated our technologies, the higher the energy cost to cope with the waste products that result. The cost of radioactive and chemically toxic waste will be with us and with future generations long after we have consumed the energy. To dispute the validity of the limits-to-growth thesis is to gamble with the future. Some do so, disingenuously, because they stand to profit from business as usual. Others refuse to recognize the practical implications of entropy. In future years our grandchildren may look back on us and say, "How could they have been so blind!? How could they not see that limits to growth are inherent in their society and its economic and technological principles?"

How, indeed? This kind of thinking is best illustrated in the following story. A skillful trader is intent upon selling his horse. The beast appears to be a prime physical specimen, tall and strong, who can run like the wind. His only defect is that he is blind as a stone. But the trader, a man of P.T. Barnum-like commercial convictions, does not despair. He invites a prospective buyer to examine and observe the horse in the paddock. All goes well until the horse begins to gallop around the field. Crash! He runs into a tree. Dazed, he gets up and gallops off, heading straight for an enormous boulder in the middle of the field. "Why, that horse is blind as a bat!" yells the prospective customer. "No sir," replies the trader. "He's not blind. He just don't give a damn."

Are we blind or do we not give a damn? It's often hard to tell. Some of the problems we face in accepting the concept of limits to growth are understandable. When traveling across the North and South American continents, and even in Western Europe, one sees vast stretches of forest and farmland. When we in the affluent, modern world want something material, it's always available. Even the "energy crisis" of the early 1970s was a relatively minor inconvenience in the grand scheme of things. We naturally assume that our children will have all that we have, if not more.

Is conventional economic thinking terminally ill?

Heidegger explored the proposition that one never becomes truly aware of life until one profoundly accepts the inevitability of nonbeing, the idea that one will cease to exist. Often, people who have had a brush with death experience renewed appreciation for living. Yet most of us adopt the "personal fable" (Elkind, 1980) that we are immortal, and we live each day as if our lives—like our resources—were unlimited. The enormous psychological challenge of recognizing our personal limits somehow complicates our ability to recognize societal limits. It is hard to accept the idea of our personal death, and even harder to accept the idea that our children's society will die. Just as our failure to accept the "limits-to-life" thesis distorts how we account for each day, so our failure to accept the limits-to-growth thesis distorts how we account for each economic transaction. If we accept psychologically the fact that our time on this planet is limited, we are less likely to squander our resources. A mature person gives up the personal fable of immortality on Earth; a mature society gives up the economic fable of infinite resources.

Later we will examine the assumptions behind conventional concepts of economic development. Here, suffice it to say that most conventional economic analysis operates in an ecological vacuum, not recognizing the long-term historical issues posed by the laws of entropy and the limits-to-growth thesis (Georgescu-Roegen, 1980). Only the last 300 years have been examined in any real detail by conventional economic analysis. But this "long run" is an inadequate basis for understanding the future. The next thirty years will produce more industrial economic activity than has transpired in all of human history. This is not surprising; more people will share the Earth in the latter twentieth century than in all previous centuries combined. And human economies are enormously more powerful than ever before. As we saw in Figure 1.1, the relation between economics and ecology has created a whole new ball game, and, unfortunately, conventional economic thinking has not adjusted to this new state of affairs.

The conventional economic model is not equipped to describe and analyze what we face in the long term now that the days of free resources, unlimited waste disposal, and low-impact living are gone. It simply doesn't consider the real, elemental world of material stocks, energy flows, biological systems, and human capital. If we accept the limits-to-growth thesis, we must conclude that conventional economic thinking is wrong, no matter how accurate its short-term predictions may have been or may continue to be regarding isolated issues such as domestic banking or corporate marketing. This brings to mind an aphorism attributed to the French philosopher Albert Camus: "Just because we are precise does not mean we smack of the truth." We will return to the problem of economics again (and again), but before that, in the next chapter, I want to examine human quality in relation to two issues: the concrete nature of a sustainable society and the central position of families. Both are essential steps along the path leading to an understanding of the environmental and economic foundations of social welfare systems.

NOTES

1. I shall have much to say later about the masculine gender of this "Man" who is at the center of Bronowski's vision of the human enterprise, as "he" is in conventional economic thinking as well.

2. I shall consider at a later point how this use of the lifeboat metaphor resembles and differs from Garret Hardin's (1976) concept of "the lifeboat ethic."

3. By John Martyn and James Allestry, published under the sponsorship of the Royal Society of London for Improving Natural Knowledge.

4. Meadows, Meadows, Randers and Behrens, *The Limits to Growth*, 1972.

5. Which is not to say that it is not denied. I shall discuss later Julius Simon's and Herman Kahn's challenges to the limits-to- growth thesis.

6. Bartlett's attributes the metaphor to R. Buckminster Fuller in his 1964 book *Prospect for Humanity*: "For at least two million years men have been reproducing and multiplying on a little automated Spaceship Earth." Some (e.g., Hardin) oppose the metaphor because it implies that someone is captaining the ship. But as Robert Heinlein has suggested in some of his novels, a spaceship planet might function for long periods on automatic pilot before the crew realizes its guidance responsibilities.

7. The anthropomorphic overtones involved in any discussion of this sort are nearly unavoidable, but potentially dangerous. Does the Earth "care" whether human beings (or any beings, for that matter) continue to exist? More on this later.

T W O

What is a Sustainable Society? Do We Live in One?

December 1974. Chichen Itza, the Yucatan, Mexico. I have came to the Yucatan to see the traces of Mayan culture left behind after centuries of neglect. I see the Mayans as a foreboding predecessor of our own society—indeed, of the modern way of life. The Mayans originated in what is now Guatemala, and for many centuries they thrived and dominated this part of the world. Why did such a powerful culture collapse? Our best guess is that soil erosion precipitated an agricultural crisis that incapacitated the whole society. For all our attention to the rise, decline, and fall of the Roman Empire, we have overlooked an equally important civilization here. The history of the Mayan civilization has much to tell us about our own society, so much so that perhaps instead of reading Gibbon's account of the Roman Empire, we should be examining the studies of E.S. Deevey and his colleagues on the collapse of the Mayan agricultural base and its cataclysmic consequences.

I have arrived at Chichen Itza, this ancient Mayan city, with dozens of affluent tourists from societies currently dominating the modern world. We Americans, Germans, and Japanese have much in common with each other. But with the Mayans?

With its pyramids, markets, sports arena, houses, and observatory, Chichen Itza is an architectural wonder. It's humbling, or at least it ought to be. Can any of us tourists see ourselves and our societies here? Do the Germans see in this city a reminder of Berlin, where they, like the Mayans, per-

formed human sacrifices? Do the Japanese see Tokyo, where they, like the Mayans, ran death camps for prisoners of war? Do I see Washington, where the extinction of Native Americans was ordered? Do any of us see our own societies being reduced to ghost towns because of an unsustainable relationship between the human community and nature's ecosystems?

I am excited to find three men at work reconstructing and restoring one of the original columns of what appears to have been an archway. The column is made of four pieces of stone, which the workers hoist and push into position, in the end recreating a small part of a city toppled hundreds of years ago by unknown forces. I discover the foreman speaking in Spanish to one man and in an Indian dialect to the other; the two workers communicate only through him. This dynamic adds to my excitement. Contemporary society in the Yucatan is in the midst of just this kind of task, of bridging the gap between the Indian and the Spanish. And as this occurs before me, I watch the column rise and assume its position—ancient history being literally put back together. It is a treasured moment.

But no one else is watching with me. A group of Germans pauses briefly. One says, "Nothing's happening here." The group moves on. Ironically, of course, he's right. It has already happened here. Where it is happening is in Berlin, and in Tokyo, and in Washington.

What makes a society sustainable?

In order to talk about a sustainable society is, it's important to understand what we mean by "sustainable." *Webster's* tells us that to sustain a thing means:

- to give support
- to provide for the support or maintenance of
- to cause to continue
- to support the weight; hold up
- to prevent from sinking or giving way
- to endure
- to support as true, legal, or just

To sustain, then, means to help a thing continue over time, to support something else, to legitimize. Each of these meanings is relevant to the concept of sustainable societies. They have a long life in the span of human history; they support a particular and desirable social order and way of life, one that offers more than mere survival; they have moral legitimacy, higher values. Each of these characteristics is inherent in a true sustainable society.

How long is long?

Until recently in their history, human societies were barely able to sustain themselves, barely able to endure. For most of our history as a species the issue has been whether we could carve out a large and stable enough niche that would allow us to form and function in a society, in a group larger than a traditional family or a clan. Disease, predators, climate, and limited food supply always threatened to overwhelm us, throwing into doubt the long-term survival of human communities. Only in the last few thousand years has our tenure on the planet seemed assured.

Considering social welfare systems and families against this backdrop cautions against simplistic nostalgia for "the good old days." Only about half the children born in medieval Europe survived infancy and lived until their fifth birthday. In the period before 1900 in the United States, so many women either died before marrying, or perished in childbirth, or were widowed very soon after marrying, or remained single, that only about 40% of American women were ever married for a significant period. The modern era is the first age in which human communities have laid the demographic and economic foundations for the social welfare systems that support families.

Before we glorify the good old days, we would do well to recall the account of family planning pioneer Margaret Sanger concerning life in the impoverished tenements of New York City at the turn of the twentieth century. Sanger writes:

> Each time I returned to this district, which was becoming a recurrent nightmare, I used to hear that Mrs. Cohen "had been carried to a hospital, but had never come back," or that Mrs. Kelly "had sent the children to a neighbor and had put her head into the gas oven." Day after day such tales were poured into my ears—a baby being born dead, great relief—the death of an older child, sorrow but again relief of a sort —the story told a thousand times of death from abortion, children going

into institutions. I shuddered with horror as I listened to the details and studied the reasons back of them—destitution linked with excessive childbearing. The waste of life seemed senseless. One by one, worried, sad, pensive, and aging faces marshaled themselves before me in my dreams, sometimes appealingly, sometimes accusingly. (Sanger, 1938, p. 89)

These conditions continue with a vengeance for today's American "underclass" and for much of the impoverished Third World. Poverty is hardly uplifting, rarely noble.

Today's challenges

Having established the human presence on Earth despite dangers from predators and the environment, we found ourselves facing another threat—self-destruction. The fall of the Mayan civilization was such a case. After thriving for a historically significant period, Mayan society collapsed, its agriculture unable to support its population. Some Mayan peoples endured, but without the rubric of societal order to support them, a kind of Dark Ages ensued.

As we seek to understand sustainability, we need to wrestle with the question, "How long is long?" Is a society sustainable if it can only project itself fifty years into the future? If we start by looking at the future of our own families, we must answer "no." Who is willing to say that one's children will be the last generation to live within a society's social welfare systems? Is 500 years long enough? That sounds more like it, so long as we are not speaking of the end of humanity in addition to the end of our society. Of course, our sense of historical times has withered. Adolph Hitler boasted that his Third Reich would last 1,000 years, but it was toppled in less than fifteen. The Soviet Union came to an end after only three quarters of a century. Our sense of forever has become trivialized in direct proportion to the pace of social change.

The family, however, remains the most potent means for linking today with the past and the future. It is the natural focus for analyzing and planning for social welfare. If we think of the family as not just parents and children, but also as ancestors and descendants, it a psychologically powerful answer to Groucho Marx's question "What did posterity ever do for me?" We need to celebrate the family, both our ancestors and our descendants, to counter the trivializing of history inherent in modern life, with its emphasis on transience, change, and the interchangeability of people, places, and things. A strong family focus helps us see beyond the end of our noses.

The dynamics surrounding the pricing of oil in the mid-1980s illustrate this need for a longer perspective. As the Club of Rome has made abundantly clear, oil consumption plays a large role in the world problematique. If petroleum is to continue to serve as the cornerstone of modern affluence, we need to conserve it. Because of a short-term decrease in the consumption of crude oil in the mid-1980s (which was linked more to a worldwide recession than to successful conservation efforts), OPEC and other oil "producers" lowered their prices. A collapse of the pricing structure resulted, and there was "cheap oil" again as "producers" competed for sales. The public cheered, despite the need for *higher* prices in order to encourage a more realistic approach to petroleum and other nonrenewable resources. The low price has continued into the 1990s, but it can only be temporary in the long run. The ability to save less than a dollar per gallon is a trivial gain when it means that our grandchildren will, at best, have limited access to petroleum products.

When John Maynard Keynes was asked how his pump-priming approach to government expenditure would work in the long run, he replied, "In the long run, we shall all be dead." This dismissal of the long-term problem looks more and more like a prophecy. Such a trivial manner of approaching the future will certainly lead us to our death— or at least plunge us into that social and cultural death, that "worthless state of existence" forecast by *The Limits to Growth*. Family, however, serves as a potent antidote to our inability to imagine the future, because few of us will accept the end of our children's children's children. Based on data concerning life expectancy, many of the young children who witnessed Halley's comet when it was visible from 1985 to 1986 have a good chance of seeing it again. Any concept of the sustainable society must include the prospect that our civilization will be around to witness several more visits by that venerable comet.

There is no obvious answer to the question of "how long." However, given our history and tradition, it's fair to say that a society suited to a 50–year life span is clearly not a sustainable one, but one with a 500–year life span is. The benchmark for human societies is, by most Western accounts, the Roman society that arose and continued over roughly half a millennium. Chinese society has a still longer track record, so 500 years should serve at least as some sort of minimum standard.

What is society good for?

A sustainable society offers more than the mere biological continuity of the human species. The prospect of nuclear war emphasizes this point. All but the most apocalyptic visions of nuclear holocaust conclude that the human species will survive—albeit in small numbers, in shockingly impoverished circumstances, and plagued by deformities and cancer. This hardly constitutes a sustainable society. This would plunge us into that "worthless state of existence" more quickly than any other environmental catastrophe. Recent analyses of the prospect of "nuclear winter" tell this story all too well.

Jonathan Schell's *The Fate of the Earth* (1982) pictures a human race in the wake of a limited nuclear war. He portrays it struggling to maintain a place for itself on an environmentally shattered world—a situation far different from that faced by humanity in the relatively benign world of hundreds of thousands of years ago. Schell foresees an end to civilization in all locations receiving even a small fraction of the megatonnage of nuclear weapons currently targeted at them. Formal social welfare systems would no longer exist in those areas.

The number of injuries sustained in such an attack would be astronomical; severe outbreaks of epidemics would follow. Dr. H. Jack Geiger describes the conditions that would likely result from a limited attack: "The landscape would be strewn with millions of corpses of human beings and animals. This alone is a situation without precedent in history." Water and food would be polluted, greatly increasing the risk of an outbreak of cholera and typhoid. Disease-carrying insects would thrive, feeding on the tens of millions of dead bodies. Public health facilities would be destroyed as part and parcel of the general destruction of institutional life. Radiation sickness, wounds, and depression would sap the strength and resistance of survivors. The society that survived this would be, simply, sick. Geiger paints a bleak picture.

A society thus ravaged would be unable to maintain social welfare systems, because the economy that had fed and clothed it would be shattered. As Schell puts it:

If the economy in question is a modern technological one, the consequences will be particularly severe, for then the obstacles to restoring it will be greatest. Because a modern economy, like an ecosystem, is a single, interdependent whole, in which each part requires many other parts to keep functioning, its wholesale breakdown will leave people unable to perform the simplest, most essential tasks. Even agriculture— the immediate means of subsistence—is caught up in the operations of the interdependent machine, and breaks down when it breaks down." (pp. 68–69)

We might foresee an eventual resurgence of civilization as survivors cut their losses and threw themselves into the task of constructing new institutions, new social relationships, a new economy, a new network of social welfare systems. But the grim reality of undertaking such a task amidst such devastation is too much for most of us to comprehend, let alone endorse in the name of political ideology or supposed national interests.

Nuclear conflagration aside, there is yet the prospect of a "peaceful" environmental catastrophe. The horrible events in Bhopal, India, in 1984 bear witness to this possibility. Accounts of a city devastated by the leak of toxic gas from a Union Carbide plant give us an inkling of what we would face if environmental degradation accelerates, as many fear it will. The Indian government acknowledged 1,431 deaths (although some groups claim the figure is more than 2,000). Health officials document five to ten times that number of permanently disabled persons who cannot seek employment.

The Bhopal disaster is, in some respects, a microcosm. But it fails as a model because it was an isolated event. The social welfare systems of surrounding communities and of the larger society were available and responded during the crisis. Even in an impoverished nation like India, these systems are substantial. Imagine the challenge of responding at one time to hundreds or thousands of Bhopal-like disasters. This is what we would face in the event of even the most limited nuclear war or of a dramatic environmental catastrophe. And such an event may well be the outcome of an "economic war" in which more and more of the world's people are combatants or victims.

An economic war, like a shooting war, can produce social and ecological death. The nuclear scenario is so horrific that few will risk it. However, in the pursuit of affluence, many more may accept the risk of environmental breakdown and the resulting cost to quality of life. A visit to a strip mine, toxic waste dump, or urban slum shows us that. They exist and are usually placed in close proximity to those with the least political clout. Most people survive these travesties most of the time, but such environments are hardly sustainable, because they undermine the existence and operation of essential social welfare systems.

Being "sustainable" means more than merely surviving. A sustainable society supports a way of life organized around ethical and operational principles. It implies the existence of a culture and a social network within an economic system. Our concern is, after all, with sustainable *societies*, and they are nothing if not socioeconomic organizations.

The endurance of a socioeconomic order depends upon its relation to the physical and social environment. If the United States were the only society consuming petroleum and other nonrenewable materials, our society's prospects for a long life would be much greater than they are now, when more and more societies are demanding access to the world's store of raw goods. This has been particularly evident during the last twenty-five years in the efforts of Japan and the Pacific Basin countries to become economic powers. They have demonstrated that a society's sustainability depends to an ever-increasing degree upon global context. A report by the Washington-based Environment Fund illustrates this point. According to the report, per-capita consumption of energy in the United States in 1980 was five times that of the rest of the world—333 million versus 66 million BTUs. By the year 2030, however, the massive increase in the world's population will increase demand elsewhere for energy by a factor of more than five (even without a rise in the standard of living). The sustainability of any one society depends only partly on the extent of its competition with other societies for resources, however; it also depends on the extent to which it can be self-reliant. Brazil, for example, is seeking to opt out of the competition for petroleum by switching to domestically produced alcohol. Yet, however noble, this conversion is causing its own set of social, economic, and environmental costs, not the least of which is the loss of land normally used for food production.

Some societies, which have operated on a technologically primitive, labor-intensive basis for extended periods nevertheless qualify as being sustainable. The Aleutian Inuit (the name preferred by the people commonly known as Eskimos) and the pygmies of New Guinea are two examples. However, these societies were small and geographically isolated in a way that was rarely feasible and is now virtually impossible.

Except for feudal Japan under the Tokugawa Shogunate from 1603–1867, few large societies have managed to remain closed systems, and once exposed to modern societies, small-scale premodern societies rarely remain sustainable.

The Aleutian Inuit are a case in point. Contrast the picture of Inuit life presented in the 1920s documentary *Nanuck* and that portrayed in the 1976 film *From the First People*. In the 1920s Nanuck and his family were self sufficient, although the tide of modern life was rising around them. They lived in dynamic harmony with the natural environment. The Shungnak family of the 1970s, by contrast, is tied to the modern order with all its technology—radios, processed food, snowmobiles, and electricity. If anything, the Shungnak community is so removed from its self-sufficient and sustainable past that it is now hyper-vulnerable to the costs of modernization. It depends totally upon imports to meet virtually all its basic needs, and the old skills required to live in a sustainable, self-sufficient manner are dying with the elders. The life portrayed here is "easier"—after all, Nanuck died in the winter following the filming of his story. Yet the Shungnak community serves as a metaphor, reminding us in the modern era that we have increased our power and productivity by substituting petroleum- and electricity-powered machines for human and animal power; but in doing so we have increased our vulnerability to any kind of socioeconomic disruption. We have constructed elaborate formal social welfare systems to cope with life's inherent vicissitudes and the complexities introduced by modern societies. Now we must find a way to pay for them, because we can no longer live without them.

What does it mean to be modern?

For all practical purposes, the issue of socioeconomic order boils down to this: can a particular society support its socioeconomic order over the long run? A sustainable society, as we have defined it, must endure for 500 years. Will our modern societies exist in the twenty-fifth century?

This was the question posed in 1972 by *The Limits to Growth*, in 1974 by *Mankind at the Turning Point*, and in 1982 by *Groping in the Dark*. Examining the ways in which our societies operate today, the authors of these books did not see much reason for optimism. They saw that "modernized" societies fail the 500–year test because their socioeconomic orders are unsustainable—even if current relations between technologically modernized societies and the unmodernized remain unchanged. Modern societies can continue to do well for the next half century if they're lucky and if they can keep the poor societies down. But they face an erosion of wealth in the latter half of the twenty-first century, when the children of today's youngsters will be babysitting for their grandchildren.

How do the rich and the poor societies of today contribute to each other's social welfare? Modernized societies provide money and serve as models for economic development. They also serve as models for social welfare systems. They provide technical assistance and medical care, and, in some cases, supply food. Yet, they also exploit poor societies by using them as markets and as sources of raw materials and labor. Indeed, modernized economies depend upon such societies for international trade; they are the markets that keep a modernized economy alive and allow it to reap profits, which it invests in its own social welfare systems. It is just this dynamic that is one of the concerns of this book.

The modern "way of the world" is playing an even larger role in the day-to-day life of societies all over the world, as is evidenced in the lively international trade of high technology articles for mass consumption—e.g., radios, televisions, and automobiles. Through these articles alone, modernized societies have penetrated deeply into the unmodernized world. Poor societies are ripe for this penetration; they may even desire it. But once in the industrialized export business they are hooked into a game in which someone must lose (import) if someone else is to win (export). Balance-of-trade surpluses and deficits are not the whole story, however; these will not bring about sustainability. There are basic human realities that also need to be considered.

In his introduction to Duane Elgin's *Voluntary Simplicity*, Ram Dass, a Western-style intellectual turned Eastern-style mystic, recounts the following story, presented in a narrative form compatible with its content.

> I look out over a gentle valley in the Kumoan Hills at the base of the Himalayas. A river flows through the valley forming now and again man-made tributaries that irrigate the fertile fields. These fields surround the fifty or so thatched or tin-roofed houses and extend in increasingly narrow terraces up the surrounding hillsides.
>
> In several of these fields I watch village men standing on their wooden plows goading on their slow-moving water buffalo who pull the plows,

provide the men's families with milk, and help to carry their burdens. And amid the green of the hills, in brightly colored saris and nose rings, women cut the high grasses to feed the buffalo and gather the firewood which, along with the dried dung from the buffalo, will provide the fire to cook the grains harvested from the fields and to warm the houses against the winter colds and dry them during the monsoons. A huge haystack passes along the path, seemingly self-propelled, in that the woman on whose head it rests is lost entirely from view.

At a point along the stream there is laughter and talk and the continuous slapping of wet cloth against rock as the family laundry gets done. And everywhere there are children and dogs, each contributing his or her sound to the voice of the village.

Everywhere there is color: red chili peppers drying on the roofs and saris drying by the river, small green and yellow blue birds darting among the fruit trees, butterflies and bees teasing their way from one brightly colored flower to another.

I have walked for some five miles from the nearest town to reach this valley. The foot path I have taken is the only means of exit from this village. Along the way, I meet farmers carrying squash, burros bearing firewood or supplies, women with brass pots on their heads, school children, young men dressed in "city clothes." In all of these people I find a quiet shy dignity, a sense of belonging, a depth of connectedness to these ancient hills.

It all moves as if in slow motion. Time is measured by the sun, the seasons, and the generations. A conch shell sounds from a tiny temple, which houses a deity worshiped in these hills. The stories of this and other deities are recited and sung, and they are honored by flowers and festivals and fasts. They provide a context—vast in its scale of aeons of time, rich with teachings of reincarnation and the morality inherent in the inevitable workings of karma. And it is this context that gives vertical meaning to these villagers' lives with their endless repetition of cycles of birth and death.

This pastoral vision of simplicity has much appeal to those of us in the West for whom life can be full of confusion, distraction, and complexity. In the rush of modern industrial society, and in the attempt to maintain our image as successful persons, we feel that we have lost touch with a deeper, more profound part of our beings. Yet, we feel that we have little time, energy, or cultural support to pursue those areas of life that we know are important. We long for a simpler way of life that allows us to restore some balance to our lives.

Is the vision of simple living provided by this village of the East the answer? Is this an example of a primitive simplicity of the past or of an enlightened simplicity of the future? Gradually, I have come to sense that this is not the kind of simplicity that the future holds. Despite its ancient character, the simplicity of the village is still in its "infancy."

Occasionally, people show me their new babies and ask me if that peaceful innocence is not just like that of the Buddha. Probably not, I tell them, for within that baby rest all the latent seeds of worldly desire just waiting to sprout as the opportunity arises. On the other hand, the expression on the face of the Buddha, who had seen though the impermanence and suffering associated with such desires, reflects the invulnerability of true freedom.

So it is with this village. Its ecological and peaceful way of living is unconsciously won and it is vulnerable to the winds of change that fan the latent desires of its people. Even now there is a familiar though jarring note in this sylvan village scene. The sounds of static and that impersonal professional voice of another civilization—the radio announcer—cut through the harmony of sounds as a young man of the village holding a portable radio to his ear, comes around a bend. On his arm there is a silver wristwatch that sparkles in the sun. He looks at me proudly as he passes. And a wave of understanding passes through me. Just behind that radio and wristwatch comes an army of desires that for centuries have gone untested and untasted. As material growth and technological change activate these yearnings, they will transform the hearts, minds, work, and daily life of this village within a generation or two. (1979, p.i-iii)

Ram Dass writes of the vulnerability of this unconsciously "simple" society to the calculating complexity of modernization. Elgin says the answer lies not in unconscious simplicity, but in integrating the benefits of technology with the demands of the future and the wisdom of the past. He calls this "voluntary simplicity," a kind of "informed consent" to live in a sustainable society. It takes a special band of cultural intelligence to master the forces of modernization.

The revolution of rising expectations and the tidal wave of wants and demands

Japan is being put to this test. Robert Christopher (1983) provides a timely scorecard on that country's efforts to harmonize forces of modernization with the cultural wisdom of the stable past. He chronicles the firestorm of affluent modernization that erupted in Japan in the post–World War ɪɪ era. By 1981, the number of color televisions in Japan per person was 1.4! Women are entering the paid labor force in unprecedented numbers, and the number of day care centers has followed suit. Young people emphasize individuality and personal privacy more than ever before. Christopher reports on a 1980 poll in which 71% of youth between the ages of fifteen and nineteen said they have "an individual life style," and fewer than 10% indicated a desire to lead "a life useful to society." These results reversed the findings of a similar survey done in 1960. Juvenile crime and drug abuse have risen dramatically in recent years. These changes reflect a general shift in orientation that seems to be a nearly universal response to affluence: "As commitment to work begins to diminish, the emphasis on personal desires increases" (p. 87). The average number of hours Japanese spent on the job dropped from 186 per month in 1970 to 175 per month in 1980 (still at the high end of the scale for modernized societies). Borrowing rather than saving for consumer purchases is becoming the dominant pattern.

Nevertheless, Christopher does not foresee modernization's easy and total victory over traditional Japanese culture.

> Despite the self-absorption of so many young Japanese these days, the great majority of the population finds it almost impossible to conceive that anyone can achieve real stature or success except as part of a group. . . . One of Japan's greatest strengths in its extraordinary evolution from the feudal society that it was at the time of Commodore Perry's arrival to the advanced technological one it is today has been that instead of totally accepting destabilizing and often unsuitable Western ideas and institutions, the Japanese have been remarkably successful in adapting these influences to their own needs and imperatives. (pp. 90, ff.)

However, once released upon the world, modernization is a force so far-reaching and powerful that it stands almost beyond human control. Harlan Cleveland's classic image (1949) was of a "revolution of rising expectations." With that phrase he means to convey that people, once exposed to affluence, get a new vision of material possibilities and potential for enhanced social welfare. Today this concept seems too tame to convey the intensity of this desire. Perhaps a "tidal wave of wants and demands" is nearer the mark. In any case, changed expectations following World War II have made it more difficult to conceal or rationalize the distinction between modernized "haves" and unmodernized "have-nots." How can you keep them down on the farm after they've seen TV? This change places new constraints on the third component of sustainability, namely that society be just.

The just society: spaceship earth or slaveship earth?

Modern industrialized societies are living off their capital—nonrenewable sources of energy, arable land, and drinkable water. Even worse, high-powered societies are living off the *global* capital and encouraging others to do so the same, creating an intolerable situation given the vested interest of current *and future* generations of non-modernized societies. One strategy for sustaining socioeconomic order is to live off the resources of others. But this does not meet the third condition for sustainability: moral legitimacy.

Mere physical survival of the species and maintenance of order are insufficient to make a society sustainable. A sustainable society must also be just. A society may endure, but without an ethical core, it cannot be sustainable. This ethical imperative must permeate our analysis of economic, environmental, and social welfare issues. Some foresee that the most powerful modernized states will continue to endure through exploitation and suppression. In such a worst-case moral scenario, the elites within those societies would maintain an affluent lifestyle by forcing other societies to provide the necessary resources yet forego participation in that life style (with the exception, perhaps, of co-opted managerial elites). Within powerful societies, the elites would extend affluence as widely as would be consistent with maintaining their own privileged positions, relying upon coercion to make up the difference.

One could accurately call such a world "Slaveship Earth" (Paarlberg, 1975), but certainly not a world of sustainable societies. Are the foundations laid for Slaveship Earth? The vast majority of citizens in industrialized societies seem ready to accept rationalizations for their privileged position, and the performance of many local elites in primitive societies argues that Slaveship Earth is a most persuasive metaphor for the future. But it is not the sustainable society, no matter how long it endures. One can foresee it but not accept it, for it has no moral duration, whatever its historical scope. Such a society would exist without sufficiently committing itself to the moral imperative to build and maintain the social welfare systems needed to sustain families.

Slaveship Earth already exists in the day-to-day lives of millions of Earthlings. And it exists in negative utopian literature ("dystopias," as they are sometimes called). Aldous Huxley's *Brave New World* (1948) and George Orwell's *1984* (1948) are the most well known. Harry Harrison's *Make Room, Make Room* (1962), which became the film *Soylent Green*, is perhaps most to the point, however. It portrays the political, economic, ecological, and ethical bankruptcy of a society that endures by cannibalizing the world and its people. In the book, the elite live in opulent enclaves protected by the police; the masses are destitute, often homeless. The countryside is intensively farmed using chemicals and high-tech methods, producing marginal food for the urban masses and luxuries for the elite. With the oceans dead, the marginal elite turn to high-tech cannibalism; human bodies are recycled to become a protein-rich food source called "soylent green." The state encourages suicide as a way to relieve crowding and maintain the food supply. Hardly the sustainable society we would want, but not a gross exaggeration of conditions in some contemporary societies.

Reports from Mexico City tell of pervasive crowding and destitution. Brazil's three largest cities—Sao Paulo, Rio de Janeiro, and Belo Horizonte—have *millions* of abandoned children. Brazil, with a population of 150 million (sixth largest in the world), an affluent minority, and a severely impoverished majority, offers many working models of the society envisioned by Harrison. That viewers could be horrified by the fiction of *Soylent Green* yet oblivious to the facts of life for hundreds of millions around the world argues that Slaveship Earth is a plausible, realistic model for the future. We can't take sustainability for granted; it is not an inevitable result of social evolution.

Various forms of the sustainable society are possible so long as they meet three basic conditions: historical scope, social coherence, and moral legitimacy. Some may last longer than others. Some may have traditional class structures; others may be more egalitarian. Some may be primarily rural, while others will be urban. Some may be richer than others. But all will live long and prosper, to nurture the best humanity has to offer, and to respect the human spirit. All will establish social welfare systems upon a sensible economic and environmental basis. All will sustain the wealth of families.

Do we live in a sustainable society?

Having said all this, we find ourselves facing these questions: Do we North Americans, Europeans, and Japanese live in sustainable societies? Could most societies around the world readily become sustainable? Let's assume that everyone is committed to the long life of the human race, to a coherent social order, and to justice. Many doubt the validity of the benign assumption of these universal good intentions, and for good reason. But for the sake of argument, let's suppose it is true, and that current debates over nuclear power, conservation of natural resources, population, and economic development are debates of means rather than ends. What then?

Then we must look at our society and the world to see whether our situation is indeed sustainable. Those who believe it is propose four arguments: First, the population "problem" is self-correcting. Second, technological innovation eliminates constraints on natural resources by substituting abundant resources for scarcer ones. Third, the cluster of life styles in an urban industrialized society is suitable to human development over the long haul. And fourth, the current situation offers the best long-term prospects for justice. Let's look at each one of these assumptions in detail.

Population: It is commonly argued that rising affluence and a declining birth rate go hand in hand. As societies mature economically, so the analysis goes, family size shrinks. Proponents of this view cite as evidence case studies from around the world—but clustered, of course, in modern industrialized/urbanized societies. This view offers demographic hope rather than despair. It evokes the image of a population computer rather than a population bomb, as people adjust (calculatingly) to the joint phenomena of lowered mortality rates and capital-intensive life styles that make children more costly.

In 1982 the United States Census Bureau projected zero population growth for the United States by the 2050s, with a peak population of 309 million (*New York Times*, 4 November 1982). The population in 2050 would be older (22% age 65 or over versus 11% in 1981), and the ratio of elderly to working-age members would shift from 5.4 to 1 (in 1982) to 2.6 to 1. Such a society could be feasible within limits set by available resources, provided assumptions hold about industrial productivity and accessibility of resources—that is, that the world order regarding who gets to use what remains roughly intact, that potential sources of energy pan out, and that immigration does not grow significantly. In fact, the low national birth rate has led one observer to argue that we have overcorrected ourselves demographically and that we need to *increase* the birth rate among affluent modernized populations.

Looking beyond the United States, analysts who say sustainability is here project that increases in population will level off to *within acceptable limits* through a variety of automatic processes. In the already and soon-to-be affluent nations, Western attitudes toward economics and family size will do the trick. Parents will choose to have fewer children and will act upon that decision effectively because of the availability of reliable contraception. In less affluent countries (whose numbers vary depending on the estimate), the population boom of the post–World War II era will prove to be a relatively short-lived phenomenon. How? Some analysts see an end to the "demographic euphoria" that greeted declining death rates. These death rates had declined due to improved basic health care and an upsurge in the availability of food (because of improved agricultural practice and aid programs). A policy of demographic restraint will take hold and stabilize population within limits set by the planet's ecology, according to this view, and we will avoid overshooting the mark. Thus, our current situation is already sustainable, given the inevitable trends built into the social system. This view has been well publicized in the writings of economist Julius Simon (*The Ultimate Resource*, 1983), the late think-tanker Herman Kahn (*Global 2000 Revisited*, 1983, and *The Coming Boom*, 1982), and Ben Wattenberg (*A Dearth of Children*, 1987).

Technological Innovation: An economic analog to the self-correcting model of demography is the self-sustaining trend of technological innovation. In this view, each economic breakthrough of the past has arisen from new organizing technology, which permitted and even stimulated beneficial economic transformation. Some (e.g., Kondratieff) have gone so far as to plot "long waves" of continued economic development that is directly linked to the interplay of technological innovation and the investment of capital. Hydro-powered machinery, steam engines, railroads, petroleum-based industry—each technological breakthrough created economic reorganization that increased society's wealth. Economic historian Walter Rostow integrates these developments into a coherent picture in *Stages of Economic Development* (1964).

In this view, high tech microelectronics will stimulate the next advance. Just as the burning of coal solved the energy problem in a deforested England in the seventeenth century, so too will new technologies overcome the problem of declining oil reserves in the twenty-first century. This view relies on historical extrapolation and profound confidence in our scientific and engineering ability. The attitude is best expressed in the slogans, "If we did it before we can do it again," and "If we *need* to create a solution we *will*." It's a reworking of the familiar adage: "Necessity is the mother of invention."

Most of these analyses focus on the industrial sector and therefore emphasize the root problem of finding enough energy to fuel the transformation of raw materials into goods. The new energy technologies are typically high-tech, industrialized power generation ranging from nuclear fission to nuclear fusion to the large-scale capturing of solar energy. For nuclear fission, the answer is breeder reactors to generate power and atomic fuel, although few experts now see this as an option beyond the year 2025.

For nuclear fusion the key is to find a way to transform globally abundant hydrogen into usable energy. For solar energy, it is the construction of vast installations on Earth (or in orbit around the Earth) to collect sunshine and transform it into usable energy. Perhaps nuclear fusion has the greatest appeal, as is evidenced by the following public service advertisement from Gulf, under the heading "Gulf People: Energy for Tomorrow." In the ad, Tihiro Ohkawa, vice president for fusion power research at Gulf's General Atomic Company, says:

> Our research programs, sponsored by the Department of Energy and others, could lead to construction of an experimental fusion reactor within a decade. . . . Both fusion and conventional fission reactors produce heat, which can, for instance, generate electricity. But fusion produces less radioactive waste than fission. It can't get out of control. And it uses cheaper fuel—hydrogen instead of uranium. In fact, fusion reactors can make fuel for fission reactors, and possibly will even burn the fission reactor's wastes. . . . It's a tremendous technological challenge, but the reward is tremendous, too: inexhaustible energy.

The modern life style: Modern industrialized/urbanized societies provide successful individuals with an unprecedented wide range of options concerning how and where to live. Indeed, one justification for these societies is that they free people from the constraints of the past and offer mobility in all its senses. Yet, despite their apparent diversity, it is fair to say that these societies, when contrasted with past societies and with nonmodernized, nonindustrialized societies, offer only one life style.

This life style is founded upon a wide range of consumer goods for homemaking (food-related and cleaning appliances), recreation and entertainment (television and water skiing), and travel (automobiles and airplanes). In this life style, capital- and energy-intensive activities are substituted for labor-intensive activities—a vacuum cleaner substitutes for a broom, a video game for a walk in the woods, a snowmobile for a pair of snowshoes. Those who claim our society is a sustainable one argue that this life style can be a permanent feature of human life. Some, like Alvin Toffler, may see humans themselves changing, becoming more adapted to this life style, but in any case they see it as the wave of the future. They see it penetrating more and more societies and becoming the basis for a world culture. What is more, they see a life style dominated by consumer goods as being consistent with basic human needs and thus psychologically sustainable. Its demographic and ecological sustainability rests upon solutions to the population and energy problems outlined above. The "American way" that Alan Potter (1954) described nearly four decades ago as the natural destiny of a "people of plenty" will become common worldwide. This is already evident. One can drink Coca-Cola in China, eat a Big Mac in Brazil, play PacMan in Nigeria, and telephone home direct from Khartoum.

Justice: Those who claim our modern society is sustainable say it meets the criterion of justice. Because they assume population and resource problems are being solved "automatically" by the existing socioeconomic order, they see no threat to future generations. "Use more now, have more later" is a crude rendering of this view of intergenerational justice. As for the justice of the system with respect to the current individuals on Earth, they answer that it is more just now than it was in the past, and more just than the realistically available contemporary alternatives. They also argue that it offers the greatest hope for the future, for the rest of the world as well as for the United States. Current approaches do as much as is humanly possible for as many as is humanly possible—their imperfections are just that, not fundamental flaws.

In sum then, on one side stand those who argue that we already live in a sustainable society, in a world destined to become composed of ever more similarly sustainable societies—if only everyone will keep their faith in the processes of modernization. Tinker if you must, they say. If necessary, fine tune for greater efficiency. But don't meddle with the basic mechanisms, because they are working. We have a sustainable society in the making if we only stay the course.

But do we live in a sustainable society?

But do society and the current world order predict sustainability? The answer to this question appears to come from how we interpret our most recent past. Were the 1970s and 1980s aberrations or a portent of things to come. Those who foresee sustainability see the 1970s as a temporary deviation from the course, one that was corrected in the 1980s and will give way to sustained growth and development in the 1990s. They see the 1970s and the 1990s as a temporary recession rather than a symptom of profound crisis. In the year 2000, they believe, we will look back to see continued progress from World War II toward an affluent, just, and permanent world order, the progress of which was interrupted by only brief setbacks in the 1970s and 1980s. To prove their point, they argue that policymakers responded to danger signs during those two decades as they became evident. DDT and PCBs (two dangerous toxic pollutants), for example, were the target of legislative and executive action in many modernized societies. That attention influenced a 1982 United Nations environmental program to announce that progress had been made in dealing with these pollutants globally, and to conclude that the world's oceans were successfully withstanding contamination from waste dumping and agricultural runoff.

In contrast, those who disagree that we are living in sustainable societies argue that we will regard the 1970s and 1980s as the beginning of a decisive downturn that invalidated old models of investment and development. They conclude that environmental awareness, improvements, and control are important and positive but that they are only the beginning of necessary fundamental shifts in policy and practice. In the long run, they argue, many of the improvements noted so far are not of sufficient magnitude to stabilize human communities. Slowing a runaway truck from sixty to forty miles per hour is almost meaningless if a dead end awaits you 100 yards down the road. There are indeed many grounds for disputing the notion that sustainability is upon us. Let's reexamine more critically those four criteria of a sustainable society.

Population: Official estimates made in the late 1970s by the United

Nations and the World Bank do project that the world's population will stabilize at below ten billion early in the twenty-first century. According to the Environment Fund, the low estimate (based upon reaching replacement level fertility by 2000 to 2005) projected an addition by 2075 of 3.9 billion people to the 1983 figure of 4.6 billion. The high estimate (replacement by 2040 to 2045) was for 8.9 billion by 2151. By 1988, however, global population had already reached 5.1 billion! What is more, some demographers maintain that the connection between affluence and decreased birth rates does not automatically and necessarily hold. In Brazil, for example, the booming economy and dramatically increased per-capita income of the 1960s were accompanied by an equally large population increase and (through the 1970s) actual declines in basic social welfare for 80% of the population.

Are the estimated upper limits for population sufficient reassurance that the population problem is solved? Perhaps not. The estimates project massive population increases in some of the societies least equipped to deal with them in a humane and dignified manner. Already the Indian subcontinent can only marginally meet basic needs for a population of roughly 850 million. What will it be like with 2.3 billion, the estimate of the middle range? The same is true of Central America and Africa. Even China, which has already exceeded the one billion mark, is concerned, although it has an aggressive population control program. With 22% of the world's people on only 7% of the available land, even China—with its high level of governmental commitment and its ability to exert social control—is struggling to stabilize population at a sustainable level.

All this leads Lester Brown (1980) of the Worldwatch Institute to conclude that the population problem is not "solved" simply because under existing trends and policies population will stabilize at about ten billion. Ten billion may be a level at which we can survive, although that is debatable considering the demands such a population, even if most of it lived in poverty, would make on the Earth. But it is hardly sustainable if it means giving up justice and a humane life style. Brown and others argue that a population of ten billion will exact those costs and will not endure for long, because it will require cannibalizing the planet for maintenance, even if technological innovation leads to new economic wealth. Brown argues instead for a goal of six billion, a modest proposal.

> Supporting even six billion people at acceptable consumption levels will not be possible without widespread rationing, more careful management

of biological systems, stringent energy-conservation measures, materials recycling programs, and a more equitable distribution of vital resources both within and among societies. On the other hand, stabilizing world population at six billion will not require any country to do what several countries have not already done. (Brown, 1980, p. 146)

To achieve that goal and to attain a life expectancy of seventy years would require birth and death rates to balance out at about thirteen per thousand. Current death rates range from about six to about fifteen per thousand; birth rates vary from about ten to nearly fifty per thousand.

Is the population problem solved? With the world population already exceeding five billion, certainly not. But, of course, there can be no permanent solution in one sense. Birth and death rates can always vary. There are upper limits on birth rates, set by the physiology of fertility, of course, but they are much too high to be of any practical value. We need birth rates that must eventually work out to about two per woman, although biological limits do not usually begin to operate until we reach a figure that is higher by a factor of five. Active, comprehensive contraception is fundamental to any plan for stabilizing population. Access to contraception is a key feature of the social welfare of the individual family and for the community.

A growth rate of zero is possible, but extremely improbable. Rarely in history have birth rates declined below replacement levels and stayed there. The 1980 rate of 1.8 is historically noteworthy and, of course, doesn't include the effect of immigration. The price of population stability will be eternal vigilance. One aspect of a sustainable society is relative stability in birth and death rates and prompt public response when they get out of line.

The nurturing we provide to families is critical to population control. UNICEF executive director James Grant (1984) reports that health and nutrition services aimed at increasing the odds of survival in the first years of life are a consistently effective way of encouraging individuals to use birth control. *The State of the World's Children 1982–1983* concludes that if we cut the infant and child morality rate in half, we would be able to motivate parents to use birth control; this, in turn, would result in a decrease of between twelve and twenty million births each year. This estimate is based on the fact that family size decreases when parents see lowered risk to each child; when parents see this is true, they are less inclined to produce large numbers of offspring. This is particularly true in societies with few formal social welfare systems.

The impact of migration on sustainability is not yet fully appreciated. The decrease in birth rates in the United States during the 1970s has been studied in depth, but little work has been done on the impact of immigration, most notably from Mexico and Central America, during that same period. Such immigration is hard to monitor and control, and its long-range impact is unknown. With Mexico's population alone predicted to rise from 80 to 205 million by 2000, such immigration may increase dramatically. The projected economic climate in Mexico lends credence to such a prediction. No one seems to know how emigration from Mexico will affect population growth in Mexico, let alone in the United States. In any case, it seems extremely risky to believe the population problem is solved, even when the best of technological and economic conditions prevail. And optimistic forecasts concerning those conditions are themselves suspect.

Technological innovation: While those who believe that sustainability is upon us look to technological innovation as a permanent savior, others are doubtful. Few who have explored "the technology issue" foresee a return to the primitive, low-power technologies that dominated the period before the Industrial Revolution. The genuine progress offered by many technological breakthroughs is hard to deny. Umberto Colombo (1983, personal communication) for example, cites three areas in which technological innovation can help lead the way to a truly sustainable society: biotechnologies that use microorganisms and genetic engineering to reduce energy consumption and pollution; information-processing technology that facilitates decentralization and greater equity between urban and rural areas; and new materials that increase the life and utility of goods requiring fewer nonrenewable materials to produce. But the law of entropy warns against techniques that promise something for nothing. We must look at the *net* energy produced by high-tech power plants, which require massive investments of resources before they break even, and exact great maintenance and waste disposal costs after they become operational (and sometimes even after they are defunct).

Some observers have examined efforts to create an atomic breeder reactor which would generate its own plutonium to fuel fission and thus produce commercially usable energy. Billions of dollars have been invested over three decades in what some call "the dream machine," and the net result is a dead end. Even the more sensible photovoltaic cell, which transforms sunlight into electricity, must face up to the limits imposed by entropy upon its production and use. There is no perpetual motion machine, no formula for creating gold from lead. There is no free lunch. No technology will free us from the reality of limits.

Beyond the problem of entropy stands the proposition that we face a law of diminishing returns. According to Orio Giarini, the massive needs of a population numbering in the billions ensures that the costs of *any* new technology for mass use will be so large that they are probably prohibitive (Orio Giarini, p.146).

Giarini argues that the economy becomes unstable when scarcity arises because technological innovation cannot generate accelerated surplus production. In short, an investment in technology creates a crisis of diminishing returns. Giarini sees the mid-1970s as the time when the diminishing returns of technology began in earnest. Why? It is partly because new technologies are based in sophisticated science, which means it takes longer to move from idea to implementation. Fusion seems to be the worst case thus far. Just as we were told for years that policymakers could see "the light at the end of the tunnel" in the Vietnam War, so now are we told that fusion will deliver "inexhaustible energy for tomorrow" (Ohkawa, 1981). But that "tomorrow" seems always to be receding into the future, and meanwhile each today brings another cost in the form of toxic waste, fears of increased pollution, and recognition of environmental limits.

The long lead times required for technological research do not fit well with the supply–demand equilibrium of the economic process. Technological change has its own cycles, and tends to produce more waste and require more capital allocation. And sophisticated technology tends to make systems more vulnerable to human limits. This is evident in military equipment. High-tech weapons are often beyond the capacity of soldiers to operate and maintain effectively. Giarini argues that the only technological innovation not yet experiencing diminishing returns is the computer microprocessor (although others might add bioengineering). This may be one of our few aces in the hole in redirecting society towards sustainability—a bargaining chip in negotiating a way to avert disaster.

The law of diminishing returns seems to have reared its ugly head in the 1970s. The catalog is extensive: per-capita food production peaked. Most industrial applications of post–World War II technology were in place, and yet they have not delivered quick, dramatic payoffs for the masses. In the case of energy, utilities *cannot* make an adequate profit by investing in new generating plants, only by investing in conservation and efficiency. As noted before, one reviewer called Herman

Kahn's prediction of an economic boom and technological Eden "prayerful economics," in the sense that it hopes for a miracle that will transcend the normal workings of the world. All in all, the most hard-nosed, practical analyses available suggest assumptions by the "sustainability is upon us" school regarding technology are untenable.

The modern life style: Is the modern life style sustainable? Those who think it is rest their case upon two assumptions: first, that a material basis exists for consumer-oriented affluence to become the standard way of life for everyone; and, second, that consumer-oriented affluence rests upon a sound psychological foundation.

Can the modern life style continue to serve as the dominant motif for the entire world? The answer presents a dilemma of sorts, for it appears that efforts to spread the North American way of life throughout the world eventually undermines its viability in North America. Our success in Westernizing Japan, Brazil, and other societies seems to be one of the factors that depressed American industry in the 1980s. The consumer-oriented modern life style is one which truly "lives off the fat of the land." Not everyone can live this way. This kind of living requires a favorable balance of trade between the affluent and the nonaffluent, the haves and the have-nots. Our country's solution is another country's problem. The same is true *within* societies as well.

The United States is the most successful modernized nation in the world in many respects, and yet in 1986 some 25% of its children lived below the poverty line. In the 1980s, poverty grew, especially among children and single mothers. The various "economic miracles" in Latin American countries, such as Chile and Brazil, tell similar though even more dramatic stories; not 25% but 75% of the children in these countries are likely to experience real poverty amidst an outburst of what seems to be affluence. The Asian miracles (Singapore, Taiwan, South Korea) are beginning to show the same weaknesses. As the good times of the 1960s came to an end, the 1970s saw an outbreak of economic deprivation. Worldwide unemployment reached 30%, and in the United States it rose above 10%. In the 1980s basic resources and long-term planning were sacrificed to short-term greed and borrowing. The result was a short-lived boom, from which the already rich profited disproportionally, and which led to a crash in 1990s. The "normal" unemployment rate in the United States, which once was considered to be 4.5%, increased to 6% in 1990, and there is every indication that it will continue to climb, as it has done already in many modernized countries and in most Third World countries. European countries also saw ever higher "normal" levels of unemployment in the 1980s: 13% in Belgium, 11% in Britain, 9% in France, 10% in Italy, and 15% in Turkey.

By the time they reach the age of thirty-five, more and more workers will face the prospect of being unemployed for the rest of their lives, or at the age of eighteen of never holding a "real job" at all. Monetarization means that more and more families experience "modern poverty," defined as the inadequacy of cash income to meet cash expenses. If they were less tied to the cash economy, these families would not experience "classical poverty," as defined by Giarini as the inadequacy of total income to meet basic needs (Giarini, 1981). When things which were once "free" are given a cash price, those who used to be able to pay for them with their labor are then unable to obtain them because they can't pay for them with cash. This critical dynamic profoundly affects the wealth of families. Indeed, this is increasingly evident in the United States as more and more families find themselves unable to "afford" child care—because what once was outside the monetarized economy is now rapidly becoming part of it.

Families suffer casualties in the economic wars that are part of monetarizing and modernizing a society. Chronic economic deprivation results in a rise in family violence and neglect; episodes of acute deprivation precipitate still further increases in assault. Even periods of dramatic economic change typically viewed as positive (e.g., the energy boom towns of the American West) produce increases in child abuse. Families require a *stable and supportive economic climate*. Economies that jeopardize this climate jeopardize their own sustainability.

As Giarini states (1981), total welfare equals the value of the non-monetarized economy plus the value of the monetarized economy. When monetarized value increases without producing an equal or larger decrease in nonmonetary value, total welfare improves. When increases in monetary value produce offsetting decreases in nonmonetary value, total welfare remains unchanged. When costs to nonmonetary value exceed gains in monetary value, total welfare declines. This equation sets the parameters for the macroeconomy of the society and the microeconomy of the family. It finds its expression in the actual wealth of families. It defines the terms for debate about the relation of economic and social welfare systems. The modern life style seems best suited to single people and childless couples, who can run the rat race unimpeded by the day-to-day needs of children. First and foremost, children cost time and personal investment. It's the time spent listening to, talking with, caring for, playing with, and responding to children that produces good child development and family well-being. All this means little or nothing in immediate monetary payoffs. It's all too easy to borrow against this necessary but nonmonetary investment if doing so will allow a parent to earn more cash income.

It seems that the continued existence of the modern affluent life style presupposes a predatory relationship with the rest of the world and with future generations. This is true within families and in the society as a whole. The process of consuming and degrading resources to provide the material underpinnings of that life style often produces offsetting or even larger costs to those features of life outside the cash economy, most notably the intimacies of family and community. Were this life style confined to a small elite, the damage might be manageable. But widespread affluence suggests a cannibalizing of the Earth's resources needed to feed the consumer's habit, with a corresponding degradation of social life. We have already witnessed this in North America. There is reason to believe that "total welfare" of Giarini's equation may be on the way down.

In modern societies the marginal participants often use the least ecologically viable products. They rely heavily on petroplastics—cheap, nonrepairable products with a very short life and inefficient energy consumption. The high-class modern materialist is more likely to use products made from wood, glass, and gold than from materials that are more durable and efficient. Perhaps the most damning indictment of the modern life style is that only the richest can meet their desires for quantity in ways that are qualitatively sound.

Beyond the modern life style's material sustainability is the issue of its psychological sustainability. Modern affluence seems profoundly unfulfilling to many people. Particularly among marginal participants, life seems frustrating and unsatisfying. One suspects that you can fool some of the people all of the time and all of the people some of the time. But one worries (or is it hopes?) that many people realize they have been fooled when cheap affluence breaks down. Having been fooled, they are resentful. The expectations created by merchandising are very high: people take for granted what they once thought of as luxuries. If not grounded in economic reality, high expectations are socially and psychically dangerous. Observers report growing numbers of homicides because of disputes arising from minor conflicts. Senseless violence is a problem in boom towns where expectations are grossly high and in bust towns where previously high expectations have set people up for severe disappointment. Much of this turmoil derives from frustrated expectations and the stress that comes with it. Material-ism literally drives people crazy, and both the social and physical envi-ronments pay the price.

Justice: Certainly most premodern or unmodernized societies were and are unjust; justice is not the sole province of traditional societies. But does modernization bring justice? Is the current world order just? Modernization offers the *prospect* of justice, the prospect of replacing exploitive relationships with more humane ones. The wealth of the modern economy makes possible extensive formal social welfare sys-tems. Professional human services—in the form of teachers, day care providers, nurses, psychologists, and social workers—can be provided. Yet modern society can become an engine of social injustice if it devel-ops a standard of living that is too materialistic. In such a case, the indi-gent are likely to become worse off as the gap widens between them and the rest of society. In such a climate a growing perception arises that "society" (meaning affluent taxpayers) cannot afford to support so-cial welfare systems. This is painfully ironic, of course: the incredible wealth of North America belies the claim that basic social welfare sys-tems are beyond its means.

As daily life moves more and more within the constraints of a cash economy, marginal elements fall into an ever more degraded position. One sure sign of this is when elite groups retreat to enclaves of afflu-ence and rely upon security forces to protect them. We see this in both the West and the East. With the fall of communism in the former Soviet Union we see the "victory" of American-styled democracy and capital-ism, which pretends to offer equal opportunity to all, but which, in fact, is closed to those without money. In the United States there are exclusive schools, neighborhoods, tax policies, shops, and clubs that are open only to the monied classes. This was also true of the Soviet Union before its disintegration, and it will no doubt continue under de-mocracy. Both countries have stood Marie Antoinette on her head. They no longer say, "Both the rich and the poor are prohibited from sleeping under the bridges of Paris." We now say, "All are free to cross the bridge, so long as they can pay the toll."

Internationally, the justice of the modern order is suspect. Each affluent member of the modern world consumes many times the re-sources of a counterpart in the "other" world. This is not simply because some nations are better endowed with natural resources; it re-flects a policy of exploitation in which Third World elites are bought off by affluent societies. The problem is magnified in countries such as Brazil, which has an historical tradition of economic and political oligarchy. The trend in Brazil and elsewhere has led to the creation of two societies—one rich, one poor—within one nation. In the case of Brazil, we might best illustrate this situation by imagining a country such as Belgium existing within India—although using current population figures, we might do better to speak of a prosperous Canada (with a population of 26 million) existing within a desperately impoverished Bangladesh (115 million).

Justice is at a premium in the current world order. Military forces in Third World countries have doubled in the past twenty years, exceeding 20 million—almost two-thirds of the world's armed forces. Nearly half of these 113 nations are under military rule, and most routinely engage in extreme repression, including torture. More than 10 million people have died in wars since 1960. Annual world expenditures average $20,000 per soldier and $400 per school-age child. Infant mortality in some war zones (such as Afghanistan) is as much as 30 times that of modernized societies; this rate is much higher than that of poor neighboring societies at peace. By the end of the Cold War, the United States and the Soviet Union together had spent an estimated $250 billion on their military establishments. The five major possessors of nuclear devices jointly hold about 40,000 tactical and 20,000 strategic weapons. We can hope for a reduction in these numbers in the wake of the U.S.–Soviet détente, but the rise of new nuclear forces in other countries keeps the danger level high. Injustice is not new to the modern era, of course. But the struggle between self-interested competing forces and between forces of justice and injustice has never been so destructive to human life.

Are we living in a sustainable society? We are not

The population problem remains unsolved, because the point at which it would most likely level off would place too much stress on global resources. The prospect of unlimited technological innovation and economic growth is unreliable in the long run (if not the short run). The modern way of life is a material aberration; it cannot be generalized to the family of humanity across the world and through the decades. It works against the psychic needs of parents and children. And it is spiritually and psychologically risky. What is more, the current order is unjust, both within and across societies; it undermines essential social welfare systems. We do not live in a sustainable society.

What can we do to become one? First, we must suspend our belief that it is at hand. Terrible as it is to look global disaster in the face, we must not shy away. To avert our eyes now would be to deny the best of the human tradition and to surrender to what has now come clearly into focus as real danger. Ignoring this situation would lead to an ever more serious erosion of the economic and environmental foundations of social welfare systems and the wealth of families. Deathship Earth? Slaveship Earth? Spaceship Earth? Which will it be for the family of humanity, for our children, and for their brothers and sisters around the world, for those not yet born? To understand this we must understand how human families themselves operate in the human scheme of things.

THREE

The Family Lifeboat

July 1, 1983. Rio de Janeiro, Brazil. About twenty million abandoned children and youth live in Brazil, which has a total population of some 130 million. I had my first encounter with some of these kids within hours of my arrival at Rio de Janeiro. After settling in at the hotel, my companions and I set out to test the surf.

At Ipanema Beach, a group of boys who appeared to range in age from eleven to fifteen swooped down on our towels and clothes, surprising our two volunteer guards and running off with our money and valuables. We were lucky and learned our lesson cheaply; there was little there to be taken. We doubled our guard and successfully defended our property for the rest of our time there.

As we were leaving the beach, we saw again what many Brazilians call the "informal income redistribution" system. A youth ran by, fleeing from a man who shouted, "Ladron!" ("Thief!") as he pursued the boy. In an apparent ritual of negotiation, the young thief first dropped the man's ID, then his credit cards. The victim slowed, then stopped to retrieve these critical pieces of his stolen property. The bargaining completed, the thief ran off unmolested, as if to say, "I have the money and the wallet; you have the rest. Fair enough?" It almost seemed so—an informally negotiated truce between one of Brazil's haves and one of its have-nots.

Millions of Brazilian children and youth are abandoned to the streets be-

cause of family breakdown. Why else do parents give up their children? The magnitude of the problem reflects the level of social and economic stress. It recalls descriptions of the civil war that wracked the Soviet Union in the 1920s, when some nine million children and youth were left without families. Economic war destroys families now as the shooting war did then. When families dissolve, it signals a profound crisis, a breakdown in fundamental social welfare systems. Do the things I see in Brazil portend the future? With three million new Brazilians added to the population each year, the answer is critical to the family of man and to the wealth of families.

What is a family?

What is a family? Families are the thread that holds the human race together (Garbarino and Associates, 1992). Through our families we are connected to the past—the distant times and places of our ancestors—and to the future, the hope of our children's children. Although family life exacts psychological costs, families are the bedrock of human social life, a potent force for social stability and meaning. They are neither the reactionary and oppressive trap that some radicals see nor the bastions of sweetness and light that some ultraconservatives see. But they *are* our best hope in our struggle to achieve a sustainable society and guarantee the existence of social welfare systems. The challenge is to equitably balance power in families that oppress women and children, and to enhance the power of family relationships in order to teach empathy, sympathy, and ecology. Thus we may create the ethical and psychological foundations for social welfare systems in a sustainable society.

Who is not moved by the excitement of discovering one's ancestors? Who is not enriched by uncovering connections of kinship? My wife searched through old and faded archives in a small Scottish parish church and tracked down the rector, who suggested that she search among the gravestones for a relative who had been dead some two hundred years. The search was rewarded. The moment was magnificent. Equally so was the expression on her paternal grandmother's face when she saw pictures of the gravestone and of the parish records. This feeling of wholeness and connection with the past through our families is central to the human experience, and it can inspire us to build the institutions and to nurture the values we need for a sustainable society. It should guide our social welfare systems as well.

When we see a young child struggling to master a skill we now possess, we realize what enormous growth takes place in the everyday lives of our fellow human beings. Parents share the infant's unbounded glee of accomplishment. Ah, to be able to turn over! To sit unaided! To stand unassisted! And, miracle of miracles, to walk! To talk! We all can appreciate these wonders, but the special bond between parent and child goes further. To be a parent is to have a special, "irrational" feeling of responsibility for a special being. Leo Tolstoy captured these emotions in his epic *War and Peace*:

> The universal experience of the ages, showing that children grow from the cradle to manhood, did not exist for the Countess. The growth of her son had been for her at every stage as extraordinary as though millions and millions of men had not already developed in the same way. Just as twenty years before it had seemed unbelievable that the little creature lying under her heart would ever cry, nurse at the breast, or talk, so now she could not believe that this same little creature could be that strange brave officer, that paragon of sons and men, which, judging by his letter he now has. (pp. 291-292)

Definitions of family

Sociologists and anthropologists have long searched for an all- purpose, universal definition of "family"—one that would apply to all cultures and communities across time and space. In North America, recent social changes legitimizing new family forms are pushing traditional definitions to their limits and beyond. New actors have joined the efforts to define the family, as city planners, politicians, judges, legislators, the clergy, and others are asked to legitimize some relationships and not others. Three common themes are clear in most definitions. Family implies a household founded in marriage, child rearing, and kinship. Within the family, adults contract with each other to assume economic and social responsibility for each other and for children and to become part of a larger network of kinship. As much as we should be responsive to changes in family forms, we also need to retain a profound respect for the accomplishment of creating and sustaining a family. Political scientist Jean Bethke Elshtain captured this feeling when she wrote:

To throw the honorable mantle "family" over every ad hoc collection of persons who happen to be under one roof at the same time is to diminish the genuine achievements of family men and women who have retained their commitments to and for another. (1983, p. 25)

Like the concept of "sustainable society," "family" is something with such moral force and profound significance that when we apply the term to human arrangements we must do so with an appreciation for its far-reaching implications.

The poet Robert Frost spoke of the emotional significance of the family as home for the heart in "The Death of the Hired Hand":

> Home is the place where
> When you have to go there
> They have to take you in.

Anthropologist Margaret Mead spoke eloquently about family being our personal connection with history:

As in our bodies we share our humanity, so also through the family we have a common heritage . . . the task of each family is also the task of humanity. This is to cherish the living, remember those who have gone before, and prepare for those who are not yet born. (1965, p. 11)

Can we classify as families social relationships that don't stretch across generations? This is a troublesome point. Speaking of her work with the religiously oriented "Commission on Today's Families," Elizabeth Dodson-Gray (personal communication) notes that the group agreed on a definition of family as "a household joined by ties of blood or commitment." This resonates with the standard dictionary definition of family, which derives from the Latin familia—a household's members—and thus encompasses fellowship as well as kinship. Can homosexual couples form families? Surely, if they assume responsibility across generations by raising (if not necessarily bearing) children. Is a couple whose children have grown up and left the nest still a family? Yes, but it is through their connection to their children that they are one.

Who may say that someone else's relationships do not constitute a family? The answer must lie in the historical meaning of the word. Formats do change for accomplishing the basic business of forming households that create and nurture human life. But it is inappropriate to apply the label of family to any socially desirable relationship just because the label has positive connotations and conveys legitimacy. If everything is family, then nothing is family. This is particularly true because family alone does not constitute an adequate social environment. Other powerful relationships, such as friendships, are important as well. This becomes apparent as we consider the costs as well as the benefits of family.

The family is not all sweetness and light. The very intensity of family life means that breakdown within a family is likely to have a devastating impact on the development and psychological well- being of its members. This dark side of family life includes physical, emotional, and sexual abuse of children and of wives. Wife abuse, in particular, testifies to the costs of male domination (patriarchy) to families. Likewise, sexual abuse of children reveals the danger of masculine imperiousness and aggressiveness. Of course men, too, may be oppressed by the family. But when women and children are oppressed within a family, it is more likely the result of a culture that places them under male domination. And even a nice master can be oppressive. But for all its potential and actual oppression of individual members, the family remains a central facet of human experience and one of its greatest sources of meaning and value.

Families are life, and no program of social engineering will alter that. Even in the sustainable society there will be sibling rivalry, blocked relations between parent and child, conflicts between grandparents and parents over child rearing, and marital conflict. Loved ones will grow old and become sick. However, in a sustainable society, in an ecologically sane social order, we will be able to concentrate more on harmonizing family relations, on equalizing masculine and feminine power, and on directly facing basic issues of human quality, because we will not be sidetracked by the host of fundamentally irrelevant material dilemmas we deal with today. What is more, other relationships important to us will improve, complementing and augmenting families as social support systems.

Whatever definition of family we use, we need to recognize that kinship is the foundation of the family. Individuals are born into the "family of origin" and eventually may start a family of their own (the "family of procreation"). Wherever individuals may go with their lives, their actions reverberate through kinship directly. Thus, for example, whether one's parents will ever become grandparents and one's brothers and sister's become uncles and aunts, depends upon one's own childbearing—particularly in the smaller families of today. In China, under the One Child Policy, the roles of cousin, aunt, and uncle may be eclipsed in the next generation if the policy is fully implemented.

Because they embrace their families and the idea of procreation, most people spend the majority of their lives in family units and virtually all of their lives as part of an active kinship system of some sort. We rely upon families for identity, relatedness, intimacy, and growth—our most profoundly human qualities. They are the root of social welfare, and through them we share most directly in the miracles and tragedies of human experience. Even adults who are not parents themselves can play an important role in the families of which they are affiliate members, as aunts, uncles, godparents, and the like. In addition, they can support public policies and institutions that aid parents; single adults can also support these policies, recognizing that a pro-family stance is a good investment in creating and maintaining a valuable society.

Robert Frost's conception of home and Margaret Mead's idea of family are particularly relevant to North America, where traditional models of the family have deviated more and more from the realities of day-to-day life. In the United States, for example, most people traditionally define the ideal, "normal" family as consisting of a man and woman in their first marriage, who have dependent children in a household in which the man works outside the home for income while the woman manages the household and provides child care. Yet more than one-fifth of American children live in single-parent households; ninety percent of the time, that one parent is the mother. About half of all American children will spend a portion of their first eighteen years in such households or in families created by a second marriage. Thus, many adolescents have one or more stepparents. Also, one-fifth of couples forming households elect not to have children at all. And finally, more than 60% of all mothers of dependent children are employed outside the home, many full time. When all these family arrangements are put together, it becomes clear that families conforming to the traditional model are a very small minority, perhaps only 15%. The processes of modernization have displaced the traditional family—which, indeed, was never so predominant as myth would have it.

A continuum of families

The modern family is usually small—perhaps only a mother and her child. Such a small family is obviously at one end of the continuum, but, nevertheless, we need to recognize it as a family. Near the other end of the continuum stands the extended family, a composite of inter-generational relationships, including children, parents, grandparents and other relatives. Beyond that stands the clan, a confederation of re-lated families. Modernization has brought about a movement away from the clan and towards the small "nuclear" family—perhaps best called the "atomic" family or the "elemental" family, because it is the smallest unit of family possible. Modernization has also meant the growing importance of family surrogates, adults not part of a bona fide family, who want the close support a family can offer. These individu-als form attachments to families with a warmth and sense of commit-ment that is familylike. We need those connections to encourage, sup-port, and guide us. Such relationships are primary support systems, and when they are impaired we call upon social welfare systems to compensate.

With families assuming such a central position, it is little wonder that the health and welfare of the family is always a topic of discussion, a matter for concern, and an issue for debate, particularly in times when family forms and functions are changing. Social historian Colin Greer (1976) points out five common ways of viewing the condition of "The American Family":

- "The family is decaying." In this view, the traditional family is falling apart, and the security of the national community is in jeopardy as a result.
- "The family is evolving." Adherents of this view say the family, like any institution, must keep up with the times to do its job.
- "The family is not changing much at all." In this view, all the anxiety is misplaced—what is called the crisis of the family is simply a version of common intergenerational conflict.
- "There are changes in the family, but there is no need to worry about them." In this point of view, the institutional structure of society is always changing, and family changes simply reflect that.
- "The family is in retreat, defending itself against the power of the human-potential movement." From this perspective, the family is the oppressive agent of an oppressive social system that is be-ing beaten back by the positive, progressive forces freed in a postindustrial society undergoing liberation.

Obviously, family forms have changed and are still changing. Yet the essentials of a healthy, strong family remain stable and relevant to the

needs of a sustainable society—commitment, caring for the generations, creating a safe environment for children, and nurturing. Research
by Nick Stinnett and his colleagues (1979) offers a good picture of the
characteristics of families that are well equipped to meet the challenges
of the modern world. Stinnett found six elements common to strong
families:

- *Appreciation*: The members regard each other warmly, positively, and give support to each other as individuals.
- *Spending time together*: Strong families spend time together and
  enjoy it.
- *Good communication patterns*: Family members are honest, open,
  and receptive towards each other.
- *Commitment*: The family unit is important to its members, as are
  the interpersonal subsystems within the family. The family is the
  principal focus of its members' activities.
- *High degree of religious orientation*: Strong families are anchored
  by a sense of purpose that is often religious. A spiritual approach
  toward life gives family members a common belief and promotes
  family values.
- *Ability to deal with crises in a positive manner*: Strong families are
  able to deal with conflicts and band together in mutual support
  when bad times arise.

Other studies have added qualities to those mentioned above, such
as an openness to the outside world, a positive orientation toward affiliation, a fairness in allocating tasks, a feeling of esteem, and authority to
both females and males within the family. A well- functioning family
should open doors to the world, not stifle its members' development.
Most strong families excel in providing nurturance and constructive
feedback to female and male, adult and child members. This emphasis
on nurturance and feedback directs our attention to families as informal social welfare systems.

The nature of social support

Many terms exist to describe the people in one's life who provide the
meat and potatoes of social existence—whose presence, concern, and
feedback are a valued part of day-to-day life. Some researchers speak of

a range of interpersonal exchanges that provide an individual with information, emotional reassurance, physical and material assistance, and a sense of the self as an object of concern. Others just speak of "caring." The social institutions and networks of relationships that provide these critical psychological elements form the social fabric of the family and ultimately, the community. Maintaining their vitality is one of the major issues during times of social change.

The social fabric of families is determined in large part by social support systems, the sets of interconnected relationships among a group that provide its members with enduring patterns of nurturance and feedback in their efforts to cope with day-to-day life. Gerald Caplan (1974), a pioneer in outlining the importance of social support systems to mental health, defines these systems as enduring relationships that provide a sense of belonging, caring, concern, feedback, identity, and self-worth. These support systems may compensate for the impersonal character of other more formal relationships. As Caplan puts it:

> People have a variety of specific needs that demand satisfaction through enduring interpersonal relationships, such as for love and affection, for intimacy that provides the freedom to express feelings easily and unselfconsciously, for validation of personal identity and worth, for satisfaction of nurturance and dependency, for help with tasks, and for support in handling emotion and controlling impulses. (1974, pp. 5-6)

Of course, the family is our first support system, usually foremost among all others. But the family in and of itself is not enough. We need relationships outside the family. We need friends, neighbors, and colleagues. The quality of social support actively available from individuals and their families is a good indication of the human quality of the social environment. A high-quality environment enhances social competence, which we need to encourage if we are to meet the challenges of creating a sustainable society.

Mastering social competency is the joint product of personal and social resources. The help available to individuals consists both of the competence they bring to a situation themselves and the resources available to them in the social environment. Families are central to both. An effective family teaches personal competence and offers access to social resources. It is an entryway to the world.

Social support is the major currency of value in the environment; families are the chief bankers in this psychological economy. And if social support is the currency, then children are the principal "commodity," that which is of intrinsic value. Yet we know that male domination of society and its institutions leads to a devaluing of children, because children are "women's work." The patriarchal society values what men do more than what women do, and the crucial function of nurturing children suffers as a result.

Bringing men into the business of nurturing children is one way to create a more family-oriented ethic, which can then support the kind of thinking, feeling, and action needed for making the transition to a sustainable society. As Elizabeth Dodson-Gray (1982) argues persuasively in *Patriarchy as a Conceptual Trap*, until women and their work have the same status as men and theirs, social quality will take a back seat to aggressive material expansion. By putting families first, we can put *quality* of human relationships in its proper position of importance. We need to end masculine domination both in the family and in society, so that we can create a cultural climate in which the sustainable society can exist.

The fate of the family and the fate of the earth

The kind of nurturing we received at the hands of our caregivers determines the kind of care we offer, and how we nurture the world reflects how we ourselves were nurtured. Families provide the motivation for the extremely demanding role of caregiver, be it for the child or the feeble elderly. Commenting upon the realities of trying to substitute paid care for family care, a Soviet psychologist observed, "You can't pay a woman for what a mother will do for free." Of course it's not for free, and it's not just mothers. Families are bound up in an intense psychological banking system. Love and attention are invested in the hope of a large return in satisfaction, regard, and caring. All in all, the family is a blue chip psychological investment.

Family also provides the individual with a way to deal with historical time. Donella Meadows has concluded that most of us tend to look no more than seventy years into the future, the expected life span of our children. This seventy-year period is directly implicated in the world problematique and in the search for paths to a sustainable society. It forms the numerator in the equation used to compute the time it takes an environmental process to double in terms of resources and population: doubling time = 70/annual growth rate.

Family history and family future are good benchmarks to use in conveying society's memories and projections for itself, and they provide a good opening for a discussion on the sustainable society. If people are persuaded to debate the future in concrete terms of what life will be like for *their* children and *their* grandchildren, they may be able to overcome some of the narrow, limited thinking that holds us back from making the transition to a sustainable society. To do so, however, people must see that the fate of their children is bound up with the fate of other people's children at home and abroad. We must begin to create future social welfare systems for the children to come, our own and the others who will populate their world.

Population studies give us a sense of general family trends and allow us to speculate about their reasons. However, although history is usually studied on a social level, life is lived by individuals, and they are the real subjects of our attempts to understand the changing face of society. Rosa Luxemburg, the European Socialist of the early twentieth century said: "It is in the tiny domestic struggles of individual people, as they grope toward self-realization, that we can most truly discern the great movements of society." Sociologist C. Wright Mills (1963) echoed this theme when he spoke of history as biography. The real trick is to show people how their family's fate (what Mills called "personal troubles") is connected to the fate of the Earth (what Mills would call "public issues"). If we can forge this link between personal and public concerns, we will be able to harness the motivating power of the family in transforming Spaceship Earth.

Modernization and families

Modernization is contemporary historical transformation. How has it affected families? In what ways has modernization "happened to" families, and in what ways have families created it? Some say that the institution of family has only *reacted* to social change in this century and that it has been the passive victim of modernization. This theme has dominated social analysis in this century. Sociologist W.F. Ogburn (1922) concludes that the nuclear family is inappropriate to an urban industrial society and that it can only be unstable in it. Many have echoed that theme in the seven decades following his pronouncement. The problem Ogburn sees is the loss of family functions. On farms and in small businesses that once dominated the economic landscape, family members could work together—albeit in ways that were often as hard on the back as they were on the spirit. Modern technology promised to relieve us of that kind of work and to liberate women from the oppression of traditional family life. But modernization goes beyond that; it has stripped the family of its many productive and educational responsibilities. In this way families have become solely emotional and developmental centers rather than economically productive entities. As critic Ivan Illich and others have shown, women especially are limited by the modern nuclear family, because it provides them with the worst of two worlds: neither personal outlet nor opportunity to contribute to the family's material needs. One promise of the sustainable society is to restore to the family many functions, which can be performed in an energy-efficient, labor-intensive, and just manner and in a way that teaches children, encourages purposeful interaction between parents and children, and enhances the status of women. All this is possible if the transition to a sustainable society occurs in concert with an end to patriarchy. A patriarchal but sustainable society would put women back into their old homemaker roles and would thus be unacceptable to most modern women.

The American nuclear family, like the energy-intensive modern economy itself, may have reached its zenith in the 1950s. Families in earlier generations were frequently broken up by death and in later decades by divorce. Family sociologists like Andrew Cherlin (1981) point out that the 1950s were an oasis of stability. The potential economic payoffs of modern society blossomed, and many families did likewise: more people married—earlier and more permanently—and they had more children and lived more often in nuclear families than did people before or after that time. Cheap energy, new productive technology, and receptive world markets all gave rise to a Golden Age for the modern family. This history has made it all the more difficult to accept the reality of the Dark Ages envisioned in the world problematique. After having apparently solved fundamental material problems of the human condition, it seems all the more difficult to accept the need to wrestle with the prospect of profound scarcity and a "worthless state of existence." What is more, feminist gains of the last thirty years make many women rightfully suspicious of proposals that may appear as reactionary calls for a return to traditional family forms and household responsibilities. The status of women has improved markedly since the publication of Betty Friedan's *The Feminine Mystique* (1968), and many women worry that "the ecological sustainable life style" may be a code phrase for "The Total Woman"—that women may again find themselves barefoot and pregnant.

Theories that women and men are "naturally" locked into different and mutually exclusive roles are both simplistic and inaccurate. Many in the 1950s and 1960s correctly criticized as unjust family structures in which wives were confined to rigid roles and denied opportunities while husbands had only to bring home a paycheck.

Roles within marriage have begun to change, a process which sociologist Jessie Bernard (1981) characterizes as "the fall of the male good provider." In the monetarized market economy, men were judged on the basis of their ability to provide financially for their families. Emotional and domestic responsibilities were secondary. Cooperation between men and women in providing for their families was lost. Men and women were separate, but were they equal? Not quite. Each was in opposition to the other, unable to share in common tasks or concerns.

Even more "modern" families were thoroughly patriarchal, with men controlling the action and women forced into a defensive posture; choices often seemed limited to passive aggression or to withdrawal from the relationship. Bernard conveyed the hostility and resentment some felt in regards to this when she wrote: "As the pampered wife in an affluent household came often to be an economic parasite, so also the good provider was often, in a way, a kind of emotional parasite" (Bernard, 1981, p. 10).

The male's role as provider flourished as women were relegated exclusively to the home. Women have always been primarily responsible for child rearing, but only in the nineteenth and twentieth centuries has it become a full-time job which virtually excludes other economically valuable activities. Among conventional economic models, the role of homemaker only makes sense when there are many children to care for. On the other hand, the role of provider of goods only makes sense in a family in which women are totally dependent economically. Modern observers such as Bernard foresee this role diminishing as the frequency increases with which women join the labor force and raise children. As noted earlier, by 1984 more than 60% of all mothers of children under the age of eighteen were employed outside the home; by the year 2000 it could be 90%. However, a sustainable society may require fewer wage earners *outside* the household and more workers to perform tasks carried out *inside* the household. No wonder psychologists Urie Bronfenbrenner and Ann Crouter (1981) have identified the relationship between work and family as *the* human development issue of the coming years.

Family of choice

We must recognize two social innovations linked to modernization that have deeply affected the modern family: the rise in the material standard of living and the availability of birth control. The increased wealth available to the general public in modern society has tended to free the nuclear family from dependence on others—kin, neighbors, and friends. Early in this century one in three New England families had a boarder in the home. Modern affluence has decreased the financial need for such arrangements for both boarder and host. As the economy expands, there is more mobility, both within and between families. Young adults are able to move away from their parents. Adults can provide food, child care, and recreation through cash purchases rather than through social exchanges. And the elderly are more likely to be able to support themselves through purchased services rather than through goodwill and the help of their grown children. Affluence tends to increase physical and emotional distance in families and between families and their social networks. The question is, will that distance be perceived as freedom or as isolation? If isolation, the cost of this freedom is likely to be impaired mental health, for we human beings are social animals, and in isolation from our peers we often languish.

Advances in contraception have made childbearing less the destiny and more the choice of women. Child *rearing* is another matter. A woman may choose whether to bear children, but most women have little choice when it comes to rearing them. Highly publicized exceptions aside, society decrees that child care, particularly in the early years, is a feminine occupation—whether at home or in day care. Thus for most women, most of the time, the choice is limited to whether to have children. Once that decision is made, it is usually women who assume primary care for the child. Some see this as a tradition that has grown out of the different biological predispositions of males and females, while others see it as mainly the result of historical factors that have become obsolete—or at least would become so if women were liberated from patriarchal family relations.

Choice exists within a particular social context. The movement to-wards greater choice for women demands that men increase their par-ticipation in "women's work." This seems the only way to increase the range of choices available to women without stacking the deck against families, particularly against children. If men stick only to "men's work," the result will be frustrated and angry women, who will see families as oppressive (and thus opt out of them). Families will then be-come battlegrounds in which children, and ultimately all of society, will be losers. Are men up to the challenge of assuming more of the work that has traditionally been carried out by women? The answer will go far toward determining how smoothly we make the transition to a sustainable society, if we make the transition at all.

Sexual behavior, size of families, the number of women in the cash labor force, and the role of women in general are all intimately related to the ability of women to control pregnancy and to influence their re-lationships with men. Affluence and birth control have made family ar-rangements more a matter of choice than a biological or economic ne-cessity. The challenge of creating a sustainable society demands that individuals and institutions redefine affluence and make contraception more widely available. At the same time, this challenge requires that families become more economically functional in ways that respect adults who head the families. This is a tall order. In recent history, indi-viduals have been "released" or "liberated" from traditional family roles. The future may demand a return to a *greater* orientation of the family as a socioeconomic unit but in a way that emphasizes quality over quantity. In today's modernized countries, families tend to be free—free of official and unofficial pressures to be demographically re-sponsible (i.e., to limit their childbearing to replacement levels), free to pursue their goals regardless of ecological implications. Such actions will prevent the creation of a sustainable society and, in the end, lead to disaster. However, we must be careful not to discourage individuals from creating families in the first place. In some societies, men and women are deciding not to bear children for negative reasons, such as the costs and stresses of parenthood. This is occurring in Italy and in other European countries, where birth rates for the native populations have declined substantially—in some cases even below replacements rates. The lowered population rates are a good sign, but, nevertheless, we must not overlook the importance of having and nurturing families.

The expectations of freedom

Families are on their own. Family privacy, economic prosperity, and geographic mobility all separate parents and children from traditional sources of nurturance and feedback, such as the church, elders, kin, and neighbors. Isolation is contagious; we become estranged from each other, and families lose the social support of loved ones. It is increasingly difficult for family values to compete with the seductive materialism and freedom of modern commercial society. The ethic of individualism also works against the values of cooperation and mutual sacrifices that are necessary components in a stable family. This theme emerges in the analyses of modern society by Amitai Etzioni (1983) and Donald Campbell (1976), among others (e.g., Winn, 1983).

As individuals and as families, we expect a great deal from ourselves and from our society; as a consequence, we are vulnerable to frustration. Life's inevitable disappointments are magnified by what are often unrealistic standards for self-fulfillment and material aggrandizement. On an economic level, our belief that everyone should live in a single-family house—in the suburbs if possible—has led many families to overcommit themselves financially and tie themselves to environmentally dangerous patterns of transportation, land use, and household energy consumption. The result is a high level of stress and disruption of the life of the family, as well as the life of the Earth.

Futurist Alvin Toffler and others may be correct in predicting that traditional family forms will neither cease to exist nor return to a position of dominance. I believe they will coexist with surrogate families and with real families at the atomistic or elemental end of the continuum so long as contemporary modernization holds sway. As modernization causes customs and institutions formerly required for economic survival to give way to chosen and voluntary ties, we face the challenge of building social welfare systems that meet people's needs for intimacy, love, and meaning. The family will exist as long as people recognize and respond to each other's needs for close, lifelong bonds. Furthermore, a collapse of the technocratic modern order may lead to a comeback of old family forms like the clan. Collapse of modern life would result in a return to families living closer to one another, shared facilities, bartering, social recreation, more home-prepared food, home-based energy production, petroplastics, and commuting. Out of the recession of the 1980s and the 1990s in the United States have come some encouraging tales of family- and neighborhood-oriented social reforms such as these. And they usually come with refreshingly improved relationships among women and men. Strong families respond to social crisis with resilience and are often made even stronger. The community, our institutions, and all of society must move carefully around families so as not to disturb the fragile and terribly important process going on within them—creating and nurturing human beings.

Overpopulation: the dark side of the family

And yet, a demographic specter hovers over contemporary families in their creation and rearing of human beings. Each miraculous birth sets in motion a chain of events that moves the Earth's ecosystems one step closer to crisis and disaster, because the parents, community, and society that assume responsibility for that life will do what they can to clothe, feed, house, and otherwise equip that child in the style to which local economies are accustomed. The birth of each child is a moment of joy. The birth of a hundred million children in the 1990s into a world of more than five billion presents us with a sobering challenge. But the possible birth of hundreds of millions in a world of more than six billion in the year 2000 is a threat to the very integrity of the social and physical environment. Demography, not economics, is the truly dismal science of our age. We cannot escape issues of family quantity, just as we cannot neglect the issues of family quality if we hope to achieve and maintain a sustainable society.

We can call the family a human lifeboat traveling the social currents of the world problematique. The lifeboat metaphor is ambiguous, however. It suggests a haven, a vehicle for surviving catastrophe. The danger of the metaphor is that it may encourage some to advance their individual families in a selfish attempt to live in comfort while others perish in a sea of diminished prospects. There is a kind of "every man for himself" mentality that pervades much of the survivalist movement, in which affluent families seek a paramilitary solution to the world's problems by walling themselves off from society or by setting off on their own to ride out the storm. Naturally, this is not the way we interpret the metaphor. In choosing the image of the family lifeboat, we see the institution of the family as a vehicle to help us negotiate today's stormy social and economic currents and bring us safely to a sustainable society.

The current economic system, like the ocean liner *Titanic*, has struck an iceberg and is taking on water. The survivalists have already cast off in their luxury cabin cruisers. Herman Kahn, Julius Simon, and others tell the rest of us, "Don't worry. This ship is equipped with the most modern technology. It is unsinkable." Much of the world, if not sinking, is already listing seriously. We need to use our family lifeboats to reach shore, where together, we as fellow humans can create a sustainable way of living. This is the kind of "lifeboat ethic" to which we should aspire.

This perspective leads us to consider the significance of childbearing and child rearing in the historically new settings promised or threatened by the world problematique and the sustainable society. We can see three principal forces at work. The first is sociobiological.

Human beings as social animals

Aristotle and, centuries later, Spinoza conceived of human beings as "social animals." We have our biologically-based predispositions, our genetically programmed agendas, but we act out these scripts through our social selves. Nature is mediated by nurture. Those sociobiologists who see our social behavior tied to our biology remind us that our cultures and personal values, our sociology and our psychology as human beings, evolved in counterpoint to our genetic development. We should not be surprised, they argue, that our social behavior in general and as it relates to families in particular is rooted in the evolution of our biological natures.

Our genetic heritage makes some forms of social organization easier to create and maintain than others. For example, Leonard Eron's (1981) research on physical aggression suggests that males are more easily socialized into aggressive roles than are females. According to developmental psychologists such as Eleanor Maccoby, some hormonal differences appear to play a role in this. Similarly, sociobiologists argue that female hormones predispose women to such roles. In no case is social function fixed and invariant, but some patterns of social organization are more genetically plausible than others.

And what is the driving force in this evolutionary drama? It is reproduction—the successful passing along of genetic identity through one's own offspring or through the offspring of one's blood relatives. The closer the blood relationship, the more the child shares one's genes and thus the greater the value to the family of that offspring—and the greater the sacrifices the family is willing to make for that child. The greater the genetic connection the more willing one is to give one's time, resources, even one's life for that offspring. Sociobiologists are often adroitly clever in interpreting the social implications of this thesis for individuals, the family, and the community.

What Robert Trivers (1974) calls "investment" tells us that domestic relations are governed by one's genetic stake in a particular offspring. Humans' reproductive strategy generally emphasizes quality, with great investment in each of a relatively small number of offspring. Sociobiologists call this a "K" strategy, in contrast to the "r" strategy, which emphasizes many offspring into each of which little is invested. "Few" and "many" are relative terms, of course. Mammals with eight offspring per litter are "K" types compared to insects with hundreds or thousands, but they appear as "r" types when contrasted with the human proclivity for single births. Men and women differ from each other as well; men are more on the "r" side (quantity) while women incline more to the "K" side (quality).

In general, this means that women tend to value individual children more than men do, because women have relatively few children while men can have as many children as women are willing to bear them. This fact, in the sociobiological view, shaped the history of domestic relations in many ways, and it continues to influence the modern era. Men insist upon the sexual loyalty of women for whom they are responsible, because only in this way can they assure paternity and, thus, genetic success. Women trade this sexual loyalty for economic loyalty, their only way of assuring for themselves adequate support during pregnancy and childbirth. Thus, their high investment in each child pays off genetically. This need not govern modern relationships, however, because of advances in contraception, infant nutrition, and cultural standards for assigning social responsibilities.

The sociobiological foundations for the population problem

Sociobiology has something to say about most matters of kinship and community life—for example, why stepchildren are at special risk for mistreatment and why patrimony is so resistant to bureaucratic regulation and reform. It tells us to invest in social welfare systems that benefit families so that we can harness the power of genetic "investment" to motivate people. The task is to empower women to make family planning decisions on the basis of their "natural" commitment to quality over quantity in childbearing.

Females are more likely to value quality in children, males to value quantity. Evidence indicates that the birth rate would decrease 25% to 50% worldwide if women who wish to limit their offspring were fully empowered to do so. Males, with their quantitative perspective, account for most of the obstacles to resolving the demographic dimensions of the world problematique. The Club of Rome's use of the word "mankind" in the phrases the "predicament of mankind" and "mankind at the turning point" may not have been intentionally sexist, but they were right on the mark. It is man, the male, who has caused the global predicament, and it is men who are facing a turning point in their history of domination.

The role of women and of the feminine perspective in the transition to a sustainable society is considered in chapter 7. Suffice it to say here that successful population control requires that women have access to contraception. Unfortunately, it is more often the fact that it is the men who have control over contraception. Indeed, this issue of who is to control procreation and contraception may be one of the oldest of human dilemmas. It certainly is well documented in recorded history, from biblical times to the current battles between "pro-choice" and anti-abortion forces in American politics. And it may extend far into prehistory; in Jean Auel's novel *The Clan of the Cave Bear* (1979), prehistoric women practice contraception using herbs and other natural substances, but keep it secret from men, who they know would deny them that control.

The very existence of the world problematique derives in part from the success of the human species in developing a genetically sound population program. Our genetic programs tell us to "go forth and multiply." Until the last few historical moments, human population in all but a few areas has been a marginal factor in the world's physical ecology. Early in human existence, when most of our genetic programming was carried out, the challenge was not *limiting* population but *sustaining* it. The issue was quantity. Would enough humans survive? By the fourteenth century, the human population was so firmly established that there was no need to worry about it (although the Black Plague of the Middle Ages gave Europe quite a scare). Yet the size of the population was so small in relation to the Earth's ecosystems that we could operate without fear of overpopulation, except in special, localized cases. This period has come to an end, and the issue of quantity is once again paramount. Instead of worrying that our numbers are insufficient for the survival of the human species, we must worry that we will exceed the carrying capacity of the planet. According to the Environment Fund, the human population reached one billion in 1750; two billion in about 1930, two hundred years later; three billion in 1960, thirty years later; and four billion in 1974, only fourteen years later. In 1987 we reached five billion, and have grown by nearly ninety million in each successive year. What are the engines that drive population growth?

We carry within us a precultural genetic predisposition to breed. Having offspring really *is* doing what comes naturally. So, what can we do now, when we need to control and even override that genetic program? Much that we value about civilization is that it allows us to overcome problems—caring for the physically disabled, developing eyeglasses for the nearsighted, delivering babies through caesarean section for women not well suited for vaginal delivery. Biological might does not make right. This applies to population control as well.

Certainly we can resort to social engineering, including reinforcements for procreating in a responsible manner. But we must capitalize upon genetic predispositions such as investment, rather than fight them. Altruistic appeals that go against manifest self-interest don't make much evolutionary sense. The result of population control measures around the world testifies to this. When social conditions impose reinforcements that reward small families and punish large ones, population growth slows and may even stop. These reinforcements may include political policies or socioeconomic factors. The former includes recent Chinese efforts to provide special privileges and economic guarantees to one child families. The latter includes the *eventual* decrease in number of offspring a family produces, which occurs when modern societies achieve and become accustomed to affluence and when the financial costs of childbearing rise while payoffs decline or remain steady. Both create mixed emotions within societies, even when their ecological "logic" is clear. A closer look at both will shed light on how the economics and the social psychology of childbearing struggle with the sociobiology of it.

The ups and downs of population growth

U.S. Census data shed some light on historical shifts in population in twentieth-century America. The data reveal substantial variations that correspond to economic ups and downs, as well as to the availability of contraception and abortion. For women born between 1891 and 1895, 37% had fewer than two children. Forty-seven percent of women born between 1906 and 1919 had fewer than two children. Of women born between 1921 and 1925, only 28% had fewer than two children. The women in the first group were in their prime childbearing years in the second and third decades of the twentieth century and had relatively little contraceptive control by contemporary standards. Many in the second group reached prime childbearing years in the Great Depression, and the low birth rate reflects a response to economic hard times. The third group had greater contraceptive control than the others and yet produced the famous post–World War II Baby Boom. Affluence and strongly pronatal ideology resulted in the population booms of those years, a high water mark against which we will measure population trends for the rest of the twentieth century.

Nancy Davis (1982) analyzed these data to show that age of first marriage, marital disruption, and educational levels all exert a significant influence: a well-educated woman marrying late and then divorcing is most likely to be childless or to have only one child. But these demographic characteristics operate in conjunction with—and can be overridden by—socioeconomic trends. The 1950s were special in the demographic history of America, in large part because a surge in affluence and pronatal ideology produced social conditions "ripe for early marriage and rapidly paced childbearing" (Davis, 1982, p. 45).

The American experience in the twentieth century is instructive because it deals with a modernized society. But it is only part of the story. Modernization has no simple effect upon population. Its demographic significance depends largely upon when and where it occurs in socioeconomic time and space. When it does not produce widespread improvement in the conditions of day-to-day life, it may not lower the birth rate, as was evidenced by Brazil in the 1970s.

The relationship between modernization and population is complex indeed. In most respects modernization seems to produce a population boom followed by a lowering of the birth rate. In premodernized countries, most childlessness is involuntary and due to disease, while in modernized countries most childlessness is voluntary. Thus, it appears that in developing countries greater affluence brings about an increase of births, while in developed countries affluence is associated with a decrease in births.

A "rational" analysis of childbearing and family life

Authority, dogma, and mystery dominate in traditional societies, particularly where families are concerned. Modernization has tended to bring "rational" analysis to bear more and more on daily life. This usually means economic analysis, because economics is assumed to be *the* rational science of human behavior. In practice, this means assessing "costs" and "benefits" in a very narrow sense. Family life is a prime target for such analyses, with Gary Becker's *A Treatise on the Family* (1981) being the preeminent example. Replete with mathematical equations, Becker's book expresses all family relations as functions of psychic supply and demand.

This sort of analysis is applied to the dynamics of family size by Sharon Houseknecht (1983), who examines voluntary childlessness within a "social exchange framework":

> Both *career commitment* and *child rearing* can be evaluated in terms of economic costs/rewards and social costs/rewards. In general, child rearing represents an economic cost and not a reward. Economic reward comes with *not* having children, since a greater amount of money is then available for other things. On the other hand, career commitment means that there are not only economic rewards forthcoming, but all sorts of social rewards as well. (1983, pp. 462-463)

Houseknecht concludes that "the only significant cost of remaining childless . . . is the loss of those social rewards that are typically associated with child rearing" (p. 463). It is interesting and revealing that this sort of analysis has the same narrowness of concern that characterizes economic analysis in general. It does not consider the costs and benefits of human activity to the Earth's ecosystems, nor does it consider psychological or spiritual costs and benefits. The latter makes sense given the scientific and secular aspirations of economics. The former, however, is surprising. Each "career" engaged in can cost the Earth a great deal if it consumes nonrenewable energy and materials. Children are an economic benefit in the households, neighborhoods, and communities that rely upon human labor rather than nonrenewable energy and materials to produce food and provide utilities. This, of course, is one reason why many families in technologically primitive societies favor large families. Children provide labor for necessary work.

Conventional economic analysis when applied to family issues is a very circumscribed tool. It may well accurately predict behavior right up until the time when the human community either voluntarily alters its collective relationship to the Earth and generates a sustainable society or falls into that "worthless state of human existence" about which *The Limits to Growth* warned us. Indeed, one reason why we must adopt a perspective that considers the environment is that it does not endorse calculations that are divorced from the larger picture. Microanalysis may produce accurate results in a narrow sense, but it can easily produce a tragically defective aggregate picture. The "tragedy of the commons" (Hardin, 1969) is a good example, where rational self-interest brings down community well-being. Hardin's concrete example is the case of farmers who try to exploit some commonly held pasture for private gain. Their efforts unintentionally combine to overgraze and thus ruin the pasture. Proper microeconomic analysis is likewise critical in examining family life, especially when computing population and energy variables, two issues underlying the world problematique.

Ecologist Lester Brown considers this problem in *Building a Sustainable Society*:

> Until a decade or so ago, population growth reduced but did not preclude gains in per capita production of such basic commodities as forest products, seafood, and petroleum. Only as world population moved toward four billion did it begin to outpace the production of the basic commodities on which humanity depends. Now, if population growth continues as projected, a decline in material living standards the world over may be unavoidable. (1980, p. 140)

If we who live in modern societies have a goal, it is to have our cake and eat it too. Most of us have trouble recognizing when we have too much of a good thing. If one steak is good, then why not eat a steak every day? And then our overly beefy diet brings on heart disease. If we have one television, why not get a television for every room? And then our family members become estranged from one another. If one life-preserving medical device is good, why not purchase one for every person? And then our budget for medical care becomes fiscally and morally untenable. If we have one child, why not have as many children as we can bear? And then we move closer and closer to exceeding our material limits.

How do people calculate the value of children? Conventionally, they have adopted a microeconomic approach, seeking to maximize value in light of costs and resources. But how does one assess the value of children in a modern society? This is a central issue in Garrett Hardin's classic paper "The Tragedy of the Commons" (1969). His answer is that it depends on what the social environment permits and demands. If a large number of children permits an individual to reap the benefits while passing on the costs to the general public, then public resources will eventually be depleted. This is the tragedy of the commons.

In conventional microeconomics, people take into account their personal resources and needs in light of what they can get "for free" from social welfare systems. When people have unimpeded access to what they can obtain from the public sector for free, they will make irresponsible decisions about childbearing. In the modern era there is only one responsible alternative: zero population growth, at a level consistent with carrying capacity. The ghost of the demographic grim reaper Thomas Malthus sits waiting, as if to say, "You can pay me now or you can pay me later." There is no magic technological solution that will allow unlimited childbearing and population growth. The flaw identified by Hardin is that wishful thinking ignores the modern realities of population. Childbearing decisions are no longer private, because families who control sufficient "private" resources depend upon a nonsustainable social order to preserve their advantage. For those who depend more directly on the welfare state, the problem is more clearly transparent, as conventional social welfare systems (the commons) are "overgrazed." In either case, there is a compelling community interest in controlling population levels.

Population control as social welfare policy

The concept of population control is difficult for those of us who consider ourselves pro-child, pro-family. On the one hand, we want to glorify (not too strong a word) childbearing, child rearing, and family life. On the other hand, we must identify the quantitative dimensions of childbearing—and to a lesser but still quite real degree, child rearing—as a critical part of the world problematique. Controlling population is undeniably as emotionally ambiguous as it is intellectually and technically challenging.

Imagine a discussion with friends on these issues. One person says that "having more that two children is socially irresponsible." A verbal storm ensues. "No!" responds a father of two who is likely to have another child. "That's ridiculous. What matters is how well you can raise them. Limiting population is something that societies do naturally when they become developed." The discussion continues, and all the major themes are introduced. "Waste is the issue." "The poor countries need to control their population, not us." "But a child born to our way of life consumes many times more resources than a child born in a poor country." "But our society is nearly at zero population growth through natural processes, so we don't need policies that limit individual families." "But we must serve as a model." "I don't think our modeling is going to count for much in the big picture." On and on it goes.

Participating in this discussion is a young woman in her late twenties who does not have children. Her contributions are intelligent. She understands the demographic problem and sees the validity of the two-child family. But her face tells a different story. Finally she comes out with it: "I know I shouldn't want to. I know how unsound it is. But I think I might like to have three children, just like my mother did." Individuals may recognize the rational thing to do, but they don't necessarily want to follow it.

So, how do we encourage people to do the rational thing? There are several possibilities, but they all incorporate two ideas: rewarding people for choosing responsible, limited procreation or penalizing them for exceeding ecologically appropriate limits. We can limit population by encouraging people to stay out of the business of creating families in the first place. And, as noted earlier in a solution that celebrates family, we can encourage single people to ally themselves with nuclear families as informal or bloodline uncles and aunts—becoming part of familylike social arrangements. In parts of China under the One Child Policy, a man who chooses not to have children can cede his right to paternity to his brother. Limiting this to men is sexist, of course, but it does illustrate one way that unclehood (and aunthood) can meet both psychic and demographic needs.

Responsible fertility

Any realistic discussion of the number of children a family should have must acknowledge the strong—one might say primordial—feelings most of us bring to this topic. Those content with one or two children can afford the luxury of wholeheartedly endorsing population controls, just as those of us who don't smoke can see clearly the health hazards of smoking and endorse a total ban on it. We naturally see the logic of rationality when it conforms to our situation and feelings. We just as naturally accept rationalizations that let us off the hook, whether we want a big family or to smoke cigarettes. Social psychologists have produced thousands of studies that document the workings of such a "cognitive consistency model."

Is it "unnatural" to limit births within a specific family? Sociobiologist Pierce van den Berghe (1978) says yes, and he claims that those who do so are reacting to an unnatural environment, in the evolutionary sense. He argues that the "voluntary" restrictions individuals impose upon themselves don't make genetic sense. Garrett Hardin concurs and presents his agreement in a critique of appeals to conscience, which he considers unsound because they place people in a double bind. The nobler sorts respond positively and against their narrow self-interest. The others exploit the goodwill of the "suckers." The net result is population increase and a decrease in socially responsible behavior, because such behavior is not encouraged. It goes unrewarded, and people who practice it are then forced to foot the bill. Garrett Hardin (1982) puts it this way: "When we use the word responsibility in the absence of substantial sanctions are we not trying to browbeat the free man in a commons into acting against his own interest?"

Is it "unnatural" to limit population? For the individual concerned only with genetic success, the answer is often "yes"—if social conditions permit unlimited breeding and the costs can be passed on to the community. But for the community, for the collective interest as articulated and managed by public institutions, the answer is "no"—not in the modern world, when the scale of the human enterprise threatens the Earth's ecosystems and the quality of human existence. We need to transcend our genetic instructions to "go forth and multiply," because we have already accomplished that goal beyond our ancestors' wildest dreams.

Many benefits will flow from the collective action to decrease the rate of childbearing to a level consistent with available renewable energy and materials. The chief benefit will be to increase the prognosis for society as a whole. Another benefit will be to focus attention on human quality, on bearing and rearing the best possible children. Fewer children are likely to be more highly valued children, as has been observed in China and elsewhere (the ravages of a sexist preference for boys over girls not withstanding). A third benefit is that responsible individuals will be freed from the double bind they experience when faced with appeals to their conscience in a world dominated by the self-defeating, tragic dynamics of the commons.

Limiting the size of specific families may turn children into an economic commodity, if people can sell their rights to bear them. And there are a host of other moral dilemmas: what about women who exceed their allotment of pregnancies, men who exceed their allotment of impregnations, parents who have a boy but wanted a girl, and children who are born illegally? There are costs to a course of action as fundamental as limiting population. But we can contain these costs, and they are the lesser evil in any realistic moral calculus.

How many people is enough? how many is too many?

As was pointed out in chapter 2, the Environment Fund envisions that population will increase from the current 5 billion to somewhere between 8.5 and 13.5 billion in 2150. These projections derive from assumptions about declines in birth rate in countries where they once were high—assumptions that many prove invalid, either if the association between increased affluence and decreased birth rates does not hold or if the projected increase in material affluence does not take place. Both are real possibilities.

Lester Brown of the Worldwatch Institute reports that an appropriate balance in population would exist when birth and death rates stabilize at about thirteen per thousand, with a life expectancy of about seventy years. Current variation among countries runs from about six to more than twenty per thousand in the death rate and from about nine to nearly fifty per thousand in the birth rate. The task of stabilizing the population still lies before us. According to the 1980 World Fertility Study, about half the world's women do not have access to contraception, but if it were available they would use it and, in the process, significantly lower birth rates. Family planning is the most fundamental family support system, because it permits women and men to balance quality and quantity within the family.

Believing that families will choose freely to limit childbearing to within appropriate levels may be quixotic; providing free access to contraception may yield more positive results, and it is definitely the right first step. Aggressive efforts to permit and encourage contraception succeeded in substantially lowering birth rates among rural women in

Uzbekistan. However, even educated women there who work outside the home still bear an average of five children! This is hardly a sustainable rate of reproduction, and it illustrates that modernization alone—at least in the simple sense of educational and economic development—may not be enough. A stable- state population does not happen automatically. Few things do.

Population and a drain on resources are related but are not identical, of course. Per-capita use of resources varies dramatically, depending on social class and the level of modernization. A relatively poor American family typically uses less of the world's resources than an affluent American family, but it still consumes much more than an Indian family that lives at subsistence level, even if the Indian family is larger. Likewise, production per capita varies. Of course, it is only realistic to speak of "production" in terms of cultivation of renewable resources such as fish, grain, and wood. With oil wells, mines, and steel mills, where "production" is really consumption of nonrenewable resources, the disparities are perhaps even more marked between the impact of small modern families and large traditional ones.

Lester Brown has compared population trends, resource use, and production, and he sees some disturbing trends. Between 1950 and 1973, economic growth and population growth were balanced. "Since then, however, global economic growth has fallen to less than three percent per year, and the population component of the overall growth in global demand has become dominant" (1980, p. 142). Once again, we need to know whether the 1970s were simply a recession in growth or a critical turning point. If the former, we may have a prolonged period of economic ups and downs in which to work things out. If it is the latter, we may have to cope simultaneously with the problem of population growth and a net decrease in global productivity.

All this tells us that issues of human quantity and quality are not strictly separable. We cannot divorce the kind of life available to people from the number of people who are available to live that way. The image comes to mind of building a sand castle on the ocean shore. Where you build it has a lot to do with its chances of survival. Build it near the surf and all your effort will go into maintaining the most rudimentary structure, responding to the demands of each new wave—not to mention the greater challenge of the incoming tide. But if your operation is far enough back, where the waves cannot reach it, you can build for quality, for art, refining and elaborating creatively.

Which kind of world do we want—one in which we are struggling, perhaps hopelessly, to make global ends meet, or one in which we can concentrate on human quality, on helping each child become all that he or she can be? Perhaps I load the question, but I think uncontrolled population growth will force humanity to live with its back to the wall. With the specter of nuclear war, it already lives with a gun to its head. Isn't that enough?

The metaphor of the sand castle is also ambiguous. For individuals, families, communities, and even societies, it may be possible to build a castle in a protected niche, away from the tide of increasing population, of increasing demands on resources, and of growing discrepancies between the needs of families and the resources available to them. It may even be possible to profit financially from this rising tide. But are such efforts sound? Are they moral? Certainly, they seem to violate the criterion of justice required for a sustainable society. Discussions of population that consider only numbers without linking those numbers to life styles, the effect on the environment, historical prognosis, and justice are unsound at best, foolhardy in the ordinary case, and disastrous in the worst case.

The concept of carrying capacity

Until recently, it seems, much of the debate over population has taken place within a context shaped primarily by faith and assumption. Most arguments have offered projections of the number of people likely to be born and have responded to this number with either alarm or complacency, depending upon their orientation. On the one hand, there is Paul Ehrlich (1967), who refers to the population "bomb"; on the other, there is Julius Simon (1975), who speaks approvingly of population growth as "the ultimate resource." Lindsey Grant (1980) chooses to call those who warn against letting current trends continue the Jeremiads; those who predict that technological innovation will automatically solve the population/resource problem he labels Cornucopians. The Jeremiads warn that we must redirect our efforts to achieve a sustainable society or face crisis and disaster. The Cornucopians promise that business as usual will somehow solve the problems before us, including population. There is a clear tautological element in Cornucopian analysis of population. It predicts that economic modernization will lead to a steady and sustainable population worldwide, as it has done in some societies. But it does not grant that current levels of population growth in those societies have already resulted in net per-capita *decreases* in modern affluence.

Disputes exist, of course, over the mechanics of projecting population. It is hard to know how the numbers will go—except up—for most countries. The problem is that most decisions about quantity are not informed by a clear concept of quality. What kind of life is or will be available to which children? Add to this question of quality a concern "for how long?" and the list of variables grows so long it becomes intimidating.

It is therefore all the more encouraging to see the formation of a movement aimed at determining the ability of a particular environment to support populations of varying sizes and of different levels of economic activity. This movement seeks to establish the "carrying capacity" of an environment by considering both the nature and costs of a particular life style—or mix of life styles—and its impact on the environment. The concept is sound, but data are only just becoming available. Preliminary studies of the United States argue for reducing population and stabilizing it at 200 million or less to reduce stress on the environment, ensure sustainability, and increase the likelihood that agricultural and other surpluses can be used to assist other societies facing shortages.

In 1972, *The Limits to Growth* indicated that if existing population trends continued, population would exceed the carrying capacity of the Earth within a hundred years. *Mankind at the Turning Point* (1974) and *Groping in the Dark* (1982) projected that if the global order remained unchanged some regions of the world would exceed their carrying capacity in only a few decades, while others would stay within their carrying capacity for decades longer, assuming they could maintain their privileged positions. This is a vital differentiation. Carrying capacity must be calculated using assumptions about the boundaries of a particular social system. When it comes to human societies, the carrying capacity of a region is a political and moral issue, as well as a biological one.

What is our carrying capacity?

What is the carrying capacity of the Earth? No one knows for sure. The answer depends so much on the availability of resources and patterns of use that projection is subject to modification. Carrying capacity increases if consumption decreases. It increases if we slow the conversion of high entropy materials into low entropy waste. It increases if technological innovation permits substitution of plentiful or renewable resources for scarce or nonrenewable ones. The higher the estimated carrying capacity, however, the greater the risk of overshooting the actual carrying capacity. Basing agricultural projections on a period of optimal climatic conditions such as existed in the 1950s and 1960s in most of the world (as the *Global 2000* report did) is riskier than basing projections on the average climate. The latter provides a margin for error without catastrophic agricultural shortfall.

Similarly, estimates of carrying capacity for any specific society are more or less risky depending on one's assumptions about the influence of other societies. In the case of the United States, for example, the Environmental Fund has argued that projections concerning population growth reach one conclusion if they are based primarily on birth rate and quite a different conclusion if they take into account an open-door immigration policy.

In addition, the option of emigrating to the United States has an undetermined effect on the population of the country of origin. In Mexico, for example, it appears that the potential for population growth can nearly replace the numbers who emigrate. Also, as Lindsey Grant and John Tanton (1981) have shown, such emigration tends to deplete the nation sending the laborers after it has supported them through childhood, leaving it with a disproportionate number of dependent children and elderly. For these and other reasons—such as political and military responses to emigration—it is impossible to specify carrying capacity precisely. Those who seriously engage in global modeling of economic, environmental, and population trends do agree that the world is up against some tough limits to growth as conventionally defined in terms of per-capita income, energy use, and the like. This consensus forms the core of the book *Groping in the Dark* (1982), by Donella Meadows, John Richardson, and Gerhart Bruckmann.

Few who have examined the issue of global carrying capacity believe the Earth can support even the current population of five billion in the style to which Americans have become accustomed. Some estimate that carrying capacity is about seven billion, if current regional disparities in material standard of living are reduced to eliminate extravagance and desperate poverty. Lester Brown (1980) suggests six billion as a more appropriate goal, one that will provide a more secure cushion against famine and ecological catastrophe. That number requires no more dramatic reduction in population growth rates than that which some nations have already achieved. We will probably reach six billion in about the year 2000, but that will not be the end of population growth. It will serve as a momentary milepost en route to a much larger number: anywhere from 8.5 to 13.5 billion, as noted earlier.

We may be in a decisive historical period with respect to population. James Grant and John Tanton pose the issue this way:

> Along the curve of history, we are in the vicinity of the point at which human expansion forces a progressive decline in the Earth's carrying capacity, just when that capacity is needed to support the population growth which undermines it. (1981, p. 3)

James Grant examines the issue of carrying capacity in its three basic forms:

1. What population level would permit maximum consumption per capita under given assumptions about technology?
2. Given those population assumptions, may we expect to achieve a harmonious and sustainable relationship between mankind and the planet (or "this country?" "this plain?" "this valley?")?
3. What human population levels would permit such a sustainable relationship with the Earth without forcing the entire system to be engineered to human requirements?

The third method of formulating carrying capacity is the most conservative of the three because it allows for the greatest margin for error. It can accommodate surges in fertility, which frequently happen, and it is also the least arrogant. It respects other life forms, and, indeed, the Earth as an integral unit on which humans coexist with other creatures. Can we expect our families to nurture gently and teach peaceful coexistence if our societies wantonly and rapaciously devour the planet and our fellow creatures?

Conclusions

We can come away from the issue of carrying capacity with several conclusions. First, as the world's leading consumer, the United States has a special obligation to reduce its demands for resources to a level that is domestically sustainable. At the very least, we should become self-reliant so that we are no longer a negative influence upon the carrying capacity of other societies. This means we should seek a lower than maximum stable population with lower per-capita waste production. Population rarely falls below the replacement level of 2.1 children per family, but it sometimes surges above that level. Our great-grandchildren need a demographic cushion. Second, other modernized societies should do the same. Third, the international community should make humane but *feasible* assumptions regarding the carrying capacities of nonmodernized societies. These assumptions must reflect local conditions as well as the availability of international resources. Anyone who holds up the United States as a model for development fails to recognize the limits of the Earth's ecological resources. Prospects for modernization and conventional economic expansion are radically different in a world of five billion than in a world of one billion. The 1990s are not the 1770s.

Disparity between have and have-not nations is not likely to disappear, particularly given current demographic conditions. But it may be reduced within an overall picture of material adequacy and global justice. This would be a morally as well as ecologically adequate outcome. But even such a modest proposal will require enormous social and political mobilization. And at the heart of it all will be the day-to-day dynamics of population. How do we convey the vital message that our family lifeboats are roped together? Each must husband its own provisions and also recognize that if we are to make the journey comfortable and safely we must act in a socially responsible manner. This brings us closer to the original conception of the lifeboat as articulated by Garrett Hardin. Our numbers—how many there are of us—will go far toward determining how well we do.

This returns us to our friends' discussion of family size. One friend argued that it was not socially irresponsible for him and his wife to have a third (and maybe a fourth) child because they were talented, fortunate people who could nurture and support several children. And they *are* a family with many resources. In effect, he was asserting that individual parents or couples could apply the concept of carrying capacity to their individual families. He believed his family could count on an adequate supply of material resources because of technological development, his own personal productivity, the efficient household economy, the fact that others will have fewer children, and his belief that the American way of life will continue. He believes all this without ever actually using the language of carrying capacity. Cornucopians Julius Simon and Herman Kahn also believe it, aggressively so.

Based on what we have learned, it is doubtful that these assumptions will stand the test of time. If not our friend's children then his grandchildren will begin to pay the price, as people in Brazil, the Sudan, and China are already doing. The ultimate well-being of families is linked to the fate of the Earth; each depends upon the other. As Lester Brown puts it: "The challenge now is to bind the family's fate to the fate of the nations—a challenge first for governments and educators, then for individual men and women" (1978, p. 158).

There is still much to do if we are to preserve foundations of social welfare. The family, for example, is the key to the initial separation of materials for recycling, and the small family farm is the key to sustainable food production. Yet, dominant economic models denigrate the family as a productive entity. Indeed, modern industrial urbanization tends to strip families of their economic productivity while reducing them to mere consumers. The next step, then, is to look at these and other obstacles that would prevent us from making the transition to a sustainable society.

F O U R

The Dilemma of Human Wants and the Reality of Human Needs

May 1985. Wad Medani, the Sudan. I have come to the Sudan in the midst of drought and famine. Fields plowed and planted several years ago lie barren, barely distinguishable from the desert around them. The sight of animal carcasses lying along the road is commonplace. In the small villages outside the regional town of Wad Medani I see more clearly than ever the meaning of "basic human needs." In villages where an astute and enlightened private program (Foster Parents Plan International) has operated, the social fabric is intact. Children are cared for, not abandoned. One-room huts are clean and orderly, dirt floors and all. Families have convenient access to drinkable water and cook on a simple but efficient stove. One family has a cabinet with "prized possessions": a few plates, some glasses, some ceremonial items, and a few pictures. People work at irrigated vegetable gardens and tending goats; sometimes they have an opportunity to earn cash when jobs in the modern economy become available. An immunization and public health program has succeeded in cracking the infant mortality problem. More than anything else, this is a very concrete definition of "meeting basic needs." In other villages that have not felt the nurturing hand of an enlightened development agency, the drought has brought social chaos. Whole village populations are taking refuge in camps and moving to the city. I think about American shopping centers and the difference between human wants and human needs.

What are the obstacles that impede the transition to a sustainable society? One that comes to mind and stays there is our love affair with things, our pleasure in acquiring material goods, the ease with which we become addicted to buying and accumulating. When Ferdinand Marcos was deposed and fled the Philippines in 1986, the world discovered that his wife owned 2,000 pairs of shoes and 500 black brassieres. Most saw this as excessive, others said it was disgusting, and still others thought it merely humorous. But is it not simply an exaggeration of something quite common among affluent consumers? Is not shopping a popular "recreation" for most of us? Is owning ten pairs of shoes so very different from owning 2,000, when each of us has only two feet?

This is no trivial affectation of modern life. This enjoyment of owning, having, spending, buying, and consuming is a serious threat. It threatens our relationship with the Earth and our relationships with each other, particularly in our families and in our efforts to preserve the resources necessary for social welfare systems. It cannibalizes the planet, undermines the spiritual order, and leaves us scrambling to fill the social and spiritual void with possessions. It is an addiction pure and simple (although, of course, it is far from pure, and hardly simple), and our chances of making the transition to a sustainable society depend in part upon our overcoming it.

One can predict that the human race will survive the economic crisis. We will continue as a biological presence on the Earth. We might even survive nuclear holocaust, with its almost incalculable devastation. It might be—as Thornton Wilder would say—by "the skin of our teeth," but we humans are a tenacious bunch. But can and will we survive without falling into "a state of worthless existence"? Of course, existence is intrinsically worthwhile to most of us. But in order to discuss the relationship of a sustainable society to social welfare systems, we must move beyond the gross issue of mere human survival. We must consider survival in cultural terms, beyond mere physiological operations of respiration, digestion, and defecation.

The late Aurelio Peccei, founder of the Club of Rome, elaborated on this theme in *The Human Quality* (1977). As he saw it, salvation depends upon some profound shifts in orientation, away from an addiction to material things and towards a greater concern for the social, psychological, and moral texture of life. Amidst the necessary debate about population size, energy consumption, and the availability of resources is the central issue of human quality. What is "the good life"?

Perhaps the ancients faced the same issues we do, but only the elite few ever had to contend with too much of a good thing. Perhaps they saw the difficult challenge of disentangling quality from quantity, of escaping materialism yet not sinking into poverty. Perhaps not. Perhaps in our modern age we experience new challenges, challenges which we are ill equipped biologically and culturally to overcome. Perhaps issues of human quality have lain dormant until now because low-power technology and traditional forms of economic organization prevented people from ever having to struggle with the problem of having too much.

Ironically, materialism has joined the Four Horseman of the Apocalypse. As societies flee War, Famine, Pestilence, and Death, they run into the arms of a beckoning figure that promises to protect and nurture them. Instead it delivers them back into the hands of the Four Horsemen, fattened up for slaughter. That beckoning figure is Modern Affluence.

Ecologist Lester Brown, among others, sees that the seductive power of material acquisitiveness is working hand in glove with unrestrained population growth to push the Earth to the brink of disaster. Look at the world today as it experiences the ravages of modern materialism: some suffer because they are "haves," while others suffer from being "have-nots." We might recall how native Hawaiians were ravaged by diseases transmitted by visiting European explorers. Just as smallpox ran amok among the Hawaiians because they had no natural immunity to it, it seems that we as a species are defenseless against modern materialism. Once the natural limits of low-power technology are removed, our inherent and voracious appetite is whetted, and mass consumption reigns supreme. And then, even generations of well-established cultural patterns are often unable to curb this consumption; they are as insubstantial as sand castles exposed to the rising tide at the seashore. The inhabitants of South Pacific villages who had met at public gatherings each Friday evening for centuries terminated that tradition within weeks of acquiring a television. Everyone wanted to stay home and watch "Dallas"! Shirley Hazzard captures this power of modernization in a passage from her novel *The Transit of Venus*, in which the steady, conserving ethic of Depression-reared Australians surrenders to American-style mass materialism without firing a shot. The encounter between these two cultures seems a fitting parable for our times:

One morning a girl whose father had been in America for Munitions came to school with nibless pens that wrote both red and blue, pencils with lights attached, a machine that would emboss a name—one's own preference—and pencil sharpeners in clear celluloid: And much else of a similar cast. Set out on a classroom table, these silenced even Miss Holster (the teacher). The girls leaned over, picking up this and that: Can I turn it on, how do you work it, I can't get it back again. No one could say these objects were ugly, even the crayon with the shiny red flower, for they were spread on the varnished table like flints from an age unborn, or evidence of life on Mars. A judgment on their attractiveness did not arise: Their power was conclusive, and did not appeal for praise.

It was our first encounter with calculated uselessness. No one had ever wasted anything. Even the Lalique on Aunt Edie's sideboard, or Mum's Balibuntl, were utterly functional by contrast, serving an evident cause of adornment, performing the necessary, recognized role of extravagance. The material accoutrements of their lives were now seen to have been essentials—serviceable, workday—in contrast to these hard, high-colored, unblinking objects that announced, though brittle enough, the indestructibility of infinite repetition.

Having felt no lack, the girls could experience no envy. They would have to be conditioned to a new acquisitiveness.

"They would have to be conditioned to a new acquisitiveness"—and how easy it was (and is). Would that we could reverse the conditioning as easily! In 1983, newspapers reported on the deregulation of the telecommunications industry in the United States. One result, according to a Federal Communications Commission spokesman, would be competitive manufacturing and sales, making the telephone a "disposable appliance" (his words), just like any other appliance in the modern household. Imagine advertisements for "the BIC disposable phone—make one call then throw it away!" Indeed, a hotel in Hong Kong advertises precisely that. When a guest checks out, his or her personal phone is thrown away.

One need not stretch things at all to imagine warehouses full of telephones, each one (sold or not) representing the transformation of nonrenewable raw materials into incipient waste. When telephones were uniform and solely functional, did we know we *needed* to be able to choose from among the myriad alternatives we now have? Having felt no lack, did we experience any envy? Having a need only to communicate, could we have an unmet need for a designer phone? a Mickey Mouse phone? a phone in every room? Will we become better people if our phones are disposable appliances?

The same could be said of our cars, our clothes, our dwellings, our furnishings, our recreational equipment, our health care. The ease with which we as a species have accepted the principles and practices of our modern throwaway culture argues that we have some innate predilection, some vulnerability which may prove just as culturally and environmentally devastating to us as the European diseases were to the native Hawaiians.

There is an inescapable sense in which the transition to a sustainable society represents a crisis of values: "more and bigger is better" versus "small is beautiful," and "more" rather than "enough." The first quality in each pair is manifest in mass modern materialism and in planned obsolescence; we observe the latter in an emphasis on frugality, a preference for quality over quantity, a wish for a more harmonious relationship with nature. Most of us are *capable* of both. Here as elsewhere we humans live out contradictions, often knowing that our enjoyment of extravagance is wrong for the world—if not for us personally—yet seem all but powerless to resist. Listen to the central character of Paul Erdman's novel *The Crash of '79* (1976), as he expresses his preference for the "good old days" of extravagance that preceded a hypothetical collapse of the petro-based world system.

> I liked the old days when we still had airplanes and television and dry martinis and pornography. I admit it. Sure, there are lots of Latter Day Saints around these days who claim that it was hedonists like myself who were ultimately to blame for what happened . . . us being the world in general and America in particular—because we were so hell-bent upon the pursuit of pleasure and money. . . . And the truth is the we, my generation, managed to ruin our world so completely that we have no legacy to leave them but poverty and disorder. (pp. 7–8)

American debated "Plutocracy or Social Democracy?" in the nineteenth century. We are, as David Potter called us in his book, the *People of Plenty* (1954). But never before has affluence been a "problem" with such far-reaching implications for the social order, because never before has society matched the instinct for consumerism with the economic power to pursue it. Unbridled materialism is the dynamic that drives modern societies into the position of being between the rock of inflated expectations and the hard place of the limits to growth.

Shirley Hazzard's account of the Australians reared during the Depression has its parallel in John Steinbeck's American classic *The Grapes of Wrath*. Steinbeck's tour de force on the human character of the Great Depression of the 1930s focuses on the travails of the Joad family, an archetypal Oklahoma clan of dirt farmers. Forced into economic ruin by the joint forces of unusually hostile weather, unsound farming practices, and the malevolent interests of what we now call agribusiness, the Joads are evicted from their steady if subsistence agrarian life and set on a course westward to the promised land of California. En route they encounter the marshaled forces of exploitation and greed as well as glimmers of personal and institutional caring and good old-fashioned American neighborliness. They are the children of the prairie meeting both the children of darkness and the children of light.

With their arrival in California, they face still more trials and struggle on, hoping that economic deliverance is just beyond the horizon. And it is. But what of the next generation of Joads, those born and bred in post–World War ii affluence? One might envision them in the 1960s and 1970s as newly affluent consumers who come to command and expect modern material affluence. We can picture the menfolk settled around the television set, beer and pretzels in hand, in a comfortable house cluttered with disposable possessions, watching the football games after a morning out on their dirt bikes, while the womenfolk prowl the shopping plaza, buying more plastic items and eating out at McDonald's. Whatever happened to the noble poor and the heroic proletariat?

It's a reactionary question, of course. It creates a straw man. It's just the kind of thing the affluent Right might use as a ploy to justify cutting wages and feathering the nests of the upper class. The working man has dirt bikes and K-Mart; the rich have BMWs and all the amenities advertised in *New Yorker* magazine. Neither caricature is fully accurate; both are dehumanizing. But each reflects a legitimate criticism of materialism as being harmful to the ecosystems of the Earth and to the human spirit. What would Jesus Christ say to the pursuit of affluence, American style? What would the Buddha say to disposable plastic razors? What would Karl Marx say to the proletariat turning its back on social justice? What would Thomas Jefferson say to suburbia?

As a matter of fact, we can know with some assurance what each of them would say. Each in his own voice would say that "mankind does not live by bread alone." Each sees essential human quality as being beyond material affluence, although each would criticize materialism in his own way.

E.F. Schumacher, the late British proponent of "economics as if people really mattered," examined the Christian and Buddhist critiques of materialism. Of the Christian perspective he concluded "that the Christian, as far as the goods of this world are concerned, is called upon to *strive* to use them *just so far* as they help him to obtain salvation, and that he should *strive* to withdraw himself from them *just so far* as they hinder him" (1974, p. 129). This implies a preference for quality over quantity. Gross National Product (GNP) means little in itself and precious little if the criteria for evaluating it are spiritual. If a rich man has as much chance of entering Heaven as a camel has in passing through the eye of a needle, then most of us had better scout out a new home for eternity. According to Christian values of moderation, simplicity, and non-violence, modern materialism is anathema. Material "goods" are good only insofar as they help relieve physical suffering, meet basic needs so that spiritual needs can be addressed, and provide a modest vehicle for expressing human creativity.

This is not to say, however, that the Christian perspective is thoroughly in tune with the needs of the Earth's ecology. Indeed, the splitting of Man and Nature, the elevating of Man above Nature, contributes to the problem. Lynn White acknowledges this in his article "Historical Roots of Our Ecological Crisis" (1967), in which he writes: "Despite Darwin, we are not, in our hearts, part of the natural process. We are superior to nature, contemptuous of it, willing to use it for our slightest whim" (p. 1206). And we do. Blinding rabbits to test cosmetics? Shame on us.

In this respect, at least, Christianity was an ecological regression compared with the primitive animist impulse that emphasized the spiritual integrity of existence, the commonality of being, which demanded respect for the trees, the waters, the plants, the animals—for the Earth as a whole. To quote White again, "The spirits in natural objects, which formerly had protected nature from man, evaporated. Man's effective monopoly on spirit in this world was confirmed, and the old inhibitions on the exploitations of nature crumbled." Elizabeth Dodson-Gray addressed this problem in her book *Green Paradise Lost*, seeking to "go over against the whole Christian hierarchical ordering of the Creation and the whole cosmos." In this she stands with that small minority within the Christian tradition exemplified by St. Francis and Albert Schweitzer, which has sought to retain fundamental faith in a Creator yet has emphasized the gentle harmonizing voice of that Creator rather than the stern domineering voice that most Christians listen to in their dealings with the world and their fellow beings.

Primitive animism has more in common with emerging ecological science, although other religious traditions can also accommodate it. The salience of the built environment and the imperiously exploitive orientation of modern technology may blind us to our fundamental dependence upon the Earth as a physical environment—to our economic as well as our spiritual peril. Religion and science are bedfellows. Just as the body is the temple for the soul, so too are the Earth's oceans, rivers, lakes, forests, grasslands, and fields the irreplaceable foundation of our economy.

Elizabeth Dodson-Gray is correct in asserting that masculine-oriented hierarchical Christianity exacerbates rather than helps solve the problem. A softer approach is needed to justify and reinforce the attitude of wholeness and interdependence that is necessary in an ecologically sound society. The patriarchal family is a bad model on which to base ecologically appropriate relationships between humans and the rest of Earth's beings. A reformed human family emphasizing equity and harmony, on the other hand, is a good model to follow in establishing our relationship with the Earth. Here again, the family can be a training ground for the world. It is little wonder that researchers find "spiritual orientation" to be one of the qualities inherent in strong families (Stinnett et. al., 1977).

Buddhist and Christian traditions both contain themes that *should* make the believer uncomfortable with modern materialism. Both put spiritual development first. For the Buddhist, work serves several purposes. It offers an opportunity to use and develop individual characteristics, to develop a sense of fellowship in common tasks, and to achieve the sense of satisfaction that comes from producing useful objects needed to sustain life. Neither inhumane work nor indulgent leisure, as alternatives to work, make spiritual sense. The principal danger lies in seeking wealth as an end unto itself, in becoming attached to objects. It is essential that one apply simplicity and nonviolence in one's relations to the material world. Schumacher encapsulates this idea in the slogan, "amazingly small means leading to extraordinarily satisfactory results" (p. 141). In this sense, Buddhist thinking is dramatically opposed to conventional modern consumerism.

Buddhism teaches that material goods are only a means of achieving personal well-being. Consuming for its own sake has no value. Rather, one is encouraged to *minimize* consumption, to let go of objects unless they further spiritual goals. Apply this view to our culture, which urges us to see conspicuous consumption as a patriotic duty, a sacred trust. Each quarterly report on consumer spending is awaited eagerly, and if such spending declines we are accused of losing faith in the economy. If we do not purchase all that our income permits, then we are viewed with suspicion and are seen as cultural heretics or economic traitors.

In his book *An Immodest Agenda: Rebuilding America Before the 21st Century*, Amitai Etzioni castigates the 80% of the population identified by survey researcher Daniel Yankelovich which believe that needs of the self take precedence over work and the needs of others. Of course, the very existence of social welfare systems arises from a sense of responsibility for our social relations. But social responsibility is not necessarily or ethically linked to increasing material productivity in the conventional terms embraced by Etzioni, who derides concern for "quality of life" and personal fulfillment just because they stand in the way of industrial development. He rejects an orientation that is "indifferent to wealth," but yet we can see that such an attitude is vital for the establishment of a sustainable society, one that doesn't abuse the Earth and that provides for basic human needs.

In this way Etzioni links consumerism, the work ethic, and cultural patriotism. This is a linkage we must break, replacing it with a combination of passionate commitment to a humane social environment and rejection of materialism as an end rather than a very limited means. Certainly refocusing time and energy away from materialism and toward social welfare systems and productive family relations is one way to break the consumer habit. Cynthia Hollander's "My Turn" column in *Newsweek* titled "Thanks for the Recession" is worth noting. Confronted with an economic crisis when her husband lost his job, Hollander and her family found that "you can lower your standard of living and be happy. . . . I can't say that money is not important. It is. But how I spend my time is equally important." Once adequacy is achieved, the key is to do things that require the investment of time and human energy rather than that of cash and petro-energy.

It may be symbolic that the Buddhist is told to plant a tree every few years and nurture it until it is well established. This exhortation alone lends credibility to the Buddhist ethic, given the threat of deforestation in much of the world. The symbolism of planting trees to celebrate the birth of children and the social benefits of nurturing those trees as a family activity make tree-planting a model enterprise for families, one that social welfare systems should encourage. Living off nonrenewable energy is parasitic and does violence to the Earth. Planting trees is a modest gesture of repayment, a statement of family commitment to the future of the Earth that reveals ecological intelligence and spiritual elegance.

Both Christian and Buddhist principles condemn modern materialism. But the Christian can easily become puritanical, distrustful of simple worldly pleasures such as dancing and making love. The Buddhist, likewise, is tempted to become so unworldly, so uninterested in material things, that he becomes unconcerned about the physical world. Schumacher did much to outline the need for a "middle way" in our economic thinking and in development of technology. He urged us to commit ourselves to "a technology more productive and powerful than the decayed technology of the ancient East, but at the same time nonviolent and immensely cheaper and simpler than the labor-saving technology of the modern West" (p. 144).

Religion puts spirit first. This act offers a compelling alternative to material consumption *if* it avoids reinforcing human acquisitiveness, aggressiveness, and imperiousness in the name of humankind's unique position in the cosmos. Whether it be Islam, Judaism, or Zoroastrianism, religion can provide important resources in making the transition to a sustainable society.

Of course, Christian and Buddhist spiritual principles are just that, principles. When Joseph Stalin was advised to consider the Pope's views in making decisions about the shaping of Europe at the end of World War II, he asked, "How many divisions does he command?" The power of modern materialism in the Christian West and its appeal in the Buddhist East suggest that the wisdom of these principles is not enough. But it is something. Single-minded pursuit of wealth is silly at best and sinful at worst.

But how do we proceed?

But progress is slow. In *Voluntary Simplicity* Duane Elgin presents evidence that some of us are turning away from materialism and embracing a way of life more in keeping with both Christian and Buddhist principles. In volunteering for a more materially simple life, the individuals cited by Elgin are seeking a more spiritually, psychologically, and socially enriched existence. By living according to the credo "Enough is always plenty and less is often more," these people provide concrete reassurance to those who fear that the alternative to mass materialism is subsistence-level living that is brutish, nasty, and short. On the contrary: it is graceful, enriched, and sustainable. The world needs such living demonstrations to show that people can *live* according to their beliefs and values—without having to die or kill for them.

Thomas Jefferson created much of the language used in modern political and social discourse, particularly that used by those sympathetic to American-style democracy. He saw what was needed to preserve and nurture human character in a manner that would support a politically, morally, and culturally sound way of life. Jefferson realized that when people were divorced from the land, they became estranged from their essential humanness. This estrangement, in turn, made them ripe for being led down unwise political paths. If he were to look at our modern materialism, Jefferson would recognize its falseness and its cultural, spiritual, and political dangers.

Karl Marx believed that the overthrow of societies dependent on economic struggle would allow for the creation of a socialist way of life, a communal existence characterized by balance and harmony. Citizens of his state would deal with each other on equal economic terms and live in a steady state relationship with the planet. Marx's vision may have been politically naive, but its goals are still valid.

Unfortunately, socialist countries attempted to provide material goods but did not distribute them equally. Now that the Cold War is over, we must take care that the best, not the worst, of socialism survives. We must be careful to avoid becoming the society depicted in Aldous Huxley's post-nuclear holocaust parable *Ape and Essence*, in which all the worst chickens of the modern age come home to roost. A character equal to Fëdor Dostoevski's Grand Inquisitor sums it up this way: You have taken the worst of the East, its disregard for individual autonomy, and combined it with the worst of the West, with its acquisitive materialism, and created worldwide terror and a soulless existence. Perhaps this is the situation the leaders of the Club of Rome had in mind when they spoke of "a worthless state of existence."

In seeking to make the transition to a sustainable society we must first differentiate between human wants and human needs. How much do people *really* need? How much *should* they want? Can we meet our legitimate material needs in ways that increase our psychological, social, and spiritual well-being without cannibalizing the planet and lowering our morale? Almost any effort to answer these questions begins with two assertions. First, most individuals in most modern societies have an inflated perception of their real material needs, which interferes with their ability to seek greater personal fulfillment. Second, our present course, in addition to being unwise psychologically and spiritually, will prove disastrous for the well-being of the planet.

But how do we find good answers to the many questions posed by affluence? We begin by recognizing the economic context in which those needs arise and are or are not met. Let us consider the complex human issues surrounding poverty and unemployment in the modern era.

Glen Elder's study, *The Children of the Great Depression*, examines the impact of the Great Depression of the 1930s on American families by focusing on two groups of children: one group born in 1920 and 1921, the other born in 1928 and 1929. The study included middle-class and working-class families, some of which were hit hard by the Depression, and others who escaped relatively unscathed.

In families in which the husband lost his job or most of his income and in which the marital relationship was weak, the mother often blamed the husband for "his" economic failure. Girls in the family were encouraged by their mother's outspokenness, while the boys were disillusioned by their father's failure; the result was that girls had fewer personality and emotional problems than boys did. These factors were intensified if the children were of a very young age during the Depression, due to the fact that they were more dependent upon their parents and were exposed to the changed family dynamics and the lower standard of living for a longer period of time. On the other hand, the pressures of economic deprivation tended to strengthen families in which the marital bond was strong. As always, the state of the family did much to determine whether the children later sank or swam as adults. Elder's study showed that strong families are the real wealth during hard economic times.

Note that these findings describe families with a pre-Depression record of relative stability. The parents studied were married and had an adequate work history. These were not members of the "underclass," not of the "hard-core" unemployed, nor were they of single-parent households. For them, the economic deprivation was an event, not a permanent condition. This is significant, and it cautions against making simple generalizations about other groups, such as the single-parent families, which have constituted the core of the chronically poor in the United States since 1980.

As if all this complexity were not enough, we must remember that the Great Depression was followed by the economic "boom" of the post—World War II era. At that time, per-capita real income rose by 62% between 1946 and 1970. Some of the "victims" of the Depression were ready to benefit from opportunity offered by the boom, while others were not. Interestingly, the Depression led to the creation and expansion of a massive social welfare system that included unemployment insurance and Social Security, which many now consider to be part of today's problems because they foster family disintegration.

A child is more at risk during economic and social hard times than during less difficulty periods, although some communities are better than others in sheltering families from financial hardship and job loss. Whether troubled times will prove damaging to a child depends on how the difficulties facing a family are transmitted to that child. What is more, individual temperament played a role: some people treated the stress as a challenge; others responded to the threat by withdrawing. The latter strategy poses a threat to the child's well-being. Developmental psychologists have begun to speak of "stress resistant" children, who have the personal and social resources to cope with very difficult life circumstances.

Because much of a family's energy and time goes into making a good life for its children, we must consider the needs of children if we are to truly understand the psychology and ecology of affluence. What does it mean to be a child? In the modern sense, it is to be shielded from the *direct* demands of economic, political, and sexual forces. Children have a claim on their parents, and they have the right to receive support from their families and their communities, regardless of their economic value in conventional accounting terms. Usually, families want to provide this support and will do so if at all possible. But when parents cannot provide for their children, society must acknowledge some responsibility in helping them. This belief, held by most, is the moral force behind a society's efforts to eliminate poverty. And it heightens our concern when poverty increases in the lives of children, as it has in the United States, where in 1990 one in four American children was considered poor.

Similarly, children cannot compete in the political arena. They cannot vote and are not legally responsible, and thus they should not be used as pawns by competing political forces. Children can only relate to adults on a person-to-person basis, not through the organized bureaucracy of the political system.

Finally, children must not become objects of sexual interest. In their behavior, their interests, their attitudes and their bodies, children are explicitly asexual. To be sure, children can be and usually are very at-tuned to physical contact and affection, but they are not explicitly sex-ual. One of the worst crimes is the sexual abuse of a child. As David Finkelhor makes clear in *Child Sexual Abuse* (1984), children are not in a position, developmentally or socially, to give informed consent for sexual involvement with adults.

If a child is shielded from economic, political, and sexual forces, what then is childhood all about? It's about play! Children has a license to play, to explore the world. This play is distinguished from adult work in that it doesn't depend upon formal organizations, and it's dif-ferent from adult social life in that it isn't a basis for courtship. Children are shielded so that they can be at play—a fundamentally human activ-ity which Jacob Bronowski recognized as a key to the ascent of man.

The second fundamental purpose of childhood is to develop basic competence. Children must become adept at language, body control, morality, reasoning, emotional expressiveness, and interpersonal rela-tions. Unless they do, they become a burden—to their families, to our society, and even to themselves.

What do children need in order to develop basic human compe-tence? Outside of good health, the basic ingredients are the time, inter-est, and love parents and other adults give their children. Other crucial elements include access to basic health services, food, and shelter, as well as a continuity of care. Parents themselves must avoid situations which distract them from providing these necessary ingredients, things which limit essential resources, disrupt relationships, and even under-mine love. And a parent must allow a child to play, for play helps de-velop competence. For the child, play and competence are the main items on life's agenda. They are the means by which a family socializes a child and brings it into the community.

Children provide a good starting point for elucidating basic human needs—love, play, and security—because they appreciate them the most. Of course, their fantasies and their experience within their fami-lies influence their interpretation of these essentials, but they often have a good, if often unarticulated, grasp of what is important. Further-more, those who care for children likewise learn to appreciate what's really important. This may be one reason why women, who are usually the primary caregivers, tend to have a better grasp of social reality than men do. Children put economic needs into perspective for us, particu-larly when we define and assess the impact of poverty.

Few of us would choose to be poor except for didactic purposes, and most would agree with Sophie Tucker's classic statement, "I've been rich and I've been poor, and rich is better." Often, naive or disingenuous critics of the limits-to-growth thesis ask, "Would you have everyone live in poverty?" They see comprehensive impoverishment as the only alternative to modern materialism. The distinction is false, of course. Modern materialism is no panacea; indeed, it is a menace to material adequacy.

A generation of research on socioeconomic deprivation and the harm it does to human development associates the ups and downs of the American economy with disruptions in the quality of life, such as suicide, domestic violence, and illness. At first glance, it would thus appear that the best way to improve human development is to provide more money and jobs for the people affected. But a more penetrating analysis challenges such a simplistic response. As revisionist economists such as Orio Giarini have amply demonstrated, the fault lies with the economy's ecological and cultural foundations, not with a quirk in business cycles to be remedied with a quick fix or a simple cash transfer. And even if it did, money in itself would not completely solve the problem, since harmful influences do not result directly from low income *per se* but from an inherently stressful economic climate. This climate is inherently stressful because it is unstable—and becoming even more so—and because its monetarized activities have displaced its nonmonetarized ones. More and more people are more and more dependent upon the institutions of the cash economy, and as a result they are increasingly vulnerable to its ups and downs.

The intrusion of the cash economy into the life of the family jeopardizes many important family functions. The cash economy is at best indifferent, and at worst opposed, to meeting many basic human needs. The modern economy can decrease the quality of life by disturbing relationships that meet the basic human needs of children and parents, and by strengthening the relationship between low-income and an inability to meet those basic needs. When more and more cash is required to meet basic daily needs, the human costs of being cash poor increase. Many families are disturbed by giving "spending money" to adolescents. Spending by teenagers rose 50% between 1975 and 1980, a period during which the number of youth declined by 6.6%. Do teenagers feel richer?

The modern economy can also *increase* poverty by eliminating the nonmonetary outlets which individuals have relied on to meet these basic needs. In Brazil, for example, the "economic miracle" of the 1960s and 1970s actually maintained or even increased that nation's high rate of infant mortality—an important indicator of poverty—and decreased the real income of the rural populace who formed the bulk of the population.

In the long run, dependence on cash and economic institutions will add stress to the lives of future generations by generating new needs and thus increasing the size and speed of the socioeconomic treadmill. As a United Nations report so eloquently puts it: "We have not inherited the Earth from our fathers, we are borrowing it from our children." And living in this world of increasing consumerism is likely to be very stressful for our children and their children forever after.

It appears that we have a special vulnerability to modern materialism. My firsthand experience with societies other than our own has reinforced this belief. Fast-food restaurants, video games, and plastic gadgets are found everywhere in the world. The penetrating power of modern materialism is astounding. Few if any societies seem to have— or even want—the armor needed to deflect it. Airports, modern hotels, and shopping centers around the world are characterized by their sameness; they are harbingers of a worldwide trend in declining cultural diversity. The course of "cultural development" around the world seems to be moving toward a homogenization based upon the lowest common denominator of mass materialism. It is more interested in creating a sameness rather than in preserving cultural diversity, which, like genetic diversity in the realm of biology, is what will keep societies from reaching evolutionary dead ends.

In the short run, the modern way seems destined to become the way of the world, especially if the dominant economic order continues unimpeded. Abettors to this effort include multinational corporations whose very slogans (e.g., "It's a small world") extol this trend, as well as local governments and their populace, whose eagerness to become part of the modern world usually overwhelms their commitment to their own traditions. By and large, the victory of modern materialism seems assured until the physical limits to growth bring about the enactment of a global restraining order or until we reach that "state of worthless existence" feared by the Club of Rome. Or, we wise up. Even if we avoid collapse by stopping short of the upper limits to growth, we may face an ambiguous cultural landscape dominated by the fruits of affluence—or rather the pits, hulls, and skins—and the wreckage of older social systems.

In good times, the family is the "headquarters" for human development. When the environment is poisoned and society is full of stress and disruption, adults and children huddle together in their families to weather the storm. When families themselves disintegrate, then our social welfare systems are put into jeopardy. As we saw in chapter 3, the contemporary economic war in Brazil resembles the civil war that ravaged the Soviet Union during the 1920s; both left millions of children without families, creating a social catastrophe. Family is probably the most reliable and durable vehicle for the survival of the human race. As the family goes, so goes the individual. Recall the Joads. The members of the family survived because of the strength and endurance of the family.

An economic prospectus

Is the takeover of the world by modern materialism assured? Have we no resistance? Are we totally vulnerable? The answers to these questions might seem clear: Yes, the takeover is assured. No, we have no resistance. Yes, we are totally vulnerable. But there are encouraging signs that for all our cultural gullibility, for all our apparent eagerness to buy into modern materialism, that its victory is not complete. People are not satisfied by modern materialism, and that is cause for hope.

Maybe the belief that man does not live by bread alone is more than wishful thinking. Maybe it is based on some very *sound* thinking and reveals profound insight into both human nature and the way of the world. Psychological technicians such as B.F. Skinner tell us that we must abandon classic conceptions of humanity and move "beyond freedom and dignity." They argue that we need only a set of scientific principles and techniques to modify human behavior. Many of us are dubious, however, recalling what Joseph Wood Krutch said more than sixty years ago in *The Modern Temper*:

> Science has always promised two things not necessarily related—an increase first in our powers, second in our happiness or wisdom, and we have come to realize that it is in the first and less important of the two promises which it has most abundantly kept. (p. 43)

It is important to have techniques for modifying behavior, and this is science's strong suit. But if we are going to develop and use these techniques, we also need to put into place values by which we can motivate and direct them.

We should be willing to accept new cultural vehicles but not at the expense of classical conceptions of human purpose. A generation of research on the "quality of life" supports this belief. Ironically, the efforts of social scientists to measure "quality of life" has supplanted the classic philosophical search for "the good life" in the same way that philosophers have retreated to studying logic and linguistics. There is a science of the good life in the making.

As psychologist Donald Campbell has noted, as early as 1798 Sir John Sinclair described statistics in the following terms when he introduced them in his *Statistical Account of Scotland*: "The idea I answer to the term [statistics] is an inquiry into the state of the country, for the purpose of ascertaining the quantum of happiness." As Angus Campbell makes clear in *The Sense of Well-Being in America* (1981), we are still searching for a way to measure that quantum of happiness. But we have made some progress, which tells us that modern materialism cannot meet basic human needs very well. In fact, despite a rise in material affluence in the United States since the end of World War II, large-scale surveys report no increase—and in some cases even a decline—in the proportion of people claiming to be "very happy." These data complement the findings of others who report a large increase in the prevalence of serious psychological depression in America. At least one observer attributes this increase to both the unravelling of community and the rise of individualism.

The role of affluence in defining human quality of life is complex; the direct relationship between affluence and quality of life is weak, and, indeed, often contradictory. As material affluence increases in a society it becomes an ever more ambiguous indicator of human quality, frequently creating and exacerbating as many problems as it solves. The same affluence that provides people with the means of expanding and diversifying their diets also allows them to consume excessive amounts of animal fat, which, in turn, endangers their health. The industrial economy reduces backbreaking labor, but it also exposes its workers carcinogenic materials. The introduction of electricity has allowed us to reduce our physical exertion, but in doing so, it has created a need for weight reduction and physical fitness centers. No, Gross National Product is hardly a good measure of quality of life.

Beyond GNP

The most primitive efforts to move beyond GNP and systematically assess quality of life focus on the areas of public health and the economy. They measure infant mortality, life expectancy, educational attainment, employment, per-capita income, and material possessions such as telephones, radios, cars, and washing machines. This is the stuff of which most international and regional comparisons are made. The comparison works well some of the time in revealing gross differences between some human communities and socioeconomic systems. However, they seem to imply that there is a simple one-to-one correspondence between modernization and the meeting of basic human needs. Such a direct relationship is called "linear" in mathematical terms. But *is* the relationship linear? The answer is "no."

GNP measures the price of goods and services entering the social system rather than the current stock of goods available for use. It thus measures the *quantity* of goods put through the system rather than the *use* to which things are put. It values waste, not conservation. It devalues the way human beings really live at their best because it emphasizes "having" rather than "being." Ideal events, from the point of view of GNP, are those that accelerate the transformation of resources into priced goods; anything that lasts a long time or is outside the cash economy is a drag on this process. In conventional economic terms, families are a drag unless they consume products. Conventional economic measures such as GNP do not represent humankind well.

Several analyses testify to this. Robert Heilbroner's *Business Civilization in Decline* (1978) acknowledges that "economic success does not guarantee social harmony" or personal satisfaction. William Leiss followed this analytic path to fruition in *The Limits to Satisfaction* (1980). In it he examines the several ways in which the materialist ethos is flawed, and in doing so he reveals much about the anxiety, ambiguity, and dissatisfactions of modern societies. Leiss understands that most of the satisfaction that comes from possessing material goods is social in nature. We receive satisfaction from the messages our possessions convey: our social status or prestige, our monetary worth, our awareness of fashion, our good taste. Yet these impressions must be continually reaffirmed, which is achieved by our buying and displaying ever more expensive commodities. Thus, satisfaction does not increase in any reliable and sustainable fashion.

Like all addictions, the addiction to material things provides only a temporary "high" followed by an adjustment and a new desire for stimulation. Yet despite what Leiss, Campbell, and others tell us about the futility of finding happiness in material aggrandizement, few of us really seem to believe them. "Psychology applies to other people," we seem to say. And even in this we are exhibiting another negative psy-

chological trait, which David Elkind (1980) calls a "personal fable"—
the irrational belief that the regular rules of day-to-day life do not apply
to us. Consumer junkies, like all junkies, always think they can handle
their addiction. Who among us does not take for granted, or at least has
become accustomed to, each new level of material success, each new
increment in material consumption, each new possession?

Materialism is bad psychology, as Tibor Scitovsky's *The Joyless Economy* (1981) and Fred Hirsch's *Social Limitations to Growth* demonstrate.
But it is also bad sociology. Modernization disrupts traditional social
sources of meaning in human experience. Stuart Ewen's *Captains of
Consciousness: Advertising and the Social Roots of the Consumer Culture*
(1983) and Marshall Sahlins' *Culture and Practical Reason* (1982) makes
this clear. They show that increases in the national GNP or in per-
capita real income do not produce increases in happiness or personal
satisfaction; thus they fail the statistical test applied by Sir John Sinclair
in his attempts to develop ways of ascertaining "the quantum of happiness."

Furthermore, modernization, by disrupting traditional sources of
meaning, creates a void. Human nature abhors a psychological vacuum. Thus, we rush to fill the void with things. Pursuit of things and
attachment to wealth are probably the natural expression of our need
for meaning in a world increasingly stripped of traditional significance.
Erich Fromm developed this theme in *To Have or To Be* (1955), in
which he argued that people used to define themselves by *being* something in relation to others, whereas now they are more likely to define
themselves by what they have. No matter what it is, we must *have*
something to *be* someone. This is particularly true for women trapped
in stereotypical sex roles. Consigned to the role of consumer, they need
to have more possession to feel worthwhile. This lack in turn stimulates
the economy, and buying things thus becomes what John Kenneth Gal-
braith calls a "convenient social virtue."

The most complete picture of reality often comes not from social science, but from fiction, where the rough edges of incomplete factual information can be smoothed by the imagination. Some of the best thinking on the essential falseness of gross materialism and its inability to
meet emotional needs is found in Austin Tappan Wright's utopian
novel *Islandia* (1942). The novel presents a fully sustainable society in
which the pursuit of human quality totally informs and guides decisions about quantity. The economic and social unit is the family farm.
The family unit is the basis for decision making, and choices are made

with an eye toward harmonizing traditions established by past genera-tions with the needs of generations yet to come. Family members make extended visits to other farms and meet annually for their only political event, a congress of landowners. Islanders have no contact with other countries and little modern technology. They are educated in one-room schoolhouses and have only one national university. Family in-tegrity and an individual's own work pace are valued over speed and gross output. *Formal* social services are all but nonexistent; as in Marx's ideal state, these service "wither away" because they are not needed. In-formal networks provide routine help to individuals and families faced with acute problems. *Islandia* presents an alternative to our superficial materialist society. But it does so through a social organization that of-fers its members enough material technology to provide for themselves. Human quality is paramount.

Below, two characters from the novel discuss how Islandia would change if it were to become "modern" as John, the contemporary American, understands the term:

> *Dorn:* Why should I change?
>
> *John:* Progress!
>
> *Dorn:* Speed, is that progress? Anyhow, why progress? Why not enjoy what one has? Men have never exhausted present pleasures.
>
> *John:* With us, progress means giving pleasures to those who haven't got them.
>
> *Dorn:* But doesn't progress create the very situation it seeks to cure—always changing the social adjustment so that someone is squeezed out? Decide on an indispensable minimum. See that everyone gets that, and until everyone has it, don't let anyone have any more. Don't let anyone ever have any more until they have cultivated fully what they have.
>
> *John:* To be unhappy is a sign we aren't stagnating.
>
> *Dorn:* Nor are we. "Happy" wasn't the right word. We are quite as un-happy as you are. Things are too beautiful; those we love die; it hurts to grow old or be sick. Progress won't change any of these things, except that medicine will mitigate the last. We cultivate medicine, and we are quite as far along as you are there. Railroads and all that merely stir up a puddle, putting nothing new in and taking nothing out. (Wright, 1942, pp. 84-85).

E. F. Schumacher, the "small is beautiful" economist, provides us with insight into the misleading character of economic analyses. He noted that all the debate about economic indicators among the immensely rich 25% of the world's population pales into insignificance when compared to the rest of the world, which is immeasurably poor. This much is clear by any sort of qualitative standards of affluence. That many who are relatively rich monetarily and materially do not *feel* rich is part of the problem. And this problem highlights the fact that poverty is primarily a social, rather than a narrowly economic concept. It's not how much money you have but how well you are able to recognize and meet basic needs.

When considering cash income, we must resist the temptation to simply count dollars. Instead, we should consider how frequently families receive incomes that permit them to achieve qualitatively different styles and standards of living. This is the thinking behind a series of budgets generated by the U.S. Bureau of Labor Standards. The best known is the poverty budget, which defines the minimal financial needs of a family. In 1991, it was about $14,000 for an urban family of four. Less well known but of equal or greater importance are the low, intermediate, and high budgets. We may rename them as budgets for the "struggling," "comfortable," and "affluent," since they rest on corresponding assumptions about life style, principally the level of disposable income left after basic needs are met. For 1985, these three lifestyles for an urban family of four required an income of about $27,000, $41,000, and $60,000 respectively. These figures and the poverty figures, not average income or per-capita income, provide a real starting place for discussions on political economy. Looked at this way, it is easy to see that "satisfaction" and "meaningfulness" transcend income, particularly if the social and psychological costs of earning an income capable of supporting a comfortable life style increase. Indeed, because material goods depend upon social interpretation for their meaning, it is *always* risky to place emotional investment in them. Such investments are foolish at best; tragic at worst. Survey data tell us this much about human values and needs.

Gerald Gurin and his colleagues asked people what made them happy and what worried them most. They found "family life" was the most frequent answer to both questions. In the mid-1970s Angus Campbell and his colleagues investigated the correlates of satisfaction using the question: "In general, how satisfied or dissatisfied would you say you are with your life as a whole these days?" Other researchers asked a similar question, and found that six areas of life are important to people: satisfaction with self, family, standard of living, fun, housing, and government.

In *The Sense of Well-Being in America* (1981), Angus Campbell asserts that there is a connection between well-being and factors such as marriage, employment, educational attainment, and friendship. When these factors were positive (when the marriage was happy, for instance), an individual claimed to be fulfilled, because the individual was then able to fulfill social expectations and maintain intimate and supportive relationships. We might subsume these factors all under the rubric of social needs, whose main themes are social interconnectedness, physical well-being, and purposefulness. Family plays a large role in supporting all of these.

Modern materialism, on the other hand, plays an ambiguous role. First, once basic need are met, materialism often plays a subversive role in families. It robs them of productive functions and tempts family members to rely on material alternatives to family interaction. Second, materialism puts pressure on people to define their worth in financial terms and thus undermines the family by defining children as costs, causing parents to devalue nonpaid productive labor such as child care; it also causes wage earners to devalue homemakers because they participate in the cash economy only as consumers. Third, while materialism permits improvement in physical well-being by raising the standard of living, it typically does so in a gross and often self-defeating fashion. An individual may have more money but limited access to "free" resources such as clean air and water or to neighbors who are willing to provide supplementary child care. Modernization giveth with one hand and taketh away with another when it comes to meeting basic needs. Until now, most people have believed that the giving outweighed the taking away. Increasingly, however, some are wondering whether the balance may have shifted in the other direction. An analysis of basic needs may provide the Rosetta stone for deciphering the meaning of this fundamental challenge to human quality.

Basic human needs

What are basic human needs? Who would presume to answer? Many have labored to compile a list. Some make short lists of key words such as "belonging," "being," "loving," "having"; others rely upon evocative phrases such as "having control over one's life." All seek to combine an acknowledgement of human beings as physiological creatures with a respect for the finer qualities of human existence.

For most Western-style thinkers and social scientists, Abraham Maslow's (1951) needs hierarchy is the be-all (and often the end-all) of efforts to define human quality. His hierarchy begins with survival needs and extends upward through social esteem to personal fulfillment. Leiss (1979) notes that such a list is flawed because it does not place these needs within a social and ecological context. He argues that for a discussion of human needs to be useful, it must move from abstract to concrete analyses of how needs and economy are related in day-to-day practice. The way we define and meet survival needs for clothing and shelter affects the planet, such as when we deforest vast areas for raw materials to create these things (and thus violate key values). Similarly, if we seek to satisfy our need for actualization through energy-intensive activities, we may disrupt the regenerative capacity of field and stream. The raw power of industrial society should compel us to reconsider our needs and the ways we go about meeting them.

Leiss is right on the mark. Current forms of economic organization affect what human needs are. It is only marginally useful to speak of "basic human needs" without placing them within a social context. There are two alternatives to this: to accept the validity of that context by simply cataloging the needs of those within it (we might call this the "people's choice" approach), or to critique the context itself, thus permitting a specification of human needs based upon a better social context. Better in what sense? Better in that it is more in tune with the realities of human psychology *and* the global environment. We might call this the "knowing what's good for you" choice.

Modern societies are unrealistic on both counts. They falsely assume that ever greater affluence leads to ever greater satisfaction and meaning. It may not; it certainly cannot do so indefinitely. Also, they operate on economic principles that allow people to choose to do violence to the Earth's natural systems and threaten the very long-term existence of human cultures—often without being directly confronted with the ultimate consequences of their life styles.

In a saner socioeconomic system, we would live more lightly upon the Earth *and* invest our time and effort into activities that are satisfying and meaningful. This means, among other things, that we would place a greater emphasis on family life as a focal point of our social existence. Further, it means that we should restructure economic activity so that it helps create a social context in which the family is the natural focal point for human needs, not just one of several competing sets of human needs created by the materialist institutions of work place and commercial recreation.

This conception is tied closely to a definition of human development, which sees the creation of social maps of the world that reflect experience, intelligence, and insight, and then provide guidance on how to live in the world. Human beings are meaning-seeking organisms. If we establish a false environment, we generate false needs and doom individuals to developmental dead ends, because people will do all they can to achieve what society defines as meaningful. There is madness in the message of modern life.

Modernization promises to enhance human development by minimizing physical threats and by extending the power of the person to discover, sustain, or alter the environment. But it has unleashed forces that threaten to negatively impact this environment and neutralize human development by establishing "needs" that undermine the family and create unrealistic expectations. This economic order and its cultural baggage are major obstacles in the transition to a sustainable society. In *Islandia* the need for social welfare systems was diminished, yet welfare was increased by a "small is beautiful" social organization. The opposite situation plays itself out in our world: the need for a powerful social welfare system grows while the forces generating that need erode the foundation for sustaining those systems.

FIVE

The Tragedy of Conventional Economic Thinking: Does Every-thing Have a Price?

November 1982. Ft. Wayne, Indiana. I have come to the American heart-land to speak to the staff and supporters of Ft. Wayne's Mental Health Cen-ter at a seminar titled "Today's Adversity: Tomorrow's Strength." The cen-tral issue is the economy of this community and its relation to the mental health of its citizens. Most of the nation has been wallowing in a recession, but certain cities like Ft. Wayne have been experiencing Depression-like un-employment. Major industrial plants have closed or have cut back on pro-duction, forcing them to lay off workers. The move has produced a ripple ef-fect in the local economy, which is dependent upon the plants, and many area businesses themselves have been compelled to lay off employees. Ft. Wayne recently received another serious blow when International Harvester announced it would close its truck/bus body production plant located here. Over 2,000 jobs will be lost; the total job loss will be several times that when the effect on secondary businesses is determined. I am here to present a re-view of the social science research that has been done on the human conse-quences of unemployment. My focus is the impact unemployment has on family life.

During the moderator's opening remarks, I scan the worried faces in the audience. They are not the same people shown on the news shows each night, waiting in line at the unemployment insurance office, but they are worried nonetheless—some out of compassion for other families, some because they

117

themselves have been directly affected by the recession, some because they fear what may happen next. As I look at these faces, I recall my first college course in economics of nearly two decades ago.

It was called "Economics 101: Introduction to Economics." In one of the lectures, the instructor had called unemployment "a necessary part of the economic system as a way of controlling prices, demands, and production." He then continued into a discussion of the classical capitalist economics of unemployment, its functions and benefits in combatting inflation. The college I was attending was private, and most of my classmates had been raised in upperclass families; they took affluence and employment for granted. The topic of unemployment had little meaning to them. But I was there on scholarship, and I couldn't forget the period at home when my father was unemployed during one of the "minor economic dislocations" of the 1950s. I couldn't forget the human cost of that period on my family's life. Finally I spoke up and asked the professor: "Where are the real unemployed people in your lecture? What kind of discipline is economics, which views such human disasters as 'normal, even beneficial'?"

The meaning of economic development

We can begin a discussion on the relationship between economics and social welfare systems with two books: Frederick Jackson Turner's *The Frontier in American History*, originally published in 1897 and reissued in the early 1960s, and Walter Rostow's *Stages of Economic Growth*, published in 1962. For Turner, the official end of the frontier in 1890—so declared by the U.S. Census Bureau—was a pivotal event in American history. The physical frontier, he argued, had influenced the creation of an American character that was democratic and optimistic, and the end of that frontier brought about corresponding changes in that same character. Modern readers of Turner would draw parallels between the end of the physical frontier and the end of the economic frontier of unlimited growth in the 1980s. Rostow, on the other hand, analyzed the stages of economic growth and development in societies around the world. He demonstrated how some societies had passed through these economic cycles and showed how other societies were just beginning.

I read both books in 1963. Nearly two decades later, Walter Rostow came to speak at the university where I was teaching, and I attended his lecture with great anticipation. But listening to him, I was struck by how alien and out of step his message was from the new economics of development as articulated by E.F. Schumacher (*Small is Beautiful: Economics As If People Really Mattered*), Kenneth Boulding (*Evolutionary Economics*), Herman Daly (*Steady State Economics*), and Orio Giarini (*Dialogue on Wealth and Welfare: An Alternative View of the World Capital Formation*). In contrast to them, Rostow sounded somewhat anachronistic and oblivious to the ecological realities with which economic policy and practice must come to terms.

A bit of research I did in the university library revealed some intriguing historical coincidences. Rostow published *Stages of Economic Growth* in 1962. In 1972, when a second edition of the book was being published, Dennis Meadows and his colleagues were presenting to the Club of Rome their assessment of the world's economic condition in *The Limits to Growth*. In 1982, the Smithsonian Institution celebrated the tenth anniversary of the publication of *The Limits to Growth* with a conference. The ideas presented at that conference conspired to make that lecture by Rostow sound like an unfortunate plea for "business as usual—only better." All of this inspired me to reread *Stages of Economic Growth* as a counterpoint to the new ecology of economics.

In the second edition of his book, Rostow addresses questions that had been raised about points in the first edition, but essentially he left the original text intact. Like evolutionary economist Kenneth Boulding, who defines economic development as "the rate of increase of human know-how," and "the evolution of human artifacts," Rostow begins by defining economic growth as the "degree of efficient absorption of technologies" (p. xiii) rather than simply as an increase in Gross National Product. This certainly is an encouraging start, because sustainable societies will need alternatives to GNP in assessing change. In the preface to that second edition, Rostow also makes several other statements that are interesting, both for what they say about economics in general and about his book in particular.

First, he asserts that the book "is both a scientific effort and a tract for the times" (p. xiv). This raises the question: To what extent is his analysis limited to specific times and places? To what extent is it universal? Rostow believes it is the latter. He says in the 1972 revision that the 1960s produced numerous examples of societies that successfully combined rapid economic growth with a social progress congruent with national cultures "in an environment of political independence." This is an affirmation of his belief in the universality, the scientific objectivity of his approach.

In his preface to the 1972 revised edition, Rostow describes his purpose in writing the book: "... to raise a number of questions that men, societies, and governments would have to answer as they turned to explore new frontiers ..." (p. xiv). Rostow had been one of the best and brightest of John F. Kennedy's inner circle, and his use of the "new frontier" metaphor was more a reference to the former president's vision than it was an allusion to Frederick Jackson Turner. But the reference is better placed with Turner. The end of cheap energy, like the end of cheap land in the American West that Turner described, was the closing of another frontier.

A reading of this preface encouraged me to review the core text of the book itself, starting with the five stages of growth. Rostow identifies these stages as "The Traditional Society," "The Preconditions for Take-Off," "The Take-Off," "The Drive to Maturity," and "The Age of High Mass-Consumption." The Traditional Society is characterized by large numbers of people living at subsistence level; technology is primitive and agriculture is labor-intensive. Small elite classes wring their luxuries out of the sweat of the masses. "But the central fact about the traditional society was that a ceiling existed on the level of attainable output per head" (p. 4). This stage had the longest tenure, of course. But change eventually comes about when preconditions exist for that change. This is the second stage of growth.

In Rostow's view these preconditions are characterized by a shift in ideology, values, and purpose.

> The idea spreads not merely that economic progress is possible, but that economic progress is a necessary condition for some other purpose judged to be good: be it national dignity, private profit, the general welfare, or a better life for the children. (p.6)

For my purposes, it is significant that the demand for social welfare systems may motivate economic development in Rostow's scheme. The force behind this shift in economic ideology includes new and exemplary enterprises, new social policies initiated by the elites, the infusion of a new worldview that redefines human goals, and technological breakthroughs. The point is that new economic possibilities arise when people catch a glimpse of a new economic order. (Recall that the *technical* expertise for the Industrial Revolution existed in the days of the Roman Empire but wasn't harnessed for lack of an appropriate worldview.)

In "Take-Off," the third stage, the economic parts created and developed earlier become a whole greater than the sum of those parts, setting off a chain reaction.

> The take-off is the interval when the old blocks and resistances to steady growth are finally overcome. The forces making for economic progress, which yielded limited bursts and enclaves of modern activity, expand and come to dominate the society. Growth becomes its normal condition." (p. 7)

This period is one of rapid change, in which old patterns are disrupted, modified, and replaced by the institutions and facilities of the new order. As this process becomes the norm, the society enters the fourth stage, the "Drive to Maturity":

> After take-off there follows a long interval of sustained if fluctuating progress, as the now regularly growing economy drives to extend modern technology over the whole front of its economic activity. . . . This is the stage in which an economy demonstrates that it has the technological and entrepreneurial skills to produce not everything, but anything it chooses to produce." (pp. 9-10)

One can imagine a visual display of this period. Computer generated graphics would show "modern economy" in vivid color spreading over the page until the entire area was covered. This would depict the fifth stage, the "Drive to Maturity," in which economic institutions grow at unprecedented rates. What happens then? To what use do societies then put these economic machines? The answer is found in the sixth stage, "The Age of High Mass-Consumption."

In this stage, the industrial infrastructure is so effective and efficient that what by any *historical* criterion would be called luxury becomes a mass phenomenon. The economic system shifts away from building the physical plant to managing the production of consumer goods and services.

> As societies achieved maturity in the Twentieth Century two things happened: real income per head rose to a point where large numbers of persons gained a command over consumption which transcended basic food, shelter, and clothing and the structure of the working force changed in ways which increased not only the proportion of urban to to-

tal population, but also the proportion of the population working in offices or in skilled factory jobs. (p. 10)

These are the five stages of economic growth as Rostow sees them. The rest of his book deals with two sorts of questions. The first are technical questions concerning the *historical* validity of his model. Did societies really grow in this way? Where and when did it happen first. Why? Most of Rostow's updating in the second edition addresses these questions. The other kinds of questions Rostow wrestles with concern the future. What will societies do after they reach the stage of high mass consumption? When will societies still in the first four stages achieve the fifth? Our interests are with this second question—and in the apparent *lack* of interest they have generated among other economists.

How does Rostow see the future? With the benefit of hindsight, we can see that Rostow's view of the future, which is based in large measure on data from the 1950s, is positive but also fatally flawed. He recognizes that economic growth is not automatic, but he acknowledges only the social and political limits to growth, not the physical and ecological ones. This is understandable, given that economists have only recently begun to consider environmental factors.

Rostow's vision of the future does consider the fate of both the haves and the have-nots of the world. For the underdeveloped, have-not nations he foresees economic fulfillment (i.e., reaching the stage of high mass consumption)—if they can utilize technology to increase agricultural productivity, if they are given adequate capital, and if their elites can manage the population growth which occurs when modern medicine lowers death rates and when contraception is not yet widely available. This last condition is crucial. Of these elites Rostow says:

It is they who must overcome the difficulties posed by the rapid diffusion of modern medicine, and ensure that the humane decision to save lives does not lead to an inhumane society. (p. 144)

Many countries began reaching economic fulfillment in the 1960s, when global population was three billion. The size of the world's population in 1990 was over five billion. What does this say about the ability of these affluent countries to use their wealth to help control their populations? Are they in danger of creating inhumane societies?

All in all, Rostow seems optimistic about the outcome. He discusses a variety of issues connected with agricultural productivity, the availability of capital, and population control, and he foresees the world making a successful transition to a state of high mass consumption.

> Billions of human beings must live in a world, if we preserve it, over the century or so until the age of high mass-consumption becomes universal. (pp. 166–167)

And again:

> The end of all of this is not compound interest forever, it is the adventure of seeing what man can do when the pressure of scarcity is lifted from him. (p. 166)

The end of scarcity

But is scarcity on its way out? Or will it stage a comeback in the world's successful economies and continue to hold sway in the rest of the world? Rostow foresaw the modern problem as one of dealing with life beyond scarcity, and asked:

> What to do when the increase in real income itself loses its charm? Babies, boredom, three day weekends, the moon, or the creation of new inner, human frontiers in substitution for the imperatives of scarcity? (p. 16)

As we moved through the 1980s, the public rhetoric took a very different turn. Affluence was still the dominant motif in the American way of life and life in undeveloped nations, of course. Schumacher's characterization of the world as being divided into two camps—25% of which are immensely rich, 75% immensely poor—held true. But a new theme, "the new scarcity," began to enter into public discourse in the United States, and it has since figured prominently in dialogues on political economy, where one sees conventional thinking at its best.

In 1982, former Colorado Governor Richard Lamm presented his views on the country's economic climate in an essay entitled "The Economic Pie Isn't Growing, But More Americans Need Slices." He noted in the economy a decline in real income and fierce competition for public funds:

Very quietly the United States has seen its economy falter and then slide backward. Median family income in 1970 was $20,939 and by 1980 has risen only $84, to $21,023. Family income was actually less in 1980 than it was in 1973. All wage increases and benefits since 1975 have been wiped out by inflation, and in 1980 the average American saw a 5.5 percent loss in real income. The economic pie, sad but true, is not growing.

The supposed prosperity of the Reagan years that followed hardly brought an end to this scarcity, with one in four American children living in poverty, a massive deficit, a bill to bail out the savings and loan industry at a cost of $2,000 per person, and a crumbling infrastructure—roads, bridges, schools, etc.

The voices raised to deplore the new scarcity are numerous and diverse. One that has sounded loudly and has had influence in political circles is that of business policy analyst Robert Reich. In *The Next American Frontier* (1983), Reich chronicles the decline in American productivity, a situation, he believes, is the result of American business applying anachronistic methods to industrial production. His solution is the same offered by others: "Get America moving again through more production!" It is true that Reich's formula is slightly different; he locates the basis of the problem not in productive activity, but in the rise of industrialism in the Third World and in financial manipulation. Reich asks us to recognize that modern nations such as the United States cannot compete with developing nations in enterprises requiring mass production and an unsophisticated work force. Modern societies must shift their attention towards expertise-intensive enterprises, he argues. In addition, the United States must discourage "paper entrepreneurialism"—the skillful manipulation of rules and numbers which produces nothing, but which can generate a huge profit for the manipulator. Otherwise, Reich argues, wealth will become an increasingly scarce commodity in the United States and in other modern societies.

Lamm wants to solve this problem with more growth; Reich wants to shift to more productive enterprises that are better suited to a modernized economy. But what exactly *is* the problem that needs solving? Put simply, it is that productivity is declining and real income is no longer increasing—that families cannot afford to purchase greater numbers of goods and services in the marketplace. This is scarcity?

Lamm acknowledges that "yesterday's luxuries have become today's necessities," but his political orientation and adoption of a conventional economic perspective prevents him from seeing a way out of the current economic crisis. The best that Reich and others can do is devise a more efficient society, which is ultimately unsustainable. The conventional economic perspective can do nothing but urge "more growth," either indiscriminately or in a more responsible way, one that seeks to redistribute income in order to reduce poverty and that perhaps tries to reduce damage to the social and the physical environment. But no matter how innovative are the efforts to "reindustrialize America," they will falter if they are unsound. And they are.

One searches for adequate metaphors to describe this situation. The problem is that of a person who cries out in hunger because there is no junk food in the cupboard, only wholesome, nutritious food. Avoiding the healthy food, the person feels hungry, of course. But what right does that person have to use his resources to buy the kind of food that destroys his health? A heroin addict feels an undeniable craving for a high, but should he be able to use resources to support a habit that will eventually kill him? Perhaps in this is a metaphor for modern economics, founded as they are upon the corrupting dynamics of addiction.

Economics, the beautiful science?

The beauty of conventional economics is its ability to define all human activity in monetary terms. But it's a sinister beauty. We enjoy the fruits of conventional economies in a modern society. We attend films. We eat fruit grown half a continent away. We travel. We have credit. But can we eat all this cake without depriving others of their bread? Are we confident that our children's children will enjoy life and not fall into the "worthless state of existence" now experienced by many hundreds of millions of the world's already impoverished?

It seems unlikely, if conventional economics continues to reign supreme. So long as the dominant economic perspective does not discriminate between cash-money (monetarized) costs and real costs, there is nothing to lead the world away from radical deterioration. Examples abound of how deeply the conventional economic perspective is embedded in our thinking about social reality.

Let us begin with Rostow himself. He simply projects into the future the stages of economic growth that facilitated the modernization of some nations in the eighteenth, nineteenth, and twentieth centuries. Our task, as he sees it, is to hold things together politically, "over the century or so until the age of high mass-consumption becomes universal" (pp. 166–167). And just how are we to do that?

Rostow is in the mainstream when he urges the rest of the world to simulate Western-style economic "development." The 1990s, however, may come to be known as the decade when economic development in conventional terms became a bad word. The historically unusual and unusually fortuitous circumstances of the post–World War II era have come to an end. The "economic miracles" of the postwar era are turning belly up. In Brazil, for example, the years of "miraculous" growth rates in monetized GNP have ended. Default on the 100–plus-billion-dollar foreign debt that financed the miracle is a practical fact of life, even though legal fictions deny it. The Mexican oil bubble has burst. Nigeria has proclaimed a grudging austerity program. Following the first flush of freedom in Eastern Europe that proclaimed the end of communism, the hard cold facts about the costs of "free enterprise" have begun to appear. What has been the net effect of economic development in these and other societies?

The evidence in the case of Brazil is abundant and compelling. The economic miracle meant the dramatic expansion of the modernized economic sector, embracing perhaps 20% of the total population. But it was accomplished by a net *decrease* in real income and social welfare for the bulk of the rural population. The 80% living outside the modern sector became even poorer than they were before the "miracle." In many areas the infant mortality rate actually increased, and today stands at nearly 100 per 1,000 nationwide! In contrast to a country like Sweden, where the mortality rate for children under five is about 1% of all deaths, in Brazil such deaths account for nearly 50% of all deaths—a figure more medieval than modern. Sylvia Hewlett's book *The Cruel Dilemmas of Development* explores this, and places responsibility for it on the models of economic development followed by Brazil. The social chaos there exemplifies the ever more apparent flaws in conventional economic thinking about development.

It is risky and somewhat unfair to lump together all economists and economies together and claim they follow "conventional economic thinking"; I do it to contrast their type of thinking with the economics of ecological transformation. There *is* diversity within the economic community, of course. Many who criticize "conventional economics" are themselves economists. Nicholas Georgescu-Roegen, Bruce Hamin, Herbert Daly, Orio Giarini, Kenneth Boulding, and E.F. Schumacher come quickly to mind. Evidence of this diversity within economic circles is found in *The Crisis in Economic Theory*, edited by Daniel Bell and Irving Kristol, and in *Dangerous Currents*, by economist Lester Thurow.

Some say that the science of economics is neutral. The world's problems are not the fault of economics or economists, they argue. The culprit is the politically- and profit-motivated use to which self-interested individuals and groups put economics. Perhaps. But perhaps not.

As the modern equivalent of the sixteenth-century clergy, economists are no more or no less to blame for economic conditions, for the economic war that rages between the forces of wealth and the forces of basic need, than were the sixteenth-century theologians to blame for the religious wars in Europe that led to the suffering and deaths of thousands during their age. Economics and politics influence one another. In economics, there is no such thing as the separation of church and state. Unlike religion, which can be partially hidden away from public life, economics is intrinsically and inevitably in the public domain. There is no real spiritual analog to *The Limits to Growth*.

The essence of the problem is how conventional economics uses the concepts of cost, price, and value to approach reality. Major problems in these three area are becoming apparent as monetarized accounting gets further and further away from actual transactions among people, in families, and from people and the physical environment.

Of course, economists are not totally blind to this problem. They have developed the concept of "externality" to identify costs that stand outside production, marketing, and sales. Externality is a central issue in Hardin's concept of the tragedy of the commons, where each person seeks to push as much of the cost of doing business onto the general public as possible. Externality then becomes primarily a political issue, for it exists to the degree that communities tolerate it. Sound economics acknowledges its political roots and limits in the same way it recognizes its ties to the environment. The economic analysis of a sustainable society insists upon a method of accounting for costs that includes concern for future generations.

Future generations cannot "bid" for resources directly. Families must manifest their concern for the future. And there is another group that cannot speak for itself—the world's non-human beings. In Dr. Seuss' *The Lorax*, the Lorax appears before a profit-seeking, polluting businessman to declare: "I am the Lorax, I speak for the trees!" But the Lorax is economically invisible. He can influence the economic life of the community only through the political process. Who speaks for the Lorax?

An economist friend writes, "We must force firms into accounting for *all* their actions by altering the legal, political, and social environment that firms operate in so that they must price resources at their true value." Amen. But this hardly exonerates economics, because the economic process will move ahead with its analyses regardless of whether costs are internalized. Giarini argues that this approach was perhaps acceptable in the past, when human impact on the life of the planet was relatively small, but, as this human impact has grown, the approach has become ever more misleading. Conventional economics seems ready to talk price even when price is an ecological fiction.

Is economics an endangered species?

With ecology on one side and politics on the other, conventional economics has a precarious hold on reality, because it operates as if the other two were not there. Political economics? Yes. Ecological economics? Yes. But economics on its own? No. Enter system dynamics analysts such as Jay Forrester. Forrester's approach to economics incorporates the interplay of economics, ecology, and politics (not to mention demography). By constructing complex models that characterize the real world, systems dynamics is often at loggerheads with economics, which minimizes complexity through use of grand assumptions. But "assuming X" and acting "as if Y" doesn't serve us well anymore. The results are misleading at best. Witness the case of GNP.

Gross National Product is the sum total of the monetarized *transactions* for goods and services. (Some note that a more sensible approach would focus on the *stock* of goods, not on their flow.) When the scale of human economic activity was relatively small, GNP made pretty good sense. It was essentially correct to assume that increases in monetarized goods and services occurred without offsetting decreases in non-monetarized goods and services. Certainly, there were many individual decreases in the nonmonetarized sector. One cannot read Charles Dickens' accounts of economic modernization in the nineteenth century without seeing some of the costs—the enclosing of the green commons and the charging of rent, an increase in taxes, the disintegration of communities, and a changing relationship with the land. But all in all, things in the nonmonetarized side of the equation absorbed the costs of increasing the monetarized side. For modernized societies such as the United States, the turning point has come with the transformation of household economies, as the nonmonetarized family economy has been monetarized—and with a vengeance.

It appears that at one time family economies were approximately balanced between the monetarized and the nonmonetarized, because households were very labor rather than capital intensive. Food preparation, childbearing and child rearing, health care, recreation, cleaning, and repair were all very labor intensive. The big change in the economy of the family came when it substituted capital intensive technologies for labor intensive ones in performing these household duties. Rostow defines his fourth stage of growth, "The Drive to Maturity," as "the period when society has effectively applied the range of [its] modern technology to the bulk of its resources." This includes its children. The *cash* cost of bearing and rearing children has *skyrocketed*. Most childbirth occurs in hospitals, and the event has become a financial spectacle. Outfitting and training a child through adolescence requires an exorbitant amount of money.

Thus far, this line of reasoning only brings us to the threshold of the new home economics. At this point the microeconomists of family life and household management arrive upon the scene. They begin to examine the economic productivity of family members. They speak of the "opportunity costs" of child rearing: what income does a person forego by spending time and laboring in the home as a homemaker and caretaker? A 1980 estimate figured the cost at about $40,000 for a woman with clerical or blue-collar skills and about $80,000 for a woman with a graduate education. The "direct costs" of raising children for a middle class family stood at about $100,000 for eighteen years, according to Department of Agriculture and Department of Labor calculations. This focus on opportunity costs does result in greater appreciation for the productivity of women, particularly those maintaining households. But that's the only good thing about it; in the long run it's dangerous because it reinforces the idea that everything is for sale. That's bad news for today's children and for their children's children.

Some jobs are more equal than others

Monetarized exchanges form the basis for these calculations, of course. The key variable is the entrance of mothers into the labor force. Indeed, the entrance into the work world of such a large segment of the population is the dominant issue in family economics today. However, if we consider only cost, price, and value, we will not be able to see the real economic implications of such movement on families. Data on the income of mothers--25% of family income on average in the United States—do not tell the whole story.

The introduction of capital- and energy-intensive technology into the family economy has real costs that transcend mere monetary transactions. From a strictly monetary point of view, a net gain occurs when a family member purchases energy-intensive goods to replace a labor-intensive activity, as long as the cost of the items is less than the income generated by the activity it replaces. Consider the family that pays eight dollars for a highly processed meal because members of the family are employed outside the home and don't have time to cook a more healthy meal from scratch for five dollars. Conventional economic accounting asks only "How much did the family earn for that time at work?" If the answer is ten dollars, then the family has a net gain. This kind of cost-benefit accounting considers the gamut of household activities and extends beyond to the neighborhood, as in the case of walking to the shopping center versus driving there.

The point is that such calculations are flawed. Every substitution of energy- and material-intensive goods for human labor has costs that extend far beyond the dollar price in the monetary economy. If such goods rely on nonrenewable energy and materials and are used by masses of people, the costs involved are historically significant. Each substitution is a moral issue. Conventional economics is blind to all this, or at least approaches it with only one eye open. It has an invalid conception of "cost," an artificial idea of price, and an incomplete concept of value.

This is not to say that economics and economists have no way of dealing with these problems—to the contrary. Most economists seem to believe that anything and everything is possible, if we only arrange the flow of dollars correctly. Want to cut down on the use of oil? Charge more for it. Want to increase the amount of oil available? Pay more for it. Want to reduce maternal employment outside the home? Pay them less. Want to increase the number of women running households full time? Pay them more. No one would disagree that adjustments in the flow of dollars can have a significant, even dramatic influence on human behavior. Everyone and everything has a price, right?

Right—but within limits. What are those limits? That is precisely the issue before us. What are the limits to conventional economic analysis?

The physical and social environments impose limits upon economics, and we are bumping up against them with ever-increasing frequency as we move through the latter part of the twentieth century. We ignore these limits at the peril of our social selves.

Family economics and the meaning of productivity

Family economics is at the cutting edge of efforts to illuminate the dynamics of making the transition to a sustainable society. Other institutions determine much of what goes on in families, of course, but it is within families that the drama of consumption and waste is played out. That's why discussions about rising and falling family income are difficult to interpret. Do more dollars mean less waste and consumption, or more? Conventional economics doesn't recognize the difference between the "more" and the "less" of this question, and that's the problem. The task is yet more complicated because one of the main variables in the equation has many cultural connotations. That variable is the role of mothers in the monetarized labor force outside the home— "working mothers," to use a term that is a model of redundancy. How fair is an economic system that simply asks mothers to shoulder the burdens of earning an income *and* raising a family? Where is the justice in allowing fathers to work outside the home at energy- and capital-intensive activities, while women are performing the labor-intensive ones at home? A just solution, one that dignifies all kinds of human labor, bases all aspects of work and play on renewable energy and material.

We need an economics that begins such a transformation, that will put social welfare systems in harmony with planetary systems. Conventional economics just can't do it. Rostow's vision of the future as "the end of scarcity" is supported by the more recent analyses of Cornucopians Julius Simon and Herman Kahn, who seem to believe that everything really does have a price and that we can overcome *all* physical and social limits if we have enough money. These approaches rely on flawed fundamental assumptions about economic life, technology, and the Earth's ecology.

One such assumption concerns productivity. Conventional approaches assume that economic development comes from shifting financial resources *to* those who will spend or lend them more "productively" and *away* from those who will put it to less "productive" uses. As Rostow points out, this is "one of the oldest and most fundamental notions in economics" (pp. 45–47).

What is productivity?

And what are the criteria for judging productivity? That's the rub, of course. Conventional economics was built and continues to rest upon assumptions about prices, costs, and values, which is a tragic flaw in the most classic sense. As Aristotle tells us in his *Poetics*, a tragic flaw is an aspect of character that simultaneously makes for nobility, success, and worth and creates the conditions for inevitable defeat. Oedipus was a tragic figure; the very ambition and courage that brought about this success also brought about his downfall.

Conventional economics contains such a tragic flaw. Many a wag refers to economics as "the dismal science," but there is growing recognition that it might be better labeled "the immaterial science," because it operates as if its conceptual and symbolic transactions are grounded firmly in the world, when in fact they may not be. Revisionist economists Nicholas Georgescu-Roegen and Kenneth Boulding, among others, have identified and explored this tragic flaw.

Conventional economics sees the economic process as a closed system, independent of the material systems of the Earth. It admits no limits to what adjustments in the flow of dollars can achieve, as if everything really does have a price. (This leaves aside its often unrealistic social and psychological assumptions.) As Georgescu-Roegen put it: "The patent fact that between the economic process and the material environment there exists a continuous mutual influence which is history-making carries no weight with the standard economist" (p. 50). Human economic activity can change the physical and social probabilities of future possibilities. Thus, we cannot presume that what were once valid economic assumptions, models, and theories will be valid in the future.

In fact, *human activity cannot produce anything material at all.* All we do, all we *can* do, is transform and degrade materials. Our economically "productive" activity transforms one state of matter into another by capturing and focusing energy. Of course, some transformed matter is beautiful and clever; some is ugly and stupid. But all of our "products" are really just transformations. This transformed matter is, *for a period of time*, useful in economic terms. Then it becomes waste. This is the key to understanding conventional economics as an immaterial science: the thing we always "produce" is waste. At issue is only the length of time between the initial transformation and eventual degradation into waste, and the duration and magnitude of the environmental impact of this process.

Conventional economics does not recognize the material base of "production" as temporary. It ignores entropy and proceeds as if metal and wood, oil-based and solar energy, polyester and cotton, and machines and people may be manipulated equally through adjustments in the flow of dollars. A person with only the most passing acquaintance with the Earth's ecology can see the absurdity of this. Some costs do not translate into dollars.

The catchphrase "everything has a price" encapsulates the standard economic paradigm, which evolved during the seventeenth century, when the scale of human civilization in relation to nonrenewable resources made it a rough approximation of reality. That paradigm is dangerously unrealistic today.

Standard economics assumes that the production/consumption process is real apart from its material aspects. It assumes that all is in order because the books balance. This assumption reminds me of a joke I heard some years ago. A group of professors is marooned on a desert island. They discover a case of canned food that has washed ashore, but they don't have a can opener. What to do? Each professor offers a suggestion based on his academic background. The physicist suggests a complex series of pulleys to create sufficient force per square inch to open the ends of the cans. The biologist suggests growing an algae that would eat through the metal. The lawyer suggests they sue the maker of the cans. Finally, the economist announces that he has the solution. The group is all ears as he speaks: "First, assume we have a can opener. . . ."

Unfair? Not when we look at the assumptions that conventional economics makes about the world. We are on a global spaceship, left to our own devices to feed, clothe, and shelter ourselves and to build satisfying and meaningful relationships, *permanently*. Each year there are more and more passengers, many with a minimum of food, clothing, and shelter. At a gathering to discuss the problem this situation creates, a conventional economist from one of the luxury suites takes charge and announces that he has a solution. "First," he says, "assume we are not on a spaceship and not dependent on ourselves to feed, clothe, and shelter our fellow passengers from the ship's stores, but that we have an infinite source of canned food. . . . Then sell a can opener at top dollar."

The news from television, newspapers, and magazines suggests that conventional economics is more like astrology or alchemy than it is like other sciences—very accurate and complex, but basically invalid. The stock market goes up and down, and "analysts" explain why in the daily news reports. The "Crash of 1987" brought this home to even the most trusting, and the "Fall of 1988" made this point to the rest. In truth, however, the stock market itself bears only the most passing connection to the material realities of life, and the only "scientific" thing about it is that those with "inside information" can do better than if they had relied on chance, while those without that information are gambling (or worse). In the 1984 annual report of Twentieth Century Fund, executive director M.J. Rossant put it this way: "Economists and economic policy makers have distinguished themselves only by the inaccuracy of their forecasts and by the wrongheadedness of their advice." Many observers enjoyed a hearty chuckle some years back at the news that the small stock portfolio of the American Economics Association did *worse* than it would have if investment decisions had been made by a roll of the dice.

Are Lee Iacocca and William Shakespeare identical twins?

In 1982, George Stigler won the Nobel Prize in economics. Stigler opposed governmental regulation and the ethos of those who seek to control the economy for political purposes. He dismisses those who argue that the introduction of a new automobile twice a year is wasteful, because he believes that the market is the best arbiter of economic choices. Stigler suggests, tongue in cheek perhaps, that if we reject changes in automobile styles, then should we not also reject new books and newspapers? Why not continue reading only Shakespeare instead of Tennessee Williams? Why read today's newspapers when those from 1900 were good enough? A man of such intellect and wit as Stigler saw the difference between cars and plays—as a person, at least, if not as an economist. Conventional economics really doesn't see the difference, of course. It *really doesn't*, and it often seems proud of that fact. Economics doesn't see such differences in cultural terms, which is understandable and even appropriate (albeit wrong) given the goal of economics: limiting economic concerns to means rather than to ends. Nor does economics see this difference in material terms, which really is inappropriate and quite wrong, considering that economics is the study of connecting means and ends.

Stigler objects to the common casting of economics as the dismal science: "I resent the phrase, for only young children should get angry at a corpus of knowledge that prevents hopeless but costly endeavors." Endeavors such as what? Semiannual changes in automobile models that serve only fashion and accelerate the transformation of low-entropy materials into high-entropy waste? If only conventional economics *were* such a dismal science when it came to preventing ecologically "hopeless but costly endeavors," rather than a Pollyannaish "science" of basically false assumptions about the material world.

Contrast Stigler with Nicholas Georgescu-Roegen on the matter of automobiles:

> Every time we produce a Cadillac, we irrevocably destroy an amount of low entropy that could otherwise be used for producing a plow or a spade. In other words, every time we produce a Cadillac, we do it at the cost of decreasing the number of human lives in the future.   ·

And again, on fashion:

> We must also get rid of fashion. . . . It is indeed a disease of the mind to throw away a coat or a piece of furniture while it can still perform its specific service. To get a "new" car every year and to refashion the house every other is a bioeconomic crime. (p. 74)

Conventional economics dismisses such thinking as romantic, utopian, visionary, fuzzy, or worse. Conventional economics offers the much more ethereal concept of the "guiding hands" of the marketplace: "everything has a price," and "if we offer to pay for it, it will be provided." It's a socially suicidal vision at worst and prayerful thinking at best.

Is "economic man" a family man?

Conventional economics lives in an ecological fantasy world. The irony is that most conventional economists see themselves—and are seen by most others—as hard-nosed realists. There has long been criticism of the concept of "Economic Man" as a valid representation of the human being. In conventional economics, Economic Man is an "information processor" who makes rational decisions about the investment of labor and capital. This Economic Man is, of course, very masculine as opposed to being generically human, as we shall see in chapter 7. To his credit, Rostow goes beyond a simplistic concept of Economic Man and echoes the early ideas of Karl Marx. The following passage is from *Stages of Economic Growth*:

> In the stages-of-growth sequence man is viewed as a more complex unit. He seeks, not merely economic advantage, but also power, leisure, adventure, continuity of experience and security; he is concerned with his family, the familiar values of his regional and national culture, and a bit of fun down at the local tavern. And beyond these diverse homey attachments man is capable of being moved by a sense of connection with human beings everywhere, who, he recognizes, share his essentially paradoxical condition. In short, net human behavior is seen not as an act of maximization, but as an act of balancing alternative and often conflicting human objectives in the face of the range of choices men perceive to be open to them. (p. 149)

Reading this again after twenty years, I remember Rostow's appeal. His Economic Man may be male, but at least it's human. He may not go far enough, but he does show an appreciation for the human quality lacking in most conventional economics. The concept of the Economic Man recalls Noam Chomsky's critique of behavioral psychologist B.F. Skinner. Skinner's "Psychological Man," as presented in *Verbal Behavior* and *Beyond Freedom and Dignity,* is much the same one-dimensional information processing entity as the classical Economic Man. Both are correct in detail but tragically incomplete in the whole. Neither is really a family man. A mature view of human behavior recognizes multiple sources of motivation—some unconscious, some rooted in biology, and some culturally conditioned. Any simple economic model is psychologically naive.

Rostow transcends the psychological impoverishment of conventional economics, and he does consider the family as a central factor in the future of socioeconomic life. He believes it is important to deal with the quantitative aspects of family life in societies just beginning to move through the stages of growth.

Among societies already in or just reaching the age of high mass consumption, he also recognizes the critical importance of family. He recognizes that once a society overcomes the problem of scarcity, the fifth stage, it is ready to turn to other matters. Its attention shifts from problems of supply to issues of demands and "welfare in the widest sense" (p. 73). Indeed, much of the public agenda is then dominated by discussions of social welfare systems. The society in the stage of high mass consumption now has the luxury of concerning itself with such things as automobiles, the technology of entertainment, and household gadgets, as well as such issues as employee benefit packages, medical specialization, and Social Security. And family.

> Americans have behaved as if, having been born into a system that provided economic security and high mass-consumption, they placed a lower valuation on acquiring additional increments of real income in the conventional form as opposed to the advantages and values of an enlarged family. (p. 31)

Birth rates and family orientation were indeed high in the economically buoyant 1950s, the source of data upon which Rostow based his conclusion. Thirty years later, we can agree that concern with and value of family remain high, although family size has shrunk. Rostow's view is not great family history; the 1950s were an aberration in a century-long trend, as Andrew Cherlin's analysis makes clear. But Rostow's thesis falters not only as *family* history, but as economic history as well.

The debate over limits to growth is historical in its essence. The historical questions are these: Is conventional economic thinking limited in its historical validity? Will the near future, until the year 2010, be a simple extension of the recent past of 1950 to 1970? Is the current period (1970–1990) typical of the long-term trend (1900-2010)? To answer these questions we must turn to Orio Giarini's *Dialogue on Wealth and Welfare* (1981). In it Giarini examines the essential features of monetarized and nonmonetarized sectors of the human economy and their relationship to each other.

The need for an economic history that is historical

Rostow's analysis may be called economic history, but it is strangely nonhistorical in the way in which it relates the human population to the material Earth. Rostow seems to assume that the relationship is constant and will not change. Giarini, on the other hand, begins and ends his economic history with this relationship.

First, Giarini argues, the modern economic system required a technological and cultural base that would allow the Industrial Revolution to occur. He cites a report in the *New Scientist* that the Roman Empire of the fourth century possessed the *technical* knowledge necessary for the Industrial Revolution but that it lacked the cultural underpinnings for it to take place. In this respect he supports Rostow's thesis about the preconditions for take-off.

Second, Giarini argues, modern conventional economics is very much historically bound to the conditions that existed in the seventeenth and eighteenth centuries. The key assumptions during that period were that money could accurately reflect value, that monetary cost was a good measure of real cost (as in the cost of the "free" materials of the Earth), that market forces were sufficient enough to regulate economic activity, and that "production" was intrinsically good. The standard economic model of that time was a rough approximation of reality—much in the way that a child's early concepts of the world are functional so long as he or she is limited to a supervised playpen. By offering this developmental perspective Giarini is doing for economics what Jean Piaget and Lev Vygotsky did for child psychology.

Giarini argues that the match between the standard economic model and reality has become less and less perfect ever since. The model's flaws are becoming obvious in our own time (1970–1990), as human activity increases to the point at which assumptions of "free" and "unlimited" materials, production, and waste disposal are shown to be false. Standard economic thinking has become anachronistic. Such thinking is not only imprecise but wrong, because it produces "scientific" conclusions that run counter to humanity's best interests. This begins to explain why the world appears to be so economically puzzling and mysterious so much of the time, particularly to those who rightly seek to put social welfare systems at the center of their analyses. The areas that appear so puzzling include food production, the quality of the physical environment, and the social consequences of capital investment strategies. Why is there hunger? Why are the air and water filled with toxins and carcinogens? Why is life such a rat race for so many of us?

Giarini believes that we need a new economic model that will *accurately* describe and analyze the new conditions we face. In it, economics and ecology return to their natural relationship, with the former being a subsidiary of the latter. At the heart of the economic model is a better estimation of total value, one that includes both monetarized and nonmonetarized economic costs and benefits. In such a model, the meaning and relationships of labor and capital must be rethought and recalculated, with everything that it implies for industrialization and urbanization.

We began with Walter Rostow's analysis of the stages of economic growth. His very strength as an economic historian proves to be his greatest weakness as an analyst of the human condition. Ironically, his work founders because he doesn't recognize historical discontinuity between the ecological/economic relationships of the past and those of the future. History is propelling us toward the ever greater need for an ecological, transformational economics, one that recognizes that human activity produces nothing material. It only transforms energy and existing material into new forms, which exist for a shorter or longer period and then become waste—which itself may be transformed further if desire and technology permit. Conventional economics is flawed in its assumption that adjustments of cash flows ("price") have unlimited power to incorporate these transformations. These limits once were of only marginal physical significance, although their social, psychological, and spiritual significance has long been recognized. Now that human activity has increased to the point that it is physically significant to the Earth's ecosystems, limits of conventional economics are becoming ever more apparent. What were once hypothetical limits have become actual. This is manifest in the world's cities and factories, as we shall see next, where efforts to integrate social welfare and conventional economic models founder.

SIX

Industrialization and Urbanization

January 1984. Taishan, China. Viewed from the air, China's cities resemble green doughnuts. The urban centers are surrounded by greenbelts that produce food, particularly vegetables and rice. A natural and mutual interdependence is at work here. Food is grown in the greenbelt and transported a relatively short distance to the concentrated urban population. The city provides cash income, organic wastes for fertilizer, services of many kinds, and a market for labor not needed in or suited to the countryside. There is little of the long-distance transportation of food which we depend upon in the United States, where the average molecule of food travels more than 1,200 miles before being eaten.

Other modernizing societies have failed the test of stabilizing the countryside, providing a standard of living for the rural population that compares well with that of the city, and preventing an unmanageable flow of people from the country into the cities. Unlike Brazil, which reversed its rural/urban mix during the 1970s (when the urban population grew by 30% in ten years), China remains 80% rural. But the agrarian and spartan collective policies of the past appear to be changing. Recent years have seen a new national commitment to modernization, which translates into mass industrialization and increase production of consumer goods. Accompanying this change is a "new responsibility system" that favors individual initiative in economic matters and includes new pressures and rewards for agricultural

140

and manufacturing production at almost any cost. This new wave is chang-
ing the face of China. Driving into Guangzhou (Canton), a returning visitor
observes in horror land that only two years ago was devoted to vegetable
growing is now a field of high-rise apartment buildings. The green doughnut
is being split by new corridors of urbanization. China is in the midst of a re-
assessment of its physical, social, and economic foundation.

All this is on my mind as I walk the streets of Taishan, a smallish city in
southern China. New construction is rampant—some of it nibbling away at
the food-producing greenbelt. Small shops, factories, and television antennas
are visible everywhere. Motorbikes swim in the stream of bicycle traffic.
There are neon signs reminiscent of Hong Kong. In the bustling market, the
traditional items—vegetables, livestock, household crafts—are joined or even
displaced by brightly colored polyester clothes, plastic containers, cassette
tape decks, and the other accoutrements of modern life. One booth even sells
plastic shopping bags printed with all-too-familiar messages: "Souvenir of
Niagara Falls." "London Bridge." "Welcome to Disney"!

I'm hearing a new song: "How ya gonna keep them down on the farm, af-
ter they've seen Disney?" (doo wah doo wah)

If Henry Ford was the perfect symbol of industrialization in the first
half of the twentieth century, then Walt Disney, Inc. serves that function in the second half. Ford focused on basic mass production and
consumption. Disney, Inc. focuses on plastic sensations, on high-tech
environmental manipulation, and on information. Many analysts of the
American economy recommend that we adopt just this kind of business in the future; Robert Reich (*The Next American Frontier*) and Alvin
Toffler (*The Third Wave*) are foremost among them.

In 1982, Disney, Inc. opened EPCOT Center, a partner of the Disney
World Complex near Orlando, Florida. EPCOT is a vision of the postindustrial order, the "information society" that Disney has been working on for decades. In a way it succeeds. Disney World–EPCOT Center
is the modern industrial order taken to its logical but absurd end. It is
environmentally imperious and energy intensive. It lives off the basic
enterprises of others; it provides social and physical arrangements that
are deceiving; and it manifests a vision of the future that offers us bigger,
better, and more—with little or no appreciation for global needs and resources. Henry Ford move over. Walt Disney, Inc. is coming through.

The nineteenth-century English poet Samuel Taylor Coleridge told
us that the appreciation of art required a "willing suspension of disbe-
lief." A visit to Disney World–EPCOT Center, though enjoyable, re-

quires a willing suspension of *belief*—belief in the world problematique. If those concerned about the fate of the Earth become increasingly curmudgeonly as they rant and rave about shopping centers,
amusement parks, and the other accouterments of modernized society,
it is because they find it harder than ever to suspend their belief that
the world is in crisis. We *all* ought to worry about our grandchildren,
born and unborn, and their prospects for a materially and socially sustainable existence. When I look beyond my family to the larger human
family, I worry about the children I met in China, the Sudan, Ecuador,
and Brazil who are already refugees of global economic war. What will
industrialization and urbanization mean for Chun Chien Wu and Ed-
ney Marciel Cardoso, as well as for my own Joshua and Joanna?

Putting "more and more energy and machinery at the disposal of
each worker and consumer" (to use Harlan Cleveland's and Tom Wilson's phrase)—this is the essence of industrialization and urbanization
stripped of ideological content. The Europeans developed this strategy
over three centuries of trial and error, increasingly in partnership with
North America, Japan, and the former Soviet Union. The "Western
model of development" that emerged emphasizes the melding of social
and physical technology in large, complex industrial systems (of which
international conglomerates are the most mature incarnation, and
monster cities and mechanized farms the most visible symbols). This
was not accomplished without causing a great deal of disruption, suffering, and injustice in families. The result was a general increase in the
energy and machinery available to the average worker and consumer,
as well as unprecedented luxury for the elites. Even the "losers" in
modern industrialized societies have access to more energy and machinery than their peers in other places and times, no matter that they
are too demoralized to make good use of it. We must question the future value and viability of this urban industrial order, both in newly
modernizing societies and in the societies that gave birth to it. And we
must wonder about its effects on our children and grandchildren.

In this chapter we apply the abstract economics of the last chapter to
the concrete environment, the physical expression of modernization in
factories, farms, and cities. This application is necessary if we are to
move beyond the limitations of economics—the immaterial science of
"production"—and adopt the more socially sensible principles of the
economics of transformation. Industrialization and urbanization show
us how and where transformation occurs; technological sophistication
accompanies the rise of urban centers. Indeed, in *Ecological Economics*

(1981), economist Kenneth Boulding goes so far as to define civilization as "cities drawing their food from the surrounding countryside" (p. 127), a process still evident in China and elsewhere, where mass transportation of processed food has not yet obscured the fundamental dynamics of land use. With some exceptions, cities provided the critical mass that allowed cultural evolution to move into high gear and produce scientific and artistic progress.

City, factory, and farm

The grand outline of the intertwined history of industrialization and urbanization is well known. Industrialization creates and employs physical and social technologies that permit significant increases in output per worker. This means the transformation of materials and energy into products for human consumption. All aspects of human activity have come under the dominance of this basic shift.

Even agriculture has become industrial. By employing technologies that cost money, industrialization maximizes the output of each farm worker. Costs rise, but the process "frees" people from the land, and, in the process, makes them available for other industrial work, such as in city factories, where the bulk of our materials and energy are transformed into products. However, if there is to be even the semblance of justice in the process of industrialization and urbanization, it must arise out of high-yield agriculture. Without high yields there is not enough food to feed city dwellers, and without food cities either die or impoverish the countryside by extorting food from subsistence farmers. This dynamic between the city and the country is visible today in Brazil, where, for example, efforts to supply the cities with both food and grain-based fuel threaten subsistence farmers in rural areas. People in the countryside have been "freed" from the land, but the cities where they go to seek work have no jobs for them. The government follows a policy of increased urbanization based in Western models—moving people out of agriculture and into industry, from the land and into the cities—but it does so without providing for the families displaced in the process. In the cities and without assistance, these families are left to reenact the suffering chronicled by Charles Dickens during the industrialization of England in the nineteenth century. At least displaced Europeans of the eighteenth and nineteenth centuries could emigrate to the United States; the displaced families of today, however, have nowhere to go and have no real chance of joining the kind of mass industrial society that once existed but that now is extinct. Sylvia Hewlett calls this one of the "cruel dilemmas" of development, and she is right on the mark.

Cities grow rapidly as agriculture becomes more industrialized. A larger city population requires more food, which in turn requires farms to produce more food. To increase output, farms become more industrialized, replacing people with machines and thus releasing more workers into the city. This self-perpetuating cycle of greater output and greater demand degrades the environment by dumping waste into rivers, fields, and the air, and it taxes social welfare systems, which have to handle the flow of families into cities unable to accommodate them.

This process in the modernized societies of Europe during the eighteenth and nineteenth centuries was often turbulent. To permit industrialized agriculture, people were forced off the land. Industrial work was, in many cases, nasty and brutish, and life expectancy was short. The quality of life for urban families was usually low, with poor sanitation, inadequate housing, and often inconsistent employment. Children were often brutally exploited for their labor. Charles Dickens, Upton Sinclair, and others cut their literary teeth describing such conditions. Indeed, in describing the conditions of families and communities during this period, Dickens was a better historian than most of his contemporaries (and many of ours as well), because he saw the essential details (children and their parents struggling to survive physically and morally) where they saw only the big picture of industrial progress.

Industrialization and urbanization have many complex consequences for the physical environment, and they eventually affect the social environment. Soil erosion is one such problem; production of methane and carbon dioxide is another. Atmospheric scientists believe that significant increases in these gases can affect climate. At very high levels they can produce a global increase in temperature sufficient to melt glacial ice at the polar caps and thereby raise the level of the world's oceans enough to flood coastal cities. If this were to occur, it would reshape patterns of human settlement. The natural factors that produce these gases and determine their levels of concentration in the atmosphere are giving way to factors determined by human activity.

Three human sources help determine the concentration of these gases in the atmosphere. The first is the burning of hydrocarbonous fuels. Second is the increased activity of gas-producing termites, which feed on wood debris accumulated in the widespread clearing-cutting of forests. Third is the fattening of cattle, an important activity in modern food production. The massive concentrations of cattle excrement produce large amounts of methane; the amount of methane in the atmosphere increased by about 2% per year in the early 1980s. Industrialization and urbanization in the twentieth century are beginning to impact the environment on a global level, in both the physical and social domains. As Herman Daly puts it, "Until recently the economy of man was 'peanuts' in the total economy of nature" (1980, p. 245). This has changed. We are now the big kid on the environmental block.

China: Progress at what cost?

The link between modernization and scale is clear, as is illustrated in the case of China, where modernization is taking place in a population of more than one billion people. Even in this predominantly rural and marginally industrialized nation, the entire environment already seems engineered for human purposes. Every animal and plant is reserved for human consumption. Songbirds are caught for food; following the harvest, fields are cleaned so that stalks and leaves can be burned for fuel; every hillside is a potential site for terraced farming. This was true even before the efforts of the last three decades to upgrade the productivity of farms, factories, and power-generation facilities in order to increase the material comforts of a population that has doubled since 1950.

According to a report by Victor Smil, most of the fuel needs of the 800 million rural Chinese have been met by environmentally cannibalistic practices—e.g., burning wood beyond renewable levels and using vegetable matter that otherwise could serve as fertilizer. I was struck by this during my visit there. It seems every available bit of biomass is accounted for. The forest floor is literally swept clean; pine needles, leaves, and branches are collected for fuel to boil water, which is otherwise unfit for drinking.

Smil reports that agricultural development has worked hand in hand with fuel needs in deforesting huge areas. In Heilongjiang Province, supplier of 50% of the country's timber, 2% of forested areas have been cleared every year. Other areas have been cleared at the same rate over the past two decades, although there is an ongoing reforestation program which requires the participation of white-collar workers to meet planting goals.

Since 1950, the Chinese have increased grain production by 70%

(counterbalanced by population increase), but they have paid for it in soil erosion, the chemical pollution of lakes from fertilizers, and other consequences of industrialized, large-scale agriculture. Smil reports that 30% of the farmland has been lost to these forces since 1960. To make matters worse, Chinese agencies and communities have yet to implement reclamation and irrigation projects. Irrigation canals effectively deliver only about 45% of the water that enters the system, and Orville Schell reports that the new individual responsibility system provides no incentive to upgrade them. Thus, some of these facilities are rapidly deteriorating. Only about one-third of the saplings planted in reforestation programs since the 1950s have survived. Despite a massive, month-long tree planting program each year, the impoverished soil and predatory fuel needs of the population greatly slow progress in reforestation. The costs of "modernization" have been staggering, even for a society accustomed to dealing with massive challenges.

The modern economy: Who's in charge?

Modernization proceeds through families. Making economics concrete means working out the implications that changes in the techniques, organization, and side effects of production will have on families. The desire to provide for one's own family is strong, so strong that it can run the engines of the larger economy. People work to provide for their dependents. How and when they work affects the care children need and receive. Pre- or nonindustrial agriculture restricts variation in day-to-day life. Subsistence farming consumes labor at a rapid rate. Modernization dramatically increases the variation in what people do and brings new challenges to family life.

For example, the modern era permits and thus demands the expansion of the "day" into the night. Shift work is possible because of electric illumination. Nearly one-quarter of the American labor force works in the evening or on night shifts; 33% of children age fourteen or younger have at least one parent who works at night. The physiological functioning of a person who works on shifts is impaired, particularly if he or she works long hours and changes shifts frequently. However, in conventional economic thinking, shift work is necessary. Modern industrial plants have large capital investments to pay off, and they must run at *their* full capacity—regardless of the needs of the human beings who serve them.

Harriet Presser's research tells us that shift work often impacts nega-tively on families. Evening shifts take their greatest toll on parent–child relationships, and shifts that run overnight undermine marriages. But increased production boosts GNP, directly through on-the-job work and indirectly through the child care programs, processed foods, and other services that cater to the working family. And because the house-work women traditionally do is invisible in GNP, moving them into "male" jobs does not show up in calculations as an economic trade-off but only as a sign of economic growth. As such, it may be totally bogus from the perspective of the wealth of families.

The availability of modern transportation permits and thus demands expansion of the size of the family's economic environment. Work and home can be separated geographically and then linked together by commuting. The same is true for school and home and for marketing and home. The costs are enormous, but conventional economics treats the trade-off as "growth" because it adds to GNP. It is a special irony that walking to work is now a luxury few can afford. Doesn't this tell us something about modernization?

Modern machinery permits (and thus requires) a diminution of "productive" enterprises within the family. Industrialization "frees" the family from its historic need to produce and recasts it into the role of consumer (to use these terms in their conventional sense). Conven-tional economics registers more gain in GNP as families pay others to grow, transport, and prepare their food, clothing, shelter, and enter-tainment. Women, in particular, are changed in this process. Tradi-tional household work and child care are no longer simply taken for granted but are actually considered costs to be borne by the family be-cause it does not participate in the cash labor force outside the home.

All these aspects of modernization seem to have a relentless internal logic. Once they become feasible, they seem to become inevitable. We have opened Pandora's box, and old ways seem powerless before the onslaught of power, speed, efficiency, and quantity.

"Time is money." Money is the essence of modern industrialism—the standard of value and the primary criterion by which to organize and judge human endeavors. It even takes precedence over putting more and more energy and machinery at the disposal of each worker and consumer. As such it is worth exploring. For help in understanding this we can turn to Orio Giarini's insightful *Dialogue on Wealth and Wel-fare* (1981).

What does it mean to be rich?

Giarini maintains that economics "is the discipline of the industrialization process and specifically of the Industrial Revolution, which started in Europe more than two centuries ago" (p. 4). As he sees it, the basic concepts of economics grew out of the industrial modes of production. Economics is not concerned with the direct, productive work of making tools (the prehistoric world); instead, it measures the creation of capital to finance machines that increase productivity and reduce the need for human labor. Capital, not labor, is the backbone of the industrial society.

Industrial society focuses on the marshaling and management of money to organize energy and machinery. Industrial organizations create jobs, of course, but their purpose is not to create work—it is to produce things that can be sold in the monetarized economy and thereby generate more money. Each element in the system seems to assume that someone else will provide the jobs. Let Jack do it. We see the "normal" level of unemployment rising around the world as more and more economies become modern. In the United States, political rhetoric seems ready to accept a 6% unemployment rate as "normal," when the standard was less than 4% only a decade or so ago. But families need jobs, regardless of the total amount of capital around them, regardless of GNP, regardless of conventional measures of economic development.

As industrialism moves forward, the capital cost of the average job site increases. These cost averages can hide great discrepancies across and within industries and plants. A nuclear power plant costs hundreds of thousands of dollars per job site, while a bakery may only cost tens of thousands, and a small pottery studio may cost hundreds. It is almost impossible to avoid using the term "production" in our discussion, particularly when summarizing the analyses of others. These job sites are engaged not in production but in transformation. The full social and physical costs of these transformations must account for their impact on families, in the areas of child care, commuting, health care, food preparation, and simple peace of mind.

In an industrial society, the household is a work site. The cost of equipping it has increased steadily decade by decade as more technology has entered upon the scene (VCRs and dishwashers, for example) and consumer demand for it has risen. Household appliances have a rationale—they deliver benefits and save time, at least when we compare each appliance with the old method it replaced.

Where does the time go?

Time- and labor-saving household appliances present us with a paradox, however. We bought them to save us time, but if they have saved so much time, why do so many of us feel so hurried and harried? Social critic Ivan Illich argues that modern appliances require false labor from us, and while it saves us much time and energy it offers little of the satisfaction and social interaction we had in the past when lower-level technology required more *genuine* work from us. Baking bread is more satisfying than driving through crowded streets to a supermarket, waiting anonymously in line to buy a loaf of bread, and then transporting it back home. Illich is probably right. Modern urban families seem starved for time in contrast to their traditional agrarian cousins, who may labor longer but do so in ways more in harmony with natural human rhythms. Indeed, a recent survey found that our leisure time had decreased by 25% during the last decade.

Perhaps television best represents the modern paradox of time. It is always available and can consume enormous amounts of time. In the average American household, the television is turned on more than seven hours each day. Many people have insufficient time to take care of business because every day they commit nearly 25% of their waking hours to television. Is television as psychically satisfying and socially facilitating as radio, reading, games, conversation, sewing, or home repair? Probably not. Television is a "time sink"—we can pour our time into it in quantities easily disproportionate to what we receive from it. By and large, there isn't enough quality programming to fill the hours of broadcast time. And the proliferation of cable channels (to as many as 100, if promises are to be believed) will surely exacerbate the problem.

Television is now a cultural force with immense economic significance. It displaces other activities, some of which have larger social and cultural payoffs. As mentioned earlier, the introduction of a television in one South Pacific community drew so many viewers that is replaced the traditional evening get-together chaired by the village elders. Now there's no time for the meetings. Television absorbs time freed by

labor-saving devices. It provides the capital-intensive urban and industrial way of life. And yet there is enough good programming that few of
us (I include myself) would forego television totally, difficult as it is to
watch selectively and be sensitive to its costs and risks. No wonder Marie Winn calls it "the plug-in drug."

Owning or having easy access to television means we open ourselves
to being exploited by it. Like most fruits of industry, television offers
much that is genuinely attractive, however negative its consequences.
Most of us are at a competitive disadvantage in relation to the modern
industrial order; we are vulnerable to being manipulated in accepting
its growing costs in return for its actual and promised benefits. Just as
individuals are vulnerable, so too are whole societies.

Is world trade a global shell game or a chain letter?

The global nature of the current economic order allows enterprises to
exploit discrepancies among societies in labor and physical resources
more efficiently than ever before. Within the confines of conventional
economic models, it is often cheaper to produce something in one area
and ship it to another than it is to produce that item locally. Trade depends upon such differences—first among individuals and families,
then among clans, then among villages and towns within a region, and
finally throughout the world. Trade creates new markets, whose existence reinforces specialized economic enterprise. If transport costs are
relatively low, it *appears* sensible to stop growing food for just one area
and concentrate on trading it for manufactured products. This makes
good sense in principle and when confined to an ecologically sensible
scale—e.g., the "green doughnuts" mentioned earlier. But does it make
ecological sense for someone in Chicago to wear a shirt made in China
when the hometown mill could do the job? Does it make any sense to
transport rice grown in the United States to China just because Chinese
labor is cheaper than American? Why should flowers from Hawaii fly
on jumbo jets to New York every day? How will we explain to our children's children that we consumed their petroleum birthright by moving food and manufactured goods around the world when we could
have been buying most of our goods from local exchanges?

The emigration of factory jobs from the relatively affluent labor force
of the United States to other countries is already well documented. The

emigration of clerical jobs made possible by advances in data processing provides an example that may portend the future. Keypunching has
been farmed out to countries with lower labor costs, such as Korea,
since the 1960s. But the new technology of microprocessors now allows for the direct transmission of data without "hard copy" (paper).
Satellite Data Corporation of New York uses this technology to send
data entry work to Barbados, where labor costs $1.50 per hour, versus
between $4 and $12 in the United States. Interestingly, the managers
view their operation as a factory, not an office.

This is not the only example of a throwback to an earlier era, and
there soon may be many more. Many observers claim that the explo-
sion of computer-assisted word processing and information management will permit, even demand, a return to a still older economic form,
the cottage industry. If this happens, it will do much to revitalize the
family as an economic unit. Or it may allow a pernicious and exploitive
piecework system to take hold and grow. It's an interesting prospect for
the sustainable society. The new technology of microprocessors, which
makes small, relatively inexpensive computers possible, may be our
last best hope for the future of Spaceship Earth and the family lifeboat.
Or it may simply provide a more powerful way to conduct business as
usual.

If one group can sell something at a lower price in the same market
as another group and still make a profit (whatever the criteria for adequate profit), then it has a comparative advantage. The current crisis in
comparative advantage for some industrialized nations is minor compared to the issues raised by the world problematique. Like most conventional economic notions, comparative advantage disregards material costs and benefits beyond the monetary short term, because it
confines itself to price as the criterion for assessing advantage.

Transformational economics views such a formulation with suspicion and doubt. If we consider the full costs and benefits to the physical and social environment over the long run, the terms of the equation
shift. Conventional economic and *political* thinking cannot accommodate the changed equation, even when such thinking recognizes its validity. The inescapable conclusion is that most of the conventional economics behind "free trade" is bogus. This should become clearer as
more countries realize that the maxim of the modern international
economy ("export more; import less") cannot provide for a stable
global economy. It's like a chain letter; there must be losers (importers)

if there are to be winners (exporters). In the long run, the result is likely to be some combination of impoverished losers, squandered resources, and economic instability for families, communities, and nations.

Why are the roads filled with trucks transporting goods? Why are freight trains traveling the rails? Why do cargo ships and tankers criss-cross the oceans? Why do air freighters roar off runways around the world? Why is the volume of world trade measured in the trillions of dollars? The answers only make sense in conventional economic terms. The present volume of world trade is far in excess of what transformational economics tells us is appropriate to a sustainable world.

In a sustainable system, trade would be limited to two domains. The first is ideas, technology, and artistic creations and the people necessary to communicate them. The second is material goods needed to meet basic human needs or to dramatically enhance human experience in ways unavailable locally. Most world trade today fails to meet either criterion.

All trade implies costs as well as benefits. It costs the physical environment a great deal to sustain the required transport, regardless of the cash price. We often hear complaints about government subsidies that increase exports by lowering their cash price and about trade barriers in the form of cash duties raised by governments to decrease imports. But these manipulations of cash price ignore the real cost of trade: future generations unknowingly subsidizing current patterns of consumption. And these costs, even if minimized through the use of solar power, for example, do not tell the whole story.

It also costs the social environment a great deal to adjust to the disruption of local patterns. Local factories may close because they can no longer compete with foreign factories. Families face difficult adjustments, which may include changes in household composition, income, place of residence, and ability to offer continuity to the next generation. Even the winners face significant challenges, such as the need for new forms of income distribution, child care arrangements, and attitudes about family roles.

Against these costs stand the benefits: the filling of gaps between local needs and resources, invigorating cross-cultural exchanges, and increased material resources of newly industrialized societies. We must not dismiss or disregard these benefits. Visiting small factories in rural China and seeing firsthand how recent economic changes permitted people to purchase such key items as bicycles, wristwatches, and radios, I better understood the human significance of the accumulation of basic goods. But, still, we must not downplay the ecological costs of trade. Beyond accumulating essential capital, meeting local needs, and stimulating cultural exchange, modern trade mainly serves other masters: private profit, nationalistic and imperialistic politics, and the disease of modern materialist excesses.

One point bears repeating here. The goal of the industrial process is not to create or sustain work. It is to achieve the highest possible *monetary* return on the investment of capital. In the early periods of industrialization, the physical transformation of materials and energy into goods was the major monetary cost of economic enterprise—just as in preindustrial subsistence agriculture, human labor was the principal cost. In classical industrial economics, investments in anything other than the physical facilities (e.g., health insurance for employees, pollution controls, etc.) are "non-productive." They are treated as a kind of necessary evil, a cost of doing business to be minimized when possible.

Orio Giarini argues that "a product is usable not because it exists but because it is available and it works" (p. 25). This is the concept of "utilization value," which includes goods and services that are both free (available at no monetary cost) and priced (available from the market at monetary costs). This concept is critical to an understanding of industrialization and urbanization, because the historical thrust of both is to reduce the scope of "free" goods and services. Industrialization does this in two ways—one direct, the other indirect.

The industrial order reduces the availability of "free" goods and services directly by giving them a price and requiring that they be purchased. Thus, families need ever larger cash incomes to maintain the same standard of living. If swimming free in a local river becomes impossible because the water is polluted, the family may have to pay cash to swim in a pool. Both a pool or a clean river would meet the family's recreational need, but the pool creates a financial need (and increases GNP) while adding little or nothing to the family's real standard of living. In fact, if the pool is highly chlorinated and less pleasant than the river, the actual quality of the recreational experience may decrease. As Giarini sees it, industrialization frequently has the paradoxical result of giving with one hand and taking away with the other. However, every time priced experiences supplant free ones, GNP increases. This affects families in everything from child care (replacing "free" home care with priced day care) to transportation (replacing walking, which costs nothing, with driving, which requires money).

A more complete accounting is needed, one that includes both the monetarized and nonmonetarized cost and benefits of economic enterprise. Often, what appears to be an economic advance is actually only the substitution of priced for free exchanges—the transformation of nonmonetarized resources into monetarized ones. GNP goes up, but the real standard of living remains the same or even declines.

Money changes everything

Monetarization is also an indirect consequence of industrialization, however. As more and more of the activities of daily living are monetarized directly (and the cost of living increases), there is an almost inevitable tendency to want to monetarize the activities of the nonmonetarized economy. Thus, potential "developers" (a bizarre term) view an expanse of wilderness with eyes that see dollar signs. Where a hiker sees beautiful vistas, the developer sees expensive views from a condominium window. Where a naturalist sees a forest, the developer sees lumber in board feet.

The same is true of families. What parents see as children, marketing specialists see as potential consumers. What children see as parents, employers see as workers. Except through political channels that preserve wilderness as part of the nonmonetarized sector, hikers cannot outbid those who would convert vistas into views. Similarly, parents need the supportive intervention of the politically powerful to resist those who use television advertising to pressure children and create monetarized needs; they also need that help to protect the time and flexibility they must have to meet their children's needs.

Monetarization threatens families and their necessary support systems. Workers are depersonalized by the mechanistic social models most compatible with industrialization, which require that decisions be made as if capital and labor were interchangeable. Human feelings only enter the economic equation if they directly affect performance. One result is that what one can do takes precedence over who one is. Families are intrinsically and primarily concerned with who you are (my brother, your son, his daughter, her sister). As such, they offer a necessary balance to the dominant industrial orientation of what you can do.

But industrialization demands much from families. It usually demands increasing mobility, which puts stress on children and parents alike, requiring that they repeatedly dissolve attachments to neighborhood and community. Traditional forms of social control and nurturing may become obsolete, further monetarizing family life by replacing nonmonetarized exchanges of social support with priced services. This trend may reach silly proportions, as when affluent families buy services that shop for its clothes and its children's toys.

Industrialization encourages families into seeing the costs and benefits of family life from a monetarized perspective. The direct costs of bearing and rearing children increase, for example. A parent must pay money to have access to the goods and services of the child care system, the processed food system, the technological recreation system, the day care system, the health care system, and the educational system. Budgets are often published, indicating that the cost of raising a middle-class child through adolescence is in the hundreds of thousands of dollars. A big item in such budgets is the income "lost" by caregivers. Economists call this lost income "opportunity costs," because they refer to the opportunities that a parent (usually a mother) can't pursue because of child care responsibilities.

Public and professional concern with "working women" testifies to the indirect power of monetarization. Women have always worked, of course, and are not just exchanging roles now; they are adding to and expanding their roles and their work. What *is* new is the massive entry by women—particularly married mothers of young children—into the officially monetarized work force. This opportunity is a mixed blessing. Many mothers work for income to provide the margin of affluence they and their families need, or at least believe they need. Others work to avoid poverty. Some from both groups would work outside the home in any case, because they prefer it. Women earn on average about 60% of what men earn and supply about 25% of total family cash income. And they need this income mainly because the cash price of daily living has increased.

Living in an industrial society puts a cash premium on recreational leisure, which costs money because it relies increasingly on technological games or access to priced experiences. It increases the amount spent on food; families today frequently eat at restaurants (spending one-third to one-half of their food budget, according to 1983 figures) or eat highly processed and expensive food at home. Transportation, too, increases in price, because communities have evolved or have been designed in ways that discourage walking. And monetarization puts a cash price on self-esteem, because it associates personal value with financial value.

Implications for family life

Money—the need for it and its use as a measure of worth—corrodes many traditional social forms. The most obvious is the role of full-time child rearer and homemaker. Those who do not earn a cash income lose economic credence. They come to be viewed—and many come to view themselves—as "economic parasites." They are haunted by the fact that they could be earning a cash income at a job outside the home. As family size shrinks this becomes an even bigger issue.

Volunteer work, too, takes on a new meaning. When volunteer work is chosen over employment in the cash labor force, people tend to see it as a sacrifice or a rip-off (depending upon your point of view). When it is done in addition to paid employment, people view it as a marginal and expendable activity. In any case, one consequence of monetarization may well be a shortage of volunteers in services of all kinds. The United States has come to recognize this in recent years and has begun to rethink volunteerism.

Monetarization can also lead to positive results. It may give women greater social leverage, because the dollar value of their unpaid work is highlighted by analyses of opportunity costs. Testifying to this are movements to extend pension benefits to homemakers and divorce decrees that legally recognize the financial equity built up by homemakers in family assets. Indeed, if monetarization brings about a greater appreciation for the realities of households as microeconomies, it will have done women a real service. But this service may be counterbalanced or even outweighed by its disservice.

Monetarization may relieve some pressures in families that succeed financially. But it creates other pressures by influencing family members to participate in the *highly* monetarized world outside the household. For example, it requires that adolescents have money in order participate in peer activities. This in turn may produce family conflict: parents feel pressured to provide money; teenagers feel let down when they don't receive enough.

In the United States, adolescents have always been active in household work ("chores"), but since World War II they have entered the monetarized part-time work force in dramatically greater numbers. According to Laurence Steinberg, by the time they graduate from high school, nearly 80% of all American adolescents will have had some formal paid work experience. But that experience does little to enhance the development of character or improve society. Rather, it tends to be geared only to making money, and it overrepresents the worst part of modern urban life. Nearly 35% of the jobs open to adolescents are in food service, mainly fast food service involving repetitive tasks that teach very little of value. According to Steinberg's research, adolescents who work part time at such jobs become more negative about work, experiment more often with drugs, and are less involved in the socially invaluable but nonmonetarized world of family and community- and school-based extracurricular activities. In short, work for cash in the areas most available to adolescents emphasizes money and materialism, thereby decreasing their appreciation for the values and attitudes needed in a sustainable society. Do we want to reinforce the belief that "time is money" or that "the best things in life are free"?

This pattern also exists among young mothers who work for money and worry about the "opportunity costs" of family life. Industrialization and urbanization continually force us to consider the question: "Can I afford the price of doing X?" For both adolescents and parents, that "X" includes social activities of intrinsic value, such as spending time with family and friends. These difficulties derive from the increasingly monetarized nature of life, the end products of monetarization and industrialization. In industrial society, monetarization is our most important product.

Monetarization and materialism: A powerful pair

The tide of monetarization has given new significance to what we earlier speculated was an innate human impulse for acquiring material possession. The preindustrial world masked this drive for most of the people most of the time. But the modern industrial and urban world shows us for what we are. In an earlier era, things were cheaper, so we could afford to invest heavily in each object we possessed. When you could only have one wooden bowl, it made sense to have a very finely crafted one. You could "afford" to take two weeks to make it. But when the market value of your time can be priced high, then the cost of investing two weeks to make a bowl is prohibitive. Who can afford such quality? Who ever could?

Modern urbanites—particularly the most successful ones—can hardly afford to do *anything* for themselves anymore. Their time is too valuable to "waste" cooking, cleaning, taking care of children, and doing all the rest of the things that make the world go round. I asked a class of undergraduate women at an Ivy League university how they planned to balance career and home. "Get a maid!" was the most common answer. Aristotle asked, "Who will watch the watchers?"; the question in modern industrial society is, "Who will care for the caregivers' children?"

I recall an interaction I had with a newcomer to computers who had written a program that would play a card game with itself. He told me with much enthusiasm how the program enabled the computer to play three hundred rounds of cards per minute. Very efficient; but what's the point? The same misguided logic is found in much of industrialized urban life.

Fortunately, there are some counterbalancing forces. Money—unlike other objects—has no inherent quality. That is, one dollar is as good as another, putting aside for the moment cross-national speculation in currencies. The technical beauty of money and its humanistic ugliness are one and the same: it is purely quantitative. Anyone with any sense or sanity will see the futility of approaching money as if it had intrinsic value. But in a fully monetarized society, people are led to believe that anything and everything has a price. And it's only a small step (if a false one) from that assumption to the one that asserts that everything and anything is for sale, that money can buy anything—including substitutes for high quality parent–child relations.

Policymakers in the former Soviet Union once attempted to establish a coterie of people who would be paid to take over parents' child care responsibilities, liberating them for other work. The effort failed because the policymakers discovered that they couldn't "pay a woman to do what a mother will do for free." That's true, and it applies to fathers as well. But monetarization is always seducing or coercing us into believing that we *can* substitute money for time, for attention, for interaction, for investment of self—that we really can have our cake and eat it too when it comes to human relations in general and family relations in particular. The root of this evil is industrialization, and its progress tells us a great deal about the dynamics of capital in human affairs. This returns us to Giarini's concept of "utilization value"—the worth of goods or services for the duration of their life span regardless of where they came from or whether or not they have a cash price.

Can we eat the forbidden fruit of moderation?

Utilization value gives us a conceptual tool for assessing the net worth of industrialization and for determining when its undeniably real benefits begin to be outweighed by its equally demonstrable costs. It permits us to do more than simply accept industrialization unconditionally or reject it completely. The latter seems unlikely. Having tasted the fruits of the industrial order, who can really imagine giving them up completely? But the former isn't satisfactory either, for it supposes a dynamic growth in the unlimited transformation of resources.

It is difficult to criticize the modern industrial order without inviting the kind of jingoistic patriotism faced by those who criticized the Vietnam War ("America: love it or leave it") or police brutality ("Next time you have an emergency, call a hippie"). One can hear the voice (and see the bumper stickers): "The modern industrial order: love it or leave it"; "My pollution, right or wrong"; "Next time you need some money, ask a tree." This kind of attitude harkens back to the 1930s, when people welcomed Benito Mussolini because he made the trains run on time, or when people tolerated nazism because it stood as a bulwark against communism. Just as the Nazis "sold out" to the Communists by signing a nonaggression pact in 1939, so too does the modern industrial order seem to be selling out on its promise to eradicate poverty (if we just pay the price in social and environmental degradation). Industrialization is actually *increasing* impoverishment in some areas. And, if recent trends continue, the future portends more rather than less impoverishment for even more people.

We need a way of judging and saying "enough!" when conditions warrant, without having to adopt the extreme attitudes of "love it or leave it" or "throw out the baby with the bath water." Utilization value promises us that. It can warn us when an enterprise or even a whole socioeconomic order has exceeded its proper limits. It can do so in a way that GNP and other strictly monetarized measures cannot. Giarini puts it this way:

> The fundamental change occurs when economic activity measured in terms of value added, starts giving signs that this increased activity is counterbalanced by its negative effects in the overall non-monetarized sources of wealth. It is the moment when we observe the "production" of deducted values: the utilization value that starts diminishing. It is the moment at which *real* zero or negative growth starts even if the GNP indices are still positive. (Giarini, 1980, pp. 31–33)

By considering only priced values, the industrialized economy has been incomplete. Will present and future conditions make this model worse than incomplete, make it invalid? The answer as I see it is "yes." Conventional industrial economics is doomed, or the best of the human enterprise is doomed. Either it goes or we go.

Just how gross is the gross national product?

Gross National Product is the single most publicly visible manifestation of the industrial economy. It reveals the gross dynamics of the monetarized economy, but it never reveals the *value* of the nonmonetarized economy—and it hides the costs to the nonmonetarized sector. GNP does not refer to utilization value but to the cash transactions. Thus, it reflects as "value" the money spent to treat illnesses (even if they result from industrial growth), to replace consumer goods (even if those goods are created to be obsolete or are never actually used), to cope with toxic wastes (even if they are a by-product of "production"). Other things of "value" to GNP include money spent to purchase military equipment (which usually makes no direct contribution to human welfare), money spent for processed food (which could be cheaper and more nutritional if prepared at home), and money spent in other nonproductive areas. Increases in GNP make some sense in an environment where the costs of economic activity are minuscule and the nonmonetarized economy is unaffected. But GNP becomes less and less sensible as these conditions diminish. The gap between changes in GNP and changes in total utilization value grows, and industrial economics becomes more and more an exercise in deception.

As Giarini notes:

- A car that lasts for 200,000 miles has twice the utilization value of a car that lasts for 100,000 miles, despite the fact that buying two of the latter makes twice the contribution to GNP (assuming initial purchase price is the same).
- A cotton bed sheet that lasts through fifty washings has at least fifty times the utilization value of a plastic disposable sheet. It has even more than that, because the cotton will serve as a cleaning rag when retired from active service, while the disposable sheet becomes waste almost immediately, even though the price of its replacement contributes to GNP.
- The water in a polluted lake has negative utilization value (for

drinking or swimming), although the price of protecting people from it contributes to GNP.

Giarini's hypothetical examples find dramatic confirmation in actual events. The 1980s and 1990s have seen growing public concern over the management of toxic wastes—"the dark side of industrial society," as the *New York Times* once described it. Environmental Protection Agency records indicate the existence of some 12,000 hazardous sites—418 of which are so toxic that even the agency's director (a self-avowed enemy of most of the environmentalist movements and an apologist for business interests, according to many accounts) has described them as "ticking time bombs." A congressional report asserts that the government has to deal with more than one ton of toxic waste per person in the United States each year.

The costs of even minimal cleanup of these sites are staggering, including a federal government "superfund" of more than fifteen billion dollars, supplemented by hundreds of millions from state and local governments. These monies appear as part of the GNP when spent to purchase the goods and services necessary to undertake the cleanup. Add to this the money spent on health care to respond to effects of these hazards, and we have a classic illustration of how GNP is a false measure of value. Indeed, more and more GNPs in modern societies increase in attempts to ameliorate deducted values. That these activities appear as "products" in national accounting is misleading at best—and it is just plain wrong. Our accounting of what is a cost and what is a benefit is sadly out of order.

GNP drives environmental deterioration

This is bad enough in modernized societies, where the slippage is becoming evident "at the margins," as conventional economists are fond of saying. But the greatest human dangers of industrialism are most evident in the nonindustrialized societies that seek to adopt the modern way of life. They try to monetarize their economies by displacing subsistence activities that are designed to meet basic human needs. Often, they replace domestically oriented agricultural activities with those that appeal to foreign markets and thus tap into imported capital. The resulting foreign commerce forges a link with highly monetarized economies. In the wake of its new "responsibility system" to encourage private economic initiative, China reports dramatic increases in productivity for all segments of its economy. But rarely if ever do these reports include the mounting costs behind these increases, such as greater reliance on petrol-energy, growing use of chemical fertilizers, and more pollution.

The economy in most modernizing societies, however, serves a small but politically powerful group of elites. Household and community food receives low priority. Cash crops and capital-intensive agriculture displace rural society, and stimulating export to secure foreign exchange is the name of the game. Stimulating a modern economic elite in the current historical context usually causes the collapse of the basic agricultural subsistence economy in the countryside. This produces a rising tide of unemployment and a grotesque rush to the big cities, where a few get lucky but most do little more than survive.

This displacement is a matter of growing concern as land available for food production declines in amount and quality due to population pressures and urbanization. In the United States alone, three million acres of land per year are converted from agricultural to nonagricultural uses, according to a federally–funded study. Farmers who wish to stay in business believe that they must enter the monetarized economy in order to purchase chemical fertilizer and capital-intensive machinery.

Societies that are modernizing today operate under very different circumstances than did those societies that modernized in the last two centuries. On the positive side, they can leapfrog over earlier technologies to the current state of the art, including computers and genetic engineering. But they must find resources and markets and adjust their rural/urban balance in a vastly more competitive and increasingly scarcity-dominated international environment. And then how do these societies know when they have caught up? When they have produced more pollution? When they have more appliances, waste, family breakup? When their mental and physical health deteriorates?

Are these societies moving in the right direction? Are modernized societies moving in the right direction? Our goal, remember, is the creation of a more *sustainable* human community based on competent social welfare systems, just and satisfying employment, reliance on the nonmonetarized economy for meeting many needs, and a political climate that encourages cultural evolution and human dignity. When visiting a community we should first ask for answers to three questions:

What's the infant mortality rate? How many children are homeless? How many young people are on the street as prostitutes? Each answer reflects how well the community is doing to support its families.

How well are the world's modernizing societies doing in this regard? We can start by noting that *where* they are facing this challenge has much to do with *how* they are doing. And where they are doing it is in cities.

Big cities are the wave of the future

By the early 1980s, the world was about 40% urban, according to geographer Gary Shannon. In areas such as Central America, however, rural areas were nearing population saturation, at thirty-nine farm workers per square kilometer of cultivated land versus ten in the United States. Thus, population increase in Central America and in similarly saturated regions mainly reflects urban growth, as people migrate from saturated rural areas—where 54% live in "extreme poverty," according to a United Nations study—to urban areas, where "only" 27% live in "extreme poverty." The Environment Fund estimates that the urban and rural population in Central American will each equal out to about eighteen million by 1995. Population will double by 2025, to about forty-five million urban and twenty- two million rural. This has already happened in Brazil, where a mid-1980s population of approximately 140 million reflected an urban to rural ratio of about 2:1. China, on the other hand, has a 4:1 *rural to urban* ratio and is working hard to upgrade life in the countryside. And it did well in decreasing the infant mortality rate (at least until the current flare-up of female infanticide linked to the One Child Policy), in drastically reducing the number of homeless children, and in nearly eliminating adolescent prostitution. But China is unusual in this, and it has paid many social and ethical costs in doing so.

The modern era is characterized by the growth of cities as much as by any other single phenomenon. Geographers estimate that at the beginning of nineteenth century, the world was about 3% urban. By 1980 that figure was 40%, and by the year 2000 the figure is estimated to be 50%. Among the world's twenty-three or so regions, East Africa is the least urban (12%), while 86% of Australia–New Zealand is urban. The pace of urbanization is now the fastest in less modernized and industrialized societies. Geographer Gary Shannon estimates that by the year

2000 there will be six times as many cities with populations greater than one million as there were in 1950. What is more, the less developed regions' share of these cities will have grown from 32% to 64%. We see a similar trend with respect to "megacities" of five million or more inhabitants. In 1950, there were only six such cities (all but one of which were in the modernized regions); by 1980, there were twenty-six (eleven in modernized regions). The projection for the year 2000 is fifty-nine (only sixteen of which will be in currently "developed" regions)!

What about these cities as environments for families? By and large, they are difficult to the point of being destructive. Mexico City, for example, has more than 20 million people, and about 1,000 peasants migrate to the city each day from the countryside. Pollution, congestion, unemployment, inadequate water supply, and poor sanitation are problems that grow correspondingly. Some foresee that Mexico City's population will be between thirty and forty million by the year 2000, as efforts to discourage further emigration from the countryside falter. This social quagmire is caused by inappropriate industrialization and the failure to stabilize and increase quality of life in the Mexican countryside. The story of Mexico City is repeated in Lagos, Nigeria; in Bangkok, Thailand; in Cairo, Egypt; in Calcutta, India. These and other magnet cities in modernizing societies are staggering under the double whammy of increasing population and decreasing resources.

Urbanization is not totally the invention of industrialization, of course. The Mayan civilization of the pre-Columbian era is one notable example of a society with a substantial urban settlement. Indeed, numerous preindustrial cities have existed in many areas of the world. They were different from modern cities in at least four respects, however. First, they represented a relatively small proportion of their country's population, which was necessarily concentrated in the rural, agricultural sector. Second, they were small by today's standards, numbering in the tens of thousands rather than the millions. Third, they depended on low-power transportation, which prevented them from growing far beyond their agricultural base. Fourth, they depended upon a political system which used force against the nearby agricultural region to extract food for the urban population.

With industrialism, cities changed in all four ways. They became larger, accounted for a bigger proportion of the population, depended on more technologically sophisticated transport, and relied upon trade, not coercion, for food. In the twentieth century, urbanization has a decisive influence on societies around the world. In modernized societies, cities live off the fruits of industrialization. They provide a wide range of goods and services to rural areas in return for food. The monetarized economy permits this, and it relies upon industrial activity across the society. Agriculture is necessary for life, but industry is the engine that drives the economy. Mechanized transport permits new urban forms and shifts in rural life away from subsistence farming and towards cash-crop farming on a larger scale.

The industrialization of agriculture permitted (and thus demanded) increased food production with fewer workers; the industrialization of other forms of production required a concentration of workers in urban centers. The two worked hand in hand. But early in the twentieth century, urbanization still bore a strong relationship to the natural geography—rivers, bays, lakes, and other physical features that have always generated urban settlements. In the United States, growth of the old ("Snowbelt") cities was linked to the rise of the modern industrial order. As the century progressed, those cities were eclipsed by new ("Sunbelt") cities, which sprouted up quickly in the special, *historically artificial* conditions of the post–World War II boom. They were built on energy-intensive technologies that sought to override naturally occurring limits of climate and geography, the most notable of which was the availability of water. Houston is a prime example. In that city, megagrowth has drained underground aquifers and left caverns into which the city is sinking by as much as a foot every five years. These new cities also were born during the era of the automobile. Some have little or no "downtown" and only a few sidewalks in residential areas, reflecting their total preference to the automobile as a way of getting around. The Sunbelt cities rose as the Snowbelt cities declined, but they may be very short lived as the unusual (even freakish) conditions in which they grew changes. And unlike many of their Snowbelt counterparts, they lack much of the physical and social infrastructure they would need to move from being boom towns to sustainable towns. In 1979, many who lived in the Sunbelt cities were crowing about how bright their futures looked. By the end of the 1980s, the tide seemed to have turned. The Corporation for Enterprise Development, a business group, issued a "report card" that graded cities on "providing jobs and economic opportunity, vitality of businesses, capacity for expansion and state policies fostering business growth." Among the Sunbelt states, only California received an "A" while five Snowbelt states did.

Short-sighted conventional economic analyses such as these overlook important evidence. Others see the madness more clearly. For example, in 1982 the *New York Times* ran an article under the headline: "Jammed Freeways Lead Sunbelt to Mass Transit." The lead (dateline, Houston) does a good job of telling the story:

> They grew with wild abandon, metastasizing into the deserts and swamps around them. They are the great new cities of the South and West, whose very urban existence and give-me-elbow room style of life has depended upon the ubiquitous automobile. Traffic congestion? Build another freeway. Now they are beginning to choke on their cars and tangled freeways. (p. 8)

In response to this, some Sunbelt cities are returning to older forms of urban transit and adopting a more historically normal pattern of development. Houston, Atlanta, Miami, and Los Angeles all have plans for new mass transit.

One problem with this, however, is that automobile-based urbanization in these cities may interfere with the operation of rail-type mass transit. America's older cities were rail-based, and thus they naturally conformed to the needed pattern of a concentrated downtown and corridors of development, however much post–World War II automobile-based growth diluted those pure forms. A study supported by the federal government reported that of thirty major American cities without rail systems already in operation or under construction, only four had the proper configuration to handle large passenger volume: Houston, Los Angeles, Seattle, and Honolulu. The prospects of establishing mass transportation in the others are uncertain. Light rail, buses, and automobiles must do most of the job now. But in their attempts to follow more sustainable patterns, these cities should consider access for walkers and bikers.

The rise of suburbia is peculiar to the industrial era, a phenomenon of major proportions. According to 1980 U.S. Census data, the economic implications of suburbs are quite significant. Average (median) household income in cities is less than 70% of that of suburbs, and it has been declining as cities become the repository of more and more "underclass families" and as middle- class families flee to the suburbs. In some older cities the discrepancy is even greater (58% in Baltimore, for example). Suburbs are not conducive to sustainable patterns for families, because they drastically limit the possibilities of efficiently integrating home and work. They also tend to oppress women, in particular, as Betty Friedan showed us a generation ago, and they deprive youth of the socially rich environment needed for sound social development, as Ed Wynne demonstrated in *Growing Up Suburban*.

Suburbanization began with railroads. People could live in small communities outside cities and yet be transported into the city to work. This pattern was supplanted in large part by the automobile, which permitted greater flexibility in scheduling and location. The railroad needs concentrations of suburbanites in a well-defined corridor of communities; the automobile encourages suburban sprawl. But both are part of the larger phenomenon of urbanization as seen from the perspective of the ecology of land and water. Where they differ is in the role they play in bringing about the sustainable society. The railroad-based suburb is much better placed and arranged for such a transition. It is likely to supply more of the infrastructure for community self-reliance, and it offers an effective alternative to the energy-intensive and wasteful automobile. This is less true of the Sunbelt cities. And, many of the burgeoning cities in the Third World offer the worst of all worlds—the sprawl of suburbs without the personal affluence to compensate for their social impoverishment.

Overall, older cities in modern industrialized societies have reasonably sound social, economic, and physical foundations. They make sense. This is not true of many cities in the modernizing world (nor in the new automobile-based cities in modernized societies). In unmodernized societies, urbanization has proceeded rapidly without an industrial order to sustain it. Many people have left the agricultural sector, either because they have been displaced or because they hope to find better opportunities in the cities. Just like Sunbelt cities in the United States, many of the cities in the modernizing nonindustrial societies are developing "unnaturally" (using the conventional Western industrial model as the norm). First, these cities don't conform to land and water resource patterns. Second, they do not have, nor are they likely to develop, the typical urban infrastructure of services. Third, many of them lack a sustainable industrial activity. They are simply holding pens for family disintegration or staging areas for emigration, rather than birthplaces of social welfare systems.

The value of cities in a sustainable society

Using Giarini's terms, the rationale for urbanization must be found in maintaining or increasing utilization value while sustaining society's stock of useful resources. Cities fulfill this mission when they provide opportunities for ecologically sane work, when they manifest a sense of community that engenders human psychological satisfaction and meaningfulness, and when they maximize true benefits of collective residence while minimizing its true costs. But urbanization, in both industrialized and modernizing nonindustrial societies, often results in a net *decrease* in sustainability on the societal level and in family support systems at the individual level. Much of what we call urban development is antithetical to the needs of families, serving instead the monetary and political needs of the modern economic system.

We can recognize potential benefits of urbanization (economies of scale in services, culture, and work) but at the same time see the following costs:

Land use: Urbanization inevitably shifts land use patterns away from agriculture and towards industrial, commercial, transportation, and residential uses. Obviously, sustainability suffers when we transform agriculturally prime land instead of marginal land. The problem is that settlements are usually in close proximity to prime land because its agriculture can support a growing population. Urbanization thus tends to remove prime rather than marginal land from agriculture. This is one variable in the equation relating urbanization to sustainability. A second is the use of the land itself. Urban agriculture can make a real contribution to sustainability and play an important role in determining the overall impact of urbanization. Many cities have ignored this potential. Few can afford to do so in the future.

Ecological balance: Urbanization puts pressure on the entire ecology. The impulse to engineer the environment to meet human needs affects the habitats of many other species. It affects the regenerative capacities of natural water systems. It influences the balances of nature in many ways, particularly as urban areas increase in size and agricultural areas decrease. The influence can be direct (raising the temperature and increasing the carbon dioxide content of the air, for example) and indirect (opening up larger new areas to termite infestation through clear-cutting).

Human organization: Social science has yet to demonstrate any absolute, generalized effects of urbanization on psychological development and family functioning. Yet we continue to be suspicious of urbanization, and now of suburbanization. The principal cost envisioned by students of urbanization is a loss of social identity, with a resulting decline in responsible interaction. This is seen as a problem in modern industrialized cities—where the pressing issues are neighborhood in-

tegrity and human scale—and in modernizing cities as well, where traditional rural patterns such as mutual child care are breaking down.
This concern extends even to urban architecture. Does it enhance
meaningful day-to-day interaction, or does it limit social intercourse?
This is the real issue, of course. Does urban life create stress and diminish social resources? How frequently does it do so? These questions remain unanswered.

Ecological Empathy: I share with many others the fear that urban life
desensitizes us to the natural environment. E.F. Schumacher echoed
the theologian/philosopher de Jouvenal on this matter: "As the world is
ruled from towns where men are cut off from any form of life other
than human, the feeling of belonging to an ecosystem is not revived"
(1980, p. 147). Interpersonal empathy is a critical force in preserving
and enhancing the quality of the social environment. Ecological empathy serves the same function with the natural environments of field,
forest, stream, lake, and ocean. Urbanization threatens this empathetic
orientation. Children, in particular, need the countryside in order to
develop a sense of kinship with nature.

When all the elements are combined, what effect do industrialization
and urbanization have on sustainability, on the wealth of families, and
on social welfare systems? There are two. On one hand, industrialization and urbanization increase the demands on families. They increase
the stakes; they increase the potential payoffs for success and the potential costs of failures. These costs and benefits increase because of the
variety available to the city family—if they can afford it.

On the other hand, however, city life for those without access to its
monetarized resources tends to produce a state of desperate
impoverishment—what is now called being part of the "underclass."
More money is required of the city dweller than of the rural resident to
achieve the same utilization value—e.g., dollar costs of child rearing are
higher in cities, according to the U.S. Department of Agriculture. This
means that the urban family must have a wider range of competence to
"produce" the kind of people who can succeed in that environment.
School success, once optional, has become essential. In the United
States high school graduation is considered essential for full economic
personhood. Sixty years ago less than half of all youth graduated.

All this is true for individual families in modern industrial cities that
are *running smoothly.* But most cities are ecologically vulnerable; they
are not sustainable if they continue to operate on the energy, waste,
and land-use principles that are their foundation. The necessary transi-

tion challenges many political and economic sacred cows. For example, we—as a global system and particularly as the modernized world—need higher rather than lower prices on basic resources, most notably nonrenewable ones. To drive the engines of the modern industrial order toward sustainability, we need to make ecologically sensible policies and practices profitable. We can achieve this only if the monetary costs of initial transformations ("production" using natural resources) are higher than the costs of subsequent "productive" transformations (recycling, conversion to other uses, repair). Without a shift to higher prices for basic resources—prices that more accurately reflect choices we are already making for our great-grandchildren—industrial and urban policies are hopeless delusions.

The transition to sustainability will mean a shift to more labor intensive, less energy-intensive approaches that bolster the family as an economic unit—with the goal of minimizing waste through recycling and other conservation measures and becoming more efficient in renewable domains such as growing food. In all such efforts for change families must play a central role. Just as the family farm is the key to agricultural production in modernized and modernizing societies alike, so too is the family household crucial to sustainable urban living—e.g., in recycling programs that rely on conscientious activity at the "point of use." And who is to lead the way in this social and economic reformation? For this leadership we must listen to the feminine voice.

SEVEN

The Feminine Voice
and the Foundations of
Social Welfare

December 1974. Mexico City, Mexico. I have come to Mexico City to see the architecture and the museums. The city seems dominated by monuments to glorious death. What do you say of a people who seem to glorify slaughter? My own do, at Gettysburg, where thousands died in moments and tens of thousands in hours, and at the Somme, where in the first day's combat 60,000 lives were forfeited. I want to hate and dismiss that kind of wrong-headed ennobling of butchery, but something male in me balks. Somehow I can almost hear "The Battle Hymn of the Republic," and my disgust for slaughter is tempered by a grudging respect for "the cause" and the courage. A female friend tells me that when she visits Gettysburg she feels only communal sorrow.

In Mexico many monuments recognize that male impulse to slaughter and be slaughtered. I've been out to the Inca pyramids. Much slaughter. I've been to the National Cathedral, where the conquering Spanish forced Montezuma's Incas to dismantle their own temple and use the brick to build a Christian one—with incidental and purposeful slaughter. I've seen government buildings decorated with wonderful murals, many of which deal in the beautiful detail of slaughter—soldiers with loaded weapons standing guard over sightseers, alert for terrorists, reminding us that slaughter is always imminent.

And I've been to another most remarkable monument to slaughter and maleness. Beautiful Chapultepec Park in Mexico City is dominated by a steep hill, once a citadel, on which now stand the gardens and palace of Maximilian, the nineteenth-century French Emperor of Mexico. At the foot of the hill stand white pillars, monuments to the young military school cadets who in 1848 leapt to their deaths rather than surrender to the invading United States Army. These white phallic pillars eloquently affirm the male character, here in Mexico where the macho mystique is blatant, of course, but elsewhere around the world as well—in Gettysburg, at Thermopylae, at Masada. Somehow I must respect it, but I hate it too, and I fear what it means for the future in a world that desperately needs not bravado but nurturance.

Another Mexico exists in the shadow of the monuments to slaughter. Women, often with young children, sit on the sidewalk begging or selling little sacks of peanuts; they are called "the Marias." There are no grand stone monuments to them in the parks, but I do meet one in the flesh through friends who live in a village thirty miles away. They introduce me to the mother of a young family living nearby; as it turns out, she is the daughter of a sidewalk "Maria." Her mother had taken her and her brothers to the city to join other rural poor starting up the ladder. Through begging, she collected enough money to buy peanuts to sell. From their sale she was able to send her children to school, to get them on the modern track. Her mission has succeeded, it would seem. Her daughter is married to a clerk and her son works as a mechanic. Considering where they started, they have arrived. But the only monuments to such entrepreneurial mothers are the lives of their children.

I am reminded of a cartoon I saw years ago. Two men sit at a bar. One has just ordered a round of drinks on a payday stopover on the way home. His money is spread before him on the counter. He says to his drinking buddy, "I ask you, my friend, what does she do with my money? I'll tell you. She blows it all on food and clothes for the kids!"

It is difficult to write anything that contrasts females and males, women and men, feminine and masculine without running the risk of stepping on someone's toes. "We all have too much at stake," a female friend reminds me. The long history of invidious characterizations of women as being second class, deviant, inferior, and less worthy than men makes this concern understandable. Even arguments of feminine superiority are suspect in many quarters, particularly when they seem to play into the hands of traditionally sexist themes. Sociologist Alice Rossi's argument that females are superior as parental caregivers was met with much negative reaction. And yet there *are* grounds for what Ashley Montague calls "the natural superiority of women." If imitation is the sincerest form of flattery, then maybe men are unconsciously aware of their cosmically inferior position. Montague notes that men use feminine terms to refer to their creative work. In his book *The Male Machine*, Charles Ferguson airs his suspicion that the expression men use to describe their accomplishments (e.g., "that's my baby" or "my brain child") are really an elaborate defense mechanism to cope with the fact that women are intrinsically superior by virtue of their capacity to bear children. But any such argument opens one to criticism. We all have too much at stake, particularly in the modern world, where traditionally feminine contributions (such as bearing and rearing children) are often undervalued.

This chapter is open to such criticism, because it argues that one key to making the transition to a sustainable society is to replace masculine forms and themes that dominate public life with feminine concepts of power, value, and social interaction.

Females are the superior organism for the modern era. This is true biologically, of course. The ratio of men to women at conception is thought to be about 130 to 100, but the higher number declines before birth because of a higher rate at which male embryos, which are often biologically defective, spontaneously abort. (Indeed, some 75% of the 190 known congenital abnormalities affect males more than females.) In the United States, the ratio at birth is 106 males to 100 females; after age 65 it is 85 to 100; and average life expectancy for females is nearly eight years longer than for males. Females also appear to be more resistant to many modern illnesses, such as cardiovascular disease. The modern era in nations like the United States has benefitted women by reducing the number of women who die in childbirth from more than 600 per 100,000 births in 1930 to about 10 per 100,000 births in 1986. Given half a chance, women will outlive men. Women's biological superiority suggests that femininity is the logical guiding force for humankind as it wrestles with the world problematique. Traditional masculinity is on the way out—or at least it ought to be. I believe this is true, but it is a risky proposition to advance.

It is a risky message because two opposite themes dominate contemporary rhetoric. First, there is the reactionary view that women and their feminine ways should retreat from the public scene. Second, there is the progressive view that women should shed their feminine ways and act directly within the existing institutional and cultural framework established by men, of men, and for men. Neither view works to make the necessary transition to a sustainable society. The feminine perspective on work and family is a better foundation for a sustainable society than is the masculine; and masculine threats to women are threats to sustainability. Having laid these cards on the table let us examine them.

Women and feminine concepts are the key because:

- the typical socialization of females engenders qualities of caring and interdependence;
- the special relation of women to childbearing generates an orientation to family that supports the movements needed for social welfare systems;
- the economic traditions of women better equip them for the demands of steady state economies and thus the sustainable society.

As sociologist Elise Boulding puts it, "the ingenuity of women may be the most precious resource the human race has left" (1980, p. 59).

An ideology of caring and interdependence

In her landmark study *In a Different Voice*, Carol Gilligan presents the psychology underlying the characteristically feminine concepts of caring and interdependence. She contrasts feminine and masculine concepts of morality, power, and aggression, allowing that no perfect correlation exists between being female and developing a feminine orientation. From the feminine perspective, moral issues arise from conflicting *responsibilities*; moral issues in the masculine view, in contrast, are defined as conflicts of *rights*. The former implies resolving moral dilemmas by seeking to increase awareness of needs, while the latter implies a process of logical analysis without regard to "feelings."

Psychologist David McClelland reports that while men display strength through assertion and aggression, women display it through nurturance. For most men, taking what you deserve indicates personal power; for most women, personal power means giving what is needed. Women tend to see aggression as a problem born of fractured relationships. The appropriate response then is to try to mend and strengthen these relationships "by avoiding isolation and preventing aggression rather than by seeking rules to limit its extent" (Gilligan, 1981, p. 43). It is a moral imperative to care, to assume responsibility for troubled relationships. Social welfare systems need this kind of orientation more than any moral calculus of rights and cost–benefit analysis. This may have political dimensions. But it also places an enormous burden on the shoulders of the world's women, who must provide a disproportionate share of the caring and healing required. Jesus may have died for our sins, but Mary lived through them. And this burden can become psychologically overwhelming to women if they don't have public and institutionalized support.

Many of the speakers who exhort us to care are the politically active women who have contested the masculine element in society. A nineteenth-century American suffragette put it this way:

The male element is a destructive force, stern, selfish, aggrandizing, loving war, violence, conquest, acquisition, breeding in the material and moral world alike discord, disease and death. See what a record of blood and cruelty the pages of history reveal! Through what slavery and slaughter and sacrifice, through what inquisitions and imprisonments, pains and persecution, black codes and gloomy creeds, the soul of humanity has struggled for centuries, while mercy has veiled her face and all hearts have been dead alike to love and hope! The male element has held high carnival thus far, it has fairly run riot from the beginning, overpowering the feminine element everywhere, crushing out the diviner qualities in human nature. (quoted in the *Washington Spectator*, March 1, 1983, p. 3)

Even some men recognize the destructive force of masculinity. And it is the image of rape that dominates their insights. Writing about the distinctly male character of gang rape, essayist Roger Rosenblatt offered his perspective on the "male element":

Gang rape is war. It is the war of men against women for reasons easy to guess at, or for no reasons whatever, for the sheer mindless display of physical mastery of the stronger over the weaker. . . . That is male terrain, the masculine jungle. And no man can glimpse it, even at a distance, without fury and bewilderment at his monstrous capabilities. (1983, p. 98)

Rape is the lingua franca of the masculine-dominated world. Militarism is the brother of rape. The presence of soldiers means rape and prostitution for women in appalling numbers. The militarization of Africa in the 1970s brought an upsurge in the number of rapes and other assaults against women—and, of course, skyrocketing mortality rates for children. Escalation of United States military involvement in Central America in the 1980s saw the appearance of a strain of venereal disease last seen in Vietnam.

The economic analogs are visible in the conventional language used to describe economic development: it is "man's domination over Mother Nature." "Virgin" forests and lands are "violated," metaphorical language which leaves little doubt as to the parallels between the physical and the social environment. In the 1976 film *Controlling Interest*, former Secretary of Agriculture and now agribusinessman Orville Freeman speaks of the various freedoms that are essential if development and profit are to proceed hand in hand. One he mentions is "the freedom of economic intercourse." In conventional approaches to economic development, one discerns more rape, incest, seduction, and molestation of minors than union between consenting adults. The male element, in its many forms, is at work in the world. And this is the male element's worst side, of course.

Also characteristically male is the emphasis on separation, rights, and rules; on rationalizing social relations; on abstract principles over people. This stands in contrast to the feminine orientation, which emphasizes the social web, the interdependence of self and others. Carol Gilligan believes that these contrasting patterns arise in part from the different positions of females and males in relation to the world. Others argue that what Gilligan calls the feminine perspective is really just the voice of those who are physically dominated, regardless of gender. Gilligan, however, thinks the different positions of men and women in society have some basis in the biology of childbearing and temperament—that they have a sociobiological component. But they are implemented through contrasting social experiences for girls and boys. The main theme in female development is attachment, while for males it is separation. Both themes exist for each gender, of course, but we downplay separation (and thus individual self) for females and attachment (and thus social identify) for males. The result is that intimacy is a threat to masculine personalities, while feminine personalities fear separation. Neither course by itself is sufficient for fully actualized adulthood, but in a patriarchal world suffused with masculine domination, accentuating the feminine voice is a necessary corrective in the transition to a sustainable society.

The fullest human development occurs when a person acknowledges self as worthy of separate value and sees that the social web is the source of meaningful and psychic stability. Modernization works against that development by programmatically institutionalizing the masculine mode and suppressing public expression of the feminine mode. This is unfortunate, because now more than ever we need an ideology of caring and interdependence to manage the transition to a sustainable society. Despite the protests of "real men," there is little reason to fear that the masculine element will be overwhelmed. Quite to the contrary, we should fear instead the homogeneous masculinization of the population in modern societies, as the economic institutions of cash income, costs, and price penetrate more spheres of life—and in the process make women more masculine in orientation without encouraging a corresponding feminization among men.

As women's lives have become modernized, women have been denigrated by the dominant masculine ideology of "hardball" politics and economics, just when we need "soft" energy paths and a material economy that lives lightly and gently upon the Earth. The ideology and politics of modernization have worked against women and the feminine perspective in most of the world, much of the time. Irene Tinker sees it this way:

> "[D]evelopment" has been viewed as the panacea for the economic ills of all less developed countries: create a modern infrastructure and the economy will take off, providing a better life for everyone. Yet in virtually all countries and among all classes, women have lost ground relative to men; development, by widening the gap between incomes of men and women, has not helped improve women's lives, but rather has had an adverse effect upon them. (1976, p. 22)

Part and parcel of this has been the institutionalizing of Economic Man as the conceptual underpinning of efforts to stimulate and assess development. Economic Man is masculine in that he has only one primary role: rational self-interest and profit, directly or indirectly, in monetary terms. Ordinarily, women must perform two roles. They bear and rear children, and they carry out economic activities that meet basic family needs. Conventional efforts to stimulate and assess development usually operate on the simplistic conception of a one-role Economic Man;

of course, these efforts are also typically conceived of and directed by men. These efforts end up stimulating male enterprises (often to the detriment of both family and community economies) and assessing those economies in misleading terms. As we have seen before, conventional economics defines development as growth in GNP, and inherent in GNP is the sexist assumption that real work is that which is done in the cash labor force outside the home. Who can fail to see the absurdity and injustice of asking the mothers of the world if they work? Apparently many people do.

As the insightful analyses of theologian Elizabeth Dodson-Gray reveal, the concept of masculine rights contributes mightily to the world problematique. The idea that the male has a "right" to dominate women and children parallels the idea that humans have the "right" to dominate the land, the forests, the rivers, lakes and oceans, and all creatures great and small. We in general and men in particular are lacking the awareness that we have responsibilities to ourselves and to others, to home and community, to the present and the future, to the human-built and the natural. The world needs to recognize that those of the feminine persuasion have rights to the "self" and that those with a masculine perspective have more responsibilities than they are being held to. Feminine personalities are often paralyzed by the injunction to not hurt others but rather to sacrifice the self. Masculine personalities, on the other hand, often run amok in the social and physical world by serving the interest of self.

Carol Gilligan calls for the integration of feminine qualities into the dominant male ideology. This, she believes, will create a more powerful and responsible ethic:

> The concept of rights changes women's conceptions of self, allowing them to see themselves as stronger and to consider directly their own needs. When assertion no longer seems dangerous, the concept of relationship changes from a bond of continuing dependence to a dynamic of interdependence. Then the notion of care expands from the paralyzing injunction not to hurt others to an injunction to act responsibly toward self and others and thus to sustain connection. A consciousness of the dynamics of human relationships then becomes central to moral understanding, joining the heart and the eye in an ethic that ties the activity of thought to the activity of care. (Gilligan, p. 149)

This sounds promising. Indeed, the women's movement in modern societies promised just that. It arose out of a critique of male power and the costs of a lopsided patriarchy. It began with the recognition that masculine personalities are lost in a social and emotional wilderness, and it promised that the feminine approach would bring what Suzanne Gordon has called "a life that balanced love, friendships, and work" (1983, p. 143).

But has feminism delivered on that promise? Gordon, for one, worries that women in the world of work are under enormous pressure to change themselves rather than to change the world. She cites several leading "advice books" that tell women to exploit their feminine interpersonal skills for personal gain while suppressing their feminine orientation to affiliation and intimate social connectedness. Gordon summarizes the advice this way:

> In other words, the recognition that we all need intimacy is not a strength but a weakness, a holdover from childhood that must be shed by women seeking to take their places in the adult world. These friendships are inappropriate and sticking together must give way to looking out for number one, say the corporate Machiavellis. (1983, p. 146)

This is disturbing, to say the least. It implies that the humanizing insights of feminism are bankrupted when women adopt masculine models of power and influence. It should warn us not to underestimate the power of situations to shape values and behavior. The task is only partly one of empowering women in the world. Women must not simply adopt the masculine models that now stand as a barrier to a sustainable society; rather, they must reorder institutions to reflect the feminine voice.

Finding a way to use the feminine orientation to change the system poses a profound challenge. Simply placing into the system those who are attuned to it will not succeed. As always, we must use our values to shape the choices we make about social systems, keeping in mind Winston Churchill's warning that "we shape our surroundings and then our surroundings shape us." Environmental psychologists call this the "principle of progressive conformity."

Of course the principle can work for, as well as against, the shift towards feminine orientation. It can be a hope as well as a warning. When we create settings that elicit empathy, intimacy, connectedness, and caring—when we arrange for men to play an active role in the birth of their children, for example—we use the principle to our collective advantage. We also use the principle when we set up groups that elicit and reinforce emotional well-being—in participative work teams on the job, for example. Even changes in language can play a role. A university committee for rural women refers to its head as a "caretaker" rather than "chairman." Symbolism is important in shaping consciousness. Social welfare systems must be attuned to these issues.

Family orientation

Family orientation is a crucial resource for making the transition to a sustainable society. Properly motivated and supported, families can help to accomplish that transition. Recycling, conservation, producing goods and energy—all are appropriate to family-level enterprise.

Children are the currency of family life, the focal point for exchanges among kin. The interests of a sustainable society are served by a qualitative, not a quantitative, orientation to children. This means intensifying parental investment in a few rather than in many children.

Sociobiologists like Robert Trivers suggest that the concept of "investment" is a key to understanding masculine and feminine orientations. The underlying issue in family life is genetic success—ensuring the transmission of one's biological relatives. Men and women have necessarily different strategies to that end. The limiting factor for male genetic success is the total number of impregnated women. The limiting factor for females is the number of children born and raised. Seen from this sociobiological perspective, women have a greater personal investment in each child. This lead to the hypothesis that women will be receptive to social arrangements that protect and nurture this investment and limit its costs. Strong families seem to be the answer to the greatest concern of women: How can I increase the chances of success for my children?

But in many parts of the world, women who seek to make wise reproductive decisions face socioeconomic and psychological conditions that discourage small families. Rae Blumberg's persuasive cross-cultural research on this topic indicates that fertility depends largely on the social status of women, which in turn is derived from their economic power. With a few notable exceptions, men virtually monopolize power in two of the three principal domains of human communities—power of force and political power. Only in the economic domain of property do women ordinarily have a powerful or dominant position. Blumberg's research shows that differences in the economic power of women account for a substantial amount (about one-third) of the variation in fertility rates among societies. Economic power is more influential than the other two domains. Blumberg concludes that empowering women economically and educationally is a wise strategy for limiting population growth. We considered this theme in chapter 3, and we return to it here because it takes on added significance as we consider ways to encourage the adoption of a feminine perspective.

Until women have economic power—or have restored to them the traditional influence modernization has stripped from them—they will opt for large families as a compensatory investment, regardless of the long-term costs to sustainability. Why? Because children have few direct costs and bring several benefits to a woman in a position of economic powerlessness. These benefits include status in her kin network, help with housekeeping, and support in old age, which she does not view as likely to come from other sources.

> Even though for the woman's nation, her high fertility may be a greater burden than benefit, family planners will have a hard time convincing her (or her husband) that two children are the ideal number when she has objective grounds for knowing her welfare would be adversely affected if she had fewer than five or six children. (Blumberg, 1976, p. 18)

It's the tragedy of the commons in full force.

We must promote human quality by creating social arrangements that offer a good psychological, economic, and social return on a small number of children. A UNICEF study predicts that if infant mortality were cut in half in developing countries, it would motivate a reduction of twelve million births per year. Why? Mothers would be more confident about concentrating their parental investment in fewer children. But once the odds of physical survival change, there still remains the issue of whether parents will reap psychological rewards for their efforts, whether children will remember and repay their psychic debts to their parents.

We should also do all we can to improve fatherhood. Drawing men into the birth and rearing of children is one way to merge the feminine and the masculine and thus more fully humanize men. In China, it may be one way to counteract the apparently increasing problem of female infanticide that has arisen in response to the One Child Policy. One way to protect infant girls is to encourage stronger initial attachment by their fathers. Direct participation by fathers in the process of childbirth can accomplish this.

More fully humanized men are a necessary component of a sustainable society. The intimacy of the experience of childbirth and the process of early parent/infant attachment are powerful socializing influences, even for men, who are usually less suited temperamentally to empathic intimacy than women. Many a male "tough guy" has had the hard edges of his masculinity softened by becoming involved in the birth and care of his children. Social engineering is the key. Margaret Mead observed that motherhood is a biological necessity but fatherhood is a social invention, and this fact should put our social inventiveness to the test.

We shouldn't expect male behavior and female behavior to become totally indistinguishable. Temperamental and historical differences will see to that. But we have much to gain by feminizing males (creating more empathic, caring men) and masculinizing females (creating women with a greater respect for the self). The world would be more fully human, with a more qualitative rather than quantitative orientation to family. Such a population would be better suited to undertaking the transition to a sustainable society, because it would be able to concentrate on enriching interpersonal, spiritual, and aesthetic encounters outside the narrow limits of the monetary economy.

Female economic traditions

Modernization has meant industrialization, urbanization, and an ever more monetarized society. As a result, the conventional view of society is at odds with reality, because it does not recognize nonmonetarized values. Elise Boulding considers the economic implications of this for women when she speaks of their "social invisibility."

In modern accounting systems, women are economically marginal in modernizing societies and second-class citizens in the already modernized ones. They are a significant part of the cash labor force in modernized societies like the United States, but they earn only about 60% of what men earn and contribute about 25% of (cash) family income. In the modernizing societies these numbers are worse.

The problem lies in the conventional economic perspective, however, not in the supposed economic marginality of women—which, itself, is one of several historical myths about women. Other myths include the belief that economic development always improves women's lives, that women are basically irrational in their childbearing decisions, and that they have always been "nonstop breeding machines."

If we consider, as Boulding suggests, not the official labor force of conventional monetarized economics, but the actual day-to-day productive labor, the picture is dramatically different. Women dominate in the basic economy of food (production and preparation), child care, and health care. From this perspective, the basic units for economic accounting should be familial households, and the basic criteria for assessing value should be the meeting of human needs rather than the producing of services and commodities.

Fortunately for us as a species, meeting these needs and providing these basic human services is intrinsically rewarding if we are in a community in which people care for each other in sickness and in health. That women are the cornerstone of the community should be obvious, and empirically it is indisputable. It is even true in modern societies, where institutionalized service facilities are important, yet women still care for children and elderly and manage households, even if they participate in the monetarized labor force. And it is undeniable in societies where the nonmonetarized economy holds sway. Valid "development" means improving these basic human systems first and foremost. Improve them and *then* evaluate economic change—not the other way around. This puts society's goals before its instrumentalities, ends before means; it puts method in its place and gives primary importance to social welfare.

As food production has slipped away from the day-to-day control of women, its essential human function has eroded and been replaced by abstract formulations in which one-sided Economic Man is the paramount actor. Margaret Mead put it this way:

> Food today is treated as a commodity in large-scale production or as a weapon in economic negotiations. Its use at the local level as the main means of freeing human beings from hunger is being neglected. Half a harvest may be lost in a country where food is considered solely as a cash crop and where the traditional role of women in allocating part of the crop for local production is ignored. (1976, p. 10)

As Mead sees it, only if we restore the feminine voice to decision- making about food will we remember that food is about feeding people—not political and financial scheming. The large-scale industrial farm easily becomes but pawn in political and financial scheming. The small farm in which the growers are close to the land has a built-in bias towards food for feeding.

The point here is twofold. First, by focusing on the traditional economic enterprises of women, we rediscover the real meaning of goods and services and thus unmask the pretensions of the monetarized economy. This shift in perception is essential if we are to develop an economic perspective appropriate to a sustainable society. Second, traditional economic enterprises of women provide the infrastructure for the technological development we need in a sustainable society. We need better technologies to feed ourselves and others, not more powerful industrial models of agriculture that are driven by financial and political interests rather than by nutritional needs. And we need it in both modernized and unmodernized societies.

In modernized societies, the monetarized economy must harmonize with and support the nonmonetarized economy without harming the social and physical environment. In nonmodern societies we need to resist efforts to dismiss or undermine nonmonetarized enterprises, instead enhancing their efficiency and effectiveness in a manner consistent with the dignity of the people (usually women) who operate them. Viewing these goals in light of the traditional female economy makes it clear that the conventional concept of economic development (increases in industrialized and monetary enterprises as measured in dollars) is bogus. Real development is more accurately based on increasing human quality where it counts most—in the actual lives of people in family households. This directs our attention to enhancing sustainable patterns of access to resources and doing so in ways that encourage individual dignity and social connectedness.

This focus on women in development is all the more important because of worldwide demographic trends. Conventional economic development, in the rhetoric of the Cornucopians, means growing prosperity as "undevelopment" withers away. In all likelihood, however, this is a false image. More to the point is the image of developed societies becoming relatively smaller. As Elise Boulding points out, in 1950 42% of all women "workers" resided in "developed" regions, while 58% lived in "developing" regions. By 1975, these figures had changed to 36% and 64% respectively, and the International Labor Organization predicted further change to 29% and 71% by the year 2000. These disparities are even greater if we consider percentage of total world population: 34% versus 66% in 1950; 28% versus 72% in 1975; 21%

versus 79% in 2000. The quality of life in the year 2000 for that 79% will depend upon how well we meet and respect the economic needs of the women in those societies. Traditional patterns that cast women in the role of beasts of burden will not suffice, nor will conventional modern ones that cast them as financially inferior citizens.

Implications for the transition to a sustainable society

Some years ago a cartoon appeared in *New Yorker* magazine that said a great deal about the masculine and feminine perspectives. In the cartoon, two middle-aged couples are comfortably seated around a coffee table. One lady says to the other, "George handles all the big issues, like war and peace, inflation, agricultural policy, and national politics. I handle the little things, like raising the children, cooking, paying the bills, and cleaning the house." The cartoon makes fun of a characteristic dichotomy of interest, and it illustrates the improper denigration of the tasks of home and the false elevation of more abstract "macro" issues.

The historical separation of the male and female domains has obscured some fundamental similarities by introducing artificial differences that have come to represent the supposed deficiencies of women. Ten thousand years ago animals were introduced into agriculture, and using them was defined as a properly masculine activity. Likewise in the nineteenth and twentieth centuries, operation of agricultural machinery was defined as a male activity. The result has been to economically isolate and downgrade females from food producers to food processors and consumers. This trend, besides producing a decline in real prospects for sustainable agricultural productivity, has reinforced the false differentiation of men and women regarding technological competence. Of course women can operate machinery and use it to good advantage, as has been demonstrated in many countries during times of war.

For the transition to a sustainable society to proceed, we must avoid sexist preconceptions and bring the characteristically feminine perspective to bear in discussions of social policy and practice. This is not, of course, simply a matter of bringing women into public life. It is more a matter of changing the character of public life. But greater involvement of women who are confident in the validity of the feminine perspective is certainly essential. As things stand (and have long stood), females are usually forced to choose between public leadership and femininity. This is psychically unfair to women, and it is a tragic loss to the community, which needs public femininity more than ever. Carol Gilligan recognizes that masculine leaders routinely sacrifice human relations for "systematic social action," be it in the service of abstract ideology or for the glory of God. For all the glorification of Mohandas Gandhi, we should recall that he largely abandoned his interpersonal commitments to his wife and children.

At a futurist meeting, the moderator led a group through an exercise on "utopia." Each participant was asked to list a characteristic of the ideal world. The standard ideas were mentioned—truth, justice, freedom. But from one woman came the suggestion, "No diarrhea!" Keeping the world's children safe from diarrhea would go a long way towards creating a utopia; diarrhea causes the deaths of tens of millions of young children every year in impoverished communities and societies. Such a practical grasp of human realities is most likely to be found among those who change society's diapers. And, it argues that one way to improve the world's chances for sustainability is to involve men more fully in the day-to-day realities of child care, particularly infant care. As long as men are shielded from the daily realities of the household, we face the danger of critically misreading what the world needs to make a go of it in the twenty–first century.

In Ernest Callenbach's novel *Ecotopia*, the government is run by an environmentally-oriented party of women, who make decisions based on caring and nurturance. The government rules the states of the Pacific Northwest, which have seceded from the rest of the United States and established of sustainable society. One hopes such a feminine-based ideological triumph is not just wishful thinking.

In any case, a focus on women and the feminine perspective is the appropriate focus of efforts to create a sustainable society. Non-modernized societies must repeal policies that undermine household economies with low environmental impact. Instead, policy should enhance and assist these household economies. A good start, as Elise Boulding suggests, is to reform accounting schemes so that women do not appear economically invisible, a fifth world beyond the fourth world of the very poor.

> The fifth world exists invisibly, uncounted, and unassisted, on every continent, in the family farms and kitchen gardens, in the nurseries and kitchens of the planet. The fifth world also sends its fingers out to the

most poorly paid work spaces of business, industry, and the service sector. Within the rural and nonindividualized parts of that fifth world, women give birth to babies, produce milk to feed them, grow food and process it, provide water and fuel, make other goods, build houses, make and repair roads, serve as the beasts of burden that walk the roads and sit in the markets to sell what their hands have made. (1980, p. 5).

Boulding suggests creating new census categories (e.g., "home production worker") that include work done outside the cash economy in order to account for the full work load of women and men. Such an approach also bases accounting systems and social indicators on meeting basic needs. This would do much to adapt census data to the realities of social welfare systems.

Boulding also recommends using the household rather than the individual as the accounting unit, as well as focusing on the activities of the total family unit. One reason for doing this is that some (many?) women see individual recognition as a threat to their nurturing function (not to mention that it could also precipitate male sanctions). And using the household as the unit of economic analysis is in better accord with the underlying empirical realities of day-to-day life—where it is the meeting of basic needs that counts, not some abstract or narrowly monetarized accounting of financial worth. Boulding is confident that such a system would more accurately reveal a society's basic economy and would better highlight the real costs and benefits of alternative paths of "development" than conventional economic indicators do. For example, based on United Nations data, Boulding estimates that women provide 99% of health maintenance services; yet they are economically invisible and may be disrupted by processes of conventional economic development. In the United States, the efforts of women as homemakers and mothers have permitted society to go about the business of capitalism, confident that all was well on the home front.

A feminine focus would also create and maintain a social and legal climate in which family quality is paramount. This would mean relying on the feminine ethic of caring in family planning (insofar as it is compatible with the carrying capacity of the environment). By and large, women will choose to limit family size to within acceptable bounds when given the motivation (economic power) and the opportunity (reproductive control) to do so. Their incentives derive from their natural "investment" in their children and the motivation to do right by the living. Yet conventional economic development has generated pressure on many rural women to produce more rather than fewer children. Schemes that emphasize industrialization have undermined rural communities and their agricultural base. Industrialization and urbanization draw men away from farm work and leave women to tend the land alone, without the technological aids that modern engineering might provide if it focused on their activities. As a consequence, women alone on the farm must struggle without sustained male help to make ends meet. The result is often decreased production and a strong incentive to "breed her own help" (to use Boulding's phrase). Population rises and agricultural productivity declines.

This trend in the "developing" societies has its parallel in societies like the United States, where increasing numbers of economically isolated and pressured women are responsible for children whose fathers are absent. Many refer to this as the feminization of poverty. According to government data, families with one parent (a woman) have less than half the median income of all families. Single mothers account for 75% of all people living in poverty, a trend that is accelerating. About 40% of all American families headed by single parents live in poverty, versus 11% of all families. This works out to a poverty rate for children of 20%-plus—the "infantilization" of poverty.

Interestingly, this "recent" increase in the number of households headed by women may not be the modern creation many assume it to be. Legal criteria aside (e.g., the married woman whose husband is not present on a continuous basis), there have always been single- parent households. According to Boulding's calculations, between 20% and 50% of all day-to-day heads of households are women. The figure worldwide is about 38%. Modernization does place some special burdens on these women and their children, however.

History tells us that modernization has had ironically negative effects on many women in many parts of the world. It is true that modernization has often liberated women from traditional constraints. But it has not been completely beneficial, because women's traditional economic rights and contributions—most typically in partnership with men or other women in agriculture and trade—have been devalued and made invisible. What is more, the shift from subsistence agriculture to cash cropping disrupts traditional male/female partnership arrangements. Women and children may lose out in the process.

Historical evidence in many parts of the world reinforces this view. The International Labor Organization notes that many areas of Africa only began to experience food shortages in the 1960s and 1970s, apparently because urbanization and cash cropping schemes ripped away the economic base of rural women (e.g., taking their time and/or land away from kitchen gardens to service cash crops or do industrial work, the cash from which does not purchase the equivalent amount of food). In the United States, as aggregate wealth has increased and women have entered the cash labor force, conditions for children are deteriorating seriously. More and more children are placed in poor quality day care, left without adult supervision in threatening urban environments, exposed to the stress of single-parent households, and hurried into premature adolescence. More of them are slipping below the official poverty line (Garbarino, 1986). Modernization is replete with such apparent paradoxes, in which the creation of wealth and impoverishment go hand in hand.

The biggest dangers of masculine thinking is that it abstracts child—bearing, transforming it into a quantitative rather than a qualitative concern. This comes to a head in issues of contraception and abortion. The evidence suggests that we should trust the moral judgment of women in using these technologies wisely. The irony of men worrying about whether women will act responsibly is sometimes too much to bear. Of much greater concern on the whole is the ability and willingness of the male to perform responsibly—in using contraception, in transcending a bias in favor of male children, in rejecting the use of social and physical force to coerce women in childbearing decisions, and in meeting responsibilities for child support.

The One Child Policy in China has run up against serious problems on this score. The masculine bias is strong, and it places tremendous pressure on women to produce male offspring (which is perversely ironic given that it is the male who donates the chromosome that determines the child's sex). Women who give birth to daughters may be punished for their "error" by their husbands, fathers-in-law, and even misguided female relatives (most notably mothers-in-law). The specter of female infanticide has risen its ugly head (again) in China. Visitors to some remote villages have reported sex ratios of 5:1 in favor of male infants. An American demographer analyzing the 1982 Chinese census estimated that 200,000 females were "missing," presumably due to some combination of infanticide and a hiding of female births.

On a visit to China in early 1984, I saw and heard evidence to confirm all this. I also learned that the government is supporting an active campaign to bolster the value of female children, through propaganda, institutional reforms to provide greater actual economic equality for females, and prosecution of those who brutalize mothers or murder female infants. This awful situation reinforces the belief that the path to a sustainable society lies in empowering the feminine element and the females most likely to exemplify it, whether it be in China, where female infanticide is the current issue, or in India, where sexist rejection of female children is compounded by fatal burnings of brides who are unable to raise a sufficiently large dowry. One journalist reports that there are two such burnings a day in the city of Delhi alone.

The feminine perspective puts family at the center of a web of relationships. The woman is most often the "kinkeeper"; she is generally the one who most efficiently meets the needs of children. In Latin America, for example, researchers have found that a monetary supplement is translated into more nutritional calories for children if the payment is made to the mothers. If it is made to fathers, it is likely to become discretionary income for a father's personal use. Recent United Nations reports reveal that efforts to reduce malnutrition can achieve major successes simply if mothers are given paper and pencil so that they can create charts that measure the growth of their children. Once they see the effect malnutrition is having on their children's growth, they can redirect family food resources to counteract the problem, as happened in 60% of the cases in the Philippines, for example.

In the United States, middle-aged women are the primary caregivers for both children and the frail elderly. Around the world, the health of women and children is a leading indicator of how well society is doing in taking care of the most important business there is—family business. The masculine orientation threatens this. Men tend to take women's work for granted, as well as women themselves. The result is a decline in social welfare and the wealth of families.

The devaluation of women has many sources. Elizabeth Dodson-Gray has explored the theological devaluation of women in patriarchal religions that place females behind God and man. The psychological devaluation exposed by Gilligan is intertwined with economic relations. Women without a sound economic base are vulnerable to exploitation, coercion, and devaluation by men. Modernization erodes the traditional economic resources of women. A few women become marvelously independent because they are liberated and enter financially powerful careers. But many are left vulnerable, either totally dependent upon male breadwinners or left to struggle alone with a marginal income of their own. If women and children are safe and secure, we will be better able to make the transition to a sustainable society.

Lest this argument be misunderstood, let me close this discussion by reiterating that the fundamental issue is the ascendancy of the feminine perspective. This perspective is not inaccessible to males, however. Indeed, the issue before us is inextricably linked to efforts to foster the feminine orientation in men. It is the aggressive, exploitive, abstracted nature of masculinity that threatens us (as embodied in Economic Man). Masculinity, threatened by the "soft" path, fearing intimacy, seeks self-respect in the "hard" way. The soft definition of self rests upon interdependence rather than competitive individualism. It is significant then that males speak of "the role of separation as it defines and empowers the self," while females speak of "the ongoing process of attachment that creates and sustains the human community" (Gilligan, p. 156).

Just as females have a natural affinity for the feminine orientation, so too will males tend towards the masculine perspective unless conditions change and unless the models and rewards that guide action change. If the feminine perspective is not in the driver's seat, we are heading down the wrong road. But conventional models of economic development are a powerful engine, and masculinity is at the controls. The message is clear. If we are to move toward a sustainable society, we must alter our ideologies and our institutions so that they will hear the feminine voice and resonate with it. We must not permit these institutions to change that voice or drown it out. With this in mind we turn next to the world of modern private enterprise, where Economic Man feels most at home and where the feminine voice is muted, if not completely silenced.

EIGHT

Business As Unusual: Private For-profit Enterprise and The Sustainable Society

Oahu, Hawaii. October, 1982. I am here visiting the Polynesian Cultural Center. The Center was created by the Mormon church's Brigham Young University campus in Hawaii to preserve and exhibit the cultures of Polynesia (Tahiti, Hawaii, Samoa) and to provide jobs for Polynesian students who attend the University. It is thus a blend of philanthropy, enterprise, and anthropology (something at which the Mormons seem to excel). The Center itself teeters on the brink of becoming a Disneyland of the Pacific. The physical environment looks real from afar, but plastic, plastered, and fake up close. It does have real people, however. There are the student guides, who range from the enthusiastic to the blasé and often seem unsure if they should be proud of their "primitive native heritage" or embarrassed by it. And there are some human artifacts—real traditional Polynesians who demonstrate their crafts.

In the Samoan compound one such human artifact is making a bowl from a slab of wood. The old man sits without speaking, hacking away at the wood with an adz, hollowing out the center. Later, he will scrape it to create a smooth surface. Examples of the final product are on display: beautiful, smooth, richly colored brown wooden bowls used both for ceremonies and day-to-day purposes. "How long does it take to make one?" asks a visitor of the young student guide. "About two weeks from start to finish," she replies.

A man near me shakes his head and mutters, "Boy, you could turn them out in about half an hour with a good lathe. How the hell can he make a living like that?"

I was to think of this incident many times when I was in China two years later. The regime's campaign to modernize China seeks to empower Chinese workers technologically and economically. After three decades of dramatic ideological mood swings, China seems to have committed itself to harnessing the power of individual initiative to spur economic development (even though it remains opposed to democratization, as the Tiananmen Square massacre made clear). Under the Responsibility System, agricultural workers are allowed to market freely the fruits of their labor beyond the production quota established by the state (which retains ownership of the land). Furthermore, small-scale private enterprises such as shops, services, and even small factories are permitted. The result has been a boom, with incomes rising dramatically for those well positioned to profit from an eager market. This includes vegetable-growing communes near cities. If ever one needed evidence of the economic power of private initiative and enterprise one could find it in China.

But profit is not the whole story. In many areas, it seems, the Communist principle of "serve the people" is increasingly taking a back seat to "it is glorious to get rich." How will the social environment prosper when left to its own devices, in competition with the profit motive? And what about the physical environment? The goal of maximizing private profit seems to encourage increasing reliance on chemical fertilizers that contaminate groundwater, mechanized vehicles that consume fuel, and conversion to cash crops of land once used for basic food crops. Rice is *the* Chinese staple, and the government sets a fixed price for it, a price that makes it a less attractive crop than some others. As more and more people make use of the freedom offered by the New Responsibility System, they seem to be concluding: "I can make more money doing other things. Let someone else grow rice. Why should I do it?" How does a society harness the power of private enterprise and at the same time preserve the common good?

It has become a tenet of our society that "The business of America is business," and the world has listened. We've heard it over and over: "What's the bottom line?" Discussions of the sustainable society seem to run aground on the shoals of profitability. Will this measure pay off?

Will it maintain or increase dividends? Will such a program meet the payroll? No analysis of the sustainable society can proceed without accounting for the role of corporate economic enterprise—the private "for-profit" sector.

At the start, it's worth noting that private enterprise can be a powerful and marvelously humanizing force. But in a sustainable society, that power must meet basic material needs and provide satisfying work in environmentally sane ways. The task is to channel enterprise into sustainable lines of activity. Modernized societies must become self-reliant and non-exploitive. We must decrease domestic consumption so that short-term "surplus" capital and other resources can be exported to impoverished societies and stimulate there a sustainable social and economic order compatible with their resources. This is a moral and political challenge of the first order.

Private enterprise has much to recommend it. Garret Hardin's concept of the tragedy of the commons and the lifeboat ethic argue persuasively for the moral value of private initiative *when set within a sustainable social milieu.* This contrasts sharply with Adam Smith's concept of the "invisible hand," which assumes that the net result of unstructured individual initiative will be good. A sustainable society will most likely rest upon what some have called "guild socialism," in which small-scale groups compete as private enterprises. This would work, set within an economic climate in which sustainability is the net result, in which true cost rather than price is the dominant force, and in which the community is committed to maintaining access to social welfare systems for all.

Private enterprise can be a sensible, efficient, and flexible force when it provides room for individual creativity, creates a sense of identity, and offers a focal point for family activity, assuming it is directed by a sustainable set of assumptions about energy use and resource transformation. It can serve families well by providing economic continuity across generations, creating incentives to build lasting economic resources and by offering cooperative work for family members. Cottage industries and small-scale retail operations sometimes do this. Private enterprise can do all these things—and do them better than government-owned enterprises—*if* the ground rules protect the Earth and the future from unfair competition. But in the absence of an appropriate context, private enterprise is a sinister threat to social welfare and the sustainable society.

How do we assess the role of private enterprise as we currently experience it, when the distinction between "private" and "public" blurs? When some "private" enterprises are bigger and more powerful than some "public" ones? When private enterprises often seem to have all the prerogatives of persons without the moral obligations of citizenship? When private enterprise seems hell-bent on consuming our environmental birthright for short-term profit? Where does private enterprise stand in the moral order of the world? How are we to trust the Invisible Hand, when a record 1,510 new grocery products were introduced into the marketplace in the United States in 1982 alone, including such basic human staples as liqueur-flavored ice cream, kosher kielbasa, and Beverly Hills Kitty Litter made of $10,000 in shredded play money? Where is the redeeming social value in all this, when children in the United States and around the world are malnourished and lack access to adequate sanitation? If the business of America is business, then whose business is this? It's an old question, but it wears well.

As many people see it, the "genius" of private enterprise is its ability to give people what they want. Does this genius become an evil genius when it commands massive resources and when private enterprise grows so large as to operate on a public scale? Can we accentuate the capacity of private enterprise to serve the needs of the sustainable society while finding ways to prevent it from devouring the social and physical environments? And can there be global justice if private enterprise is a dominating force in the world?

And while we're asking questions, let's ask if a government-run business is any better? The environmental degradation in the former Soviet Union, Eastern Europe, and China shows us that government ownership does not guarantee better business practices. Union Carbide produced the Bhopal disaster in India, but the Soviet collective economy produced the Chernobyl nuclear disaster. Government-run industries often have no external authority to monitor their performance, and they are often responsible for the most environmentally destructive enterprises such as generating electric power and mining. Both public and private enterprises may be as geared to short-term payoffs at the expense of long-term sustainability. If we add to this the fact that imperious public works projects pursued in the name of modernization are themselves often very environmentally damaging, we can see that the issue goes beyond the simple dichotomy of public versus private ownership of the means of "production" (i.e., transformation).

The social justice of government-run business is not assured, at least when it serves masters other than the common good and a sustainable future. Social injustice in state-run enterprises in profit-oriented societies such as Brazil testifies to that. And, as we face the world problematique, we must recognize that nationalism may compromise the motivation and ability of government-run business to behave responsibly toward the world's social and physical environments.

In the interest of our moral health, we cannot accept the idea that rich nations, to sustain their affluence, must expect the rest of the world to live in abject poverty. Regional (and individual) differences in material affluence are probably inevitable, and they can be tolerated, provided each society has the material resources to meet basic human needs. Some can have fuel-efficient cars if all the others can have bicycles and buses; some can have exercise clubs if all the others have maternal and infant health care. Unless we see a radical transformation, however, this sort of diversity within the context of universal adequacy is as much as we can hope for.

Our task is to adopt an attitude towards private enterprise that is consistent with the sustainable society. Accomplishing this will provide a sound foundation for social welfare systems and will promise to harness on behalf of families the awesome force of private initiative. It will, however, require that we banish Adam Smith's Invisible Hand to the land of fairy tales to which it rightly belongs.

Moving toward a sustainable society depends on three things: short-term return on capital investment, long-term return on capital investment, and impact on resources. Understanding these three concerns can go a long way towards clarifying the opportunities and limits of the private for-profit sector of the economy.

Short-term return on capital investment

Certainly the most compelling issue within the private sector is short-term return on capital investment. The drive to accumulate wealth is the critical dynamic. Growth is the norm. In conventional analysis, the alternatives are growth or decay. Like the shark that must always keep swimming in order to maintain a flow of oxygen-bearing water through its gills, the capitalist must always be using current capital to generate more capital. To stop is to drown. In conventional analyses, steady-state capitalism is a contradiction in terms, or at least a term that applies only to those relatively brief periods of stability between growth spurts and periods of decay.

This is why we must consider compatibility of private for-profit enterprise with the needs of the sustainable society. Capitalism has an intrinsic, inherent drive that must be tamed and transformed, that must be channeled into sustainable paths lest it be world-destroying. By definition, an enterprise that does not succeed in growing and accumulating capital fails. It sounds simple, but it's actually quite complex and hinges on the questions, What is a good return on investment? and How do you calculate that return? In the modern economy, the accounting for profit has become quite arcane, in part because monetarization has inextricably linked capital to money. In simple terms, to make a profit on one's capital, one must exceed the return one could obtain by lending its cash value to another enterprise. This private enterprise tends to create an economic climate in which shrewd monetary investment displaces productive activity in a kind of economic musical chairs.

Robert Reich (1981) calls this "paper entrepreneurialism," which he says is the natural outgrowth of monetarization. The system encourages clever manipulation of rules and numbers that only in theory represent real assets and products. Paper entrepreneurialism is a creation of the highly automated accounting systems and esoteric tax structures that have evolved in modernized societies. It is socially destabilizing (encouraging such things as the closing of a financially marginal factory and calling it a tax write-off), and it undermines families and communities. It is pseudo-private enterprise at its worst, but from the perspective of the winner it is successful in the short run, because it meets the fundamental goal of accumulating money.

Actually producing something is a last resort, when it is no longer possible to profit from moving capital around. In theory, this might seem like it would help in the transition to a sustainable society since money itself doesn't degrade resources, but, in practice, it doesn't. The greedier money eventually comes to rest (if only briefly) in enterprises that physically *do* something, and then the pressure is on the enterprises performing the work to do something quickly that will feed the voracious interest of that investment. Families and communities are disrupted and stressed each step of the way.

The net effect is to encourage and reward enterprises that produce high profits over the short term. The tax structure, fiscal regulation, and monetary policy all tend to reinforce this in one way or another. Only when managers have bound up their personal identity with an enterprise are they concerned with anything beyond short-run profit. A business has more than a single dimension only if it is someone's life and livelihood in the broadest sense or if it has some vivid psychic and historical link to a particular community. On the other hand, if no one has a personal stake in an enterprise beyond a monetary investment, as is the case of many stockholders, maximizing short-term profit is usually the be-all and end-all.

Fortunately, some of the measures needed to achieve a sustainable society are consistent with short-term profitability. Either they permit an enterprise to move from unprofitability to profitability (e.g., by reducing costs or increasing sales) or they permit an already profitable enterprise to become more so. No-till farming, for example, might permit a farmer to cut planting costs and thus increase profits, while at the same time reducing soil erosion to a sustainable level. Or a successful manufacturing firm might find a market for the waste resulting from its operations and thereby add additional income without significantly increasing costs. Or a new enterprise might arise to profit from a new market created by a new technology.

Short-term profitability is a continuum. At one end stand the activities that have a direct quick payoff in conventional terms. These activities require only technological development and transmission of information. At the other end are activities that don't add to short-term profitability for existing enterprises—activities that may even exact direct costs by reducing short-term return on invested capital. Requiring investment in waste treatment and pricing nonrenewable resources higher than renewable resources exemplify this.

One way to deal with this negative end of the continuum is through what Garrett Hardin refers to as "mutual coercion mutually agreed upon"—regulation, either voluntary or enforced by the government. Either approach can cancel out the competitive disadvantage of operating in a sustainable fashion by imposing the same "penalty" on all competing parties. Emission controls on smokestacks are an example of this. If everyone must add to their costs equally, then the cause of the sustainable society advances without a *relative* decline in anyone's short-term return on investment. Of course, rarely if ever does such an effort really exact equal cost from all participants. Cheating from within the group and competition from unregulated outsiders can and often does upset the apple cart. Such regulation is only one compensation at this end of the continuum, however. Another is long-term profitability.

Long-term return on investment

A private for-profit enterprise can have more than a short-term profit orientation. It can aspire to long-term success and see that goal as a mediator of short-term interests. At the simplest level, managers must plow back some returns to maintain the physical plant in the long run. They perceive a similar need with respect to the social plant—employee benefits, staff development, and community relations.

Looking more broadly still, they may see that they can enhance their future profitability by investing in resource-conserving strategies. They may shift from petroleum-based to solar energy, for example, because they foresee a decline in future profits from a petroleum-based system (although in the short term it costs less than shifting to solar). If they enter long-term operation into their day-to-day calculations, they may perceive elements of self- interest rather than altruism in efforts to advance the transition to a sustainable society. For some enterprises the issue is long-term profit, because they can absorb short-run reverses. Fortunately, many such situations exist, and they complement the short-run profitability of other sustainable enterprises. Energy companies are one example. Some observers conclude that the statelike multinational corporations will lead the transition to a sustainable society for just such reasons. They are also so enormous that they recognize the need for addressing the big picture in corporate planning. But even here long-range planning may not extend far enough into the future to take into account today's children. And that's where the crunch comes.

Impact on resources

Conventional economics is tragically immaterial because it operates as if the monetarized economy exists apart from the resources of the material world. By and large, private for-profit enterprises do not consider their impact on resources, unless short- and long-term returns on investment dictate such a concern. The distinctions between organic and inorganic, renewable and nonrenewable, have no economic significance. Making the transition to a sustainable society hinges on just these distinctions, however. We must identify existing enterprises that can use renewable and organic resources and still maintain short-term and long-term profitability. Next, we must adopt voluntary or coerced efforts to control the processes through which monetary prices are assigned to renewable and organic versus nonrenewable and inorganic resources. These measures include government regulation, modifying the economic behavior of consumers, and invoking the altruism and humanism of managers and investors, most of whom have children and perhaps grandchildren. Each and every path must be followed if we are to make the successful transition to a sustainable society.

The activities of private for-profit enterprises exist along three axes: short-term profitability, long-term profitability, and impact on resources. Of course, the location of activities along these axes is not fixed. Their position may be changed by technological innovation, depletion and discovery of nonrenewable resources, cultural shifts, and political directives that affect costs, prices, supply, and demand.

Left to itself, will the private for-profit sector help bring about a sustainable society? To what extent do we need to restructure the economic and political environment so that it forces the for-profit sector to make that kind of contribution? Let's examine this question by focusing on several enterprises.

Electric utilities. Only twenty years ago, private for-profit electric utilities appeared to be enormous roadblocks in the path toward sustainability. According to analyses conducted by Amory and Hunter Lovins, however, electric utilities have begun to appear as potential leaders on this path, driven by the demands of long-term profitability as well as pressures of short-term costs and prices. Writing before the temporary deflation of oil prices in the mid-1980s, they note:

> Price is driving the transition. Conventional oil products now retail at about forty to fifty dollars per barrel. Energy saved by more efficient use costs about zero to twenty dollars per barrel; well-designed renewable sources can now deliver a "barrel" for about five to thirty dollars. The alternatives—such as synthetic fuels at over seventy dollars per retail barrel, and electricity from new coal or nuclear power plants at about twice that price—are even less competitive than imported oil. Efficiency and renewables are simply winning the market's sweepstakes for the best buys—the cheapest ways to do each desired task. (1982, p. 154)

This change is in the works, the Lovinses argue, but it is proceeding too slowly. The economic drain on the United States from current energy "production" and use is enormous—some ninety billion dollars per year exported to purchase imported oil in the early 1980s, before the temporary price decrease. Current patterns of consumption have paralyzed many economies, particularly those Third World countries that don't produce oil. Alternatives to the current pattern are noteworthy for their ecological sensibility, profitability, and complementarity with family concerns. They involve conservation and alternative consumption measures implemented at the family, neighborhood, and community levels in concert with the profit-driven activities of the electric utilities themselves.

Although much has already been accomplished, several factors are impeding progress. People lack information about techniques and materials. Short-term incentives at the consumer level are often not organized to motivate the kind of behavior that would speed the transition. If the landlord pays for heat, for example, the tenant has no short-term incentive to conserve energy. Local policies often stand in the way of progress, such as zoning regulations that inhibit residential use of "waste" heat from commercial enterprises. And government policies are biased against renewable resources: subsidies favor nonrenewables by a factor of ten to one. The current structure of capital investment favors concentrated rather than decentralized use of resources; the latter is required for advanced conservation measures.

The Lovinses describe a series of practical steps to dislodge these roadblocks and speed the United States down the road to energy sustainability. The key is to reverse the investment strategy of utilities—to move them away from new power generation and towards efficiency and conservation and, in the process, turn them away from financial ruin and towards profitability. The twenty-five billion dollars spent every year on new power facilities is an enormous step in the wrong direction. Such power stations are so capital-intensive that each one drains off enough resources to result in a net *decrease* of about four thousand jobs for the community, and it impoverishes other enterprises that need that capital for the future.

The Lovinses believe that electric utilities should help customers conserve energy and increase the energy efficiency of their homes, *a move that would allow the utilities to make a profit on existing generating capacity* rather than take a loss in attempts to generate new energy. The social and physical benefits of this alternative course dovetail so neatly with the financial benefits that it may be the single most dramatic example of private enterprise being in a position to lead the way to a sustainable society. But it is not guaranteed (what is?). It will depend on a regulatory climate that will nurture, even demand, the needed shift in investment strategy, and it will depend on day-to-day support of consumers who must implement the conservation measures. If all the actors play their parts, the United States could move toward an electrical system that meets all three criteria for sustainability. This system could be based on renewable resources; it could be centered in family and community; and by becoming self-reliant rather than draining resources beyond its national boundaries, it could be more than just in relation to the rest of the world. All this would be a major step in the right direction.

The Lovins' message may be getting through to the public and private decision makers. A 1982 report indicated that the New Jersey Board of Public utilities had approved a plan that would compel the Public Service Electric and Gas Company to invest in conservation. Board president Barbara Curran put it this way:

> Conservation is the safest, most reliable and least expensive source of energy New Jersey has. It is a "North Slope," an "uninterrupted pipeline" of energy supply in our own state, which this board intends to fully explore and develop.

This is a step in the right direction, albeit only one step.

Industrial product life. "Product life" refers to the period during which products and goods are used. In Orio Giarini's analysis, product life is a good's utilization value, and it governs the speed with which it must be replaced. Thus, for example, a car built and serviced to last twenty years stands in a very different relationship to the sustainable society than does a car that serves for only five years. This concept has been elaborated and explored by Walter Stahel (1982).

In Stahel's view (and its validity seems clear), the currently dominant industrial model is the "fast-replacement system," in which the whole point is to produce goods that are cheap and nonrepairable. Economic well-being thus depends on turnover. Profit becomes a kind of sales commission based on volume in which resource use is only evident in the cash price required to extract and transform raw materials into marketable objects. The results of this system have indeed threatened both the quality of human experience and society's prospects for sustainability. As Stahel sees it, instead of increasing real wealth we are devoting an ever larger proportion of our national and personal incomes to replacing products. Fashion and fast depreciation drive this system. It is the evil genius of private enterprise at its most diabolical.

Depreciation is an enemy of the sustainable society. The fact that it is encouraged by current government tax incentives makes government part of the problem rather than a leader in finding a solution. As for private for-profit enterprise, Stahel suggests that it is not ready to make the shift directly to a slow-replacement system of long-life products. But where others see despair, Stahel sees possibility, a middle, transitional course he calls "product-life extension."

This approach encourages private for-profit enterprise to take up what have been called the four Rs of appropriate technology: reuse, repair, reconditioning, and recycling. These are arranged by hierarchy: in general, repair only when reuse is impossible; repair until reconditioning becomes necessary; and recycle a product after it has worn out its use. Such a strategy can be ecologically sound, in both the physical and social senses. Furthermore, this strategy can be profitable in both the short and long runs. Specifically, it:

- is available to small-scale enterprises and builds upon interpersonal initiative;
- results in a reconditioned product considerably below the cash price of a new product (even under the ecologically unsound cost criteria of current industrial societies);
- leaves room to technologically upgrade existing products as part of the reconditioning process;
- shifts activity from capital-intensive, extractive, and industrially productive enterprises to small-scale, labor-intensive, decentralized enterprises.

Stahel goes on to review the available data on product-life extension. These data argue persuasively for the strategy's soundness. Stahel found that about 75% of all energy consumption in industrial enterprises is used to extract or produce materials like steel and cement. In contrast, the transformation of materials into finished goods consumes only about 25%. Thus, Stahel argues, the longer we keep the materials (and the finished goods) "in play," the more compatible to the goals of the sustainable society are the enterprises that produce them. Keeping the materials and goods in play is labor intensive, and that is good for families, because families need jobs to function and to sustain *informal* social welfare systems, while, at the same time, they need to limit demands on *formal* social welfare systems.

Stahel offers several illustrative examples, including the following:

- Rebuilding tractor engines and other parts preserves resources and produces tractors that last almost as long as new tractors and at half the price.
- It costs 60% less to modernize a residential building than it does to build a new one (in the narrowest sense, not including the cost of a new location).
- It cost 50% less to modernize a DC-8 jet and equip it with new engines than it does to buy a new one.
- Societies at different stages of modernization can allow products to work their way "down" through the world's systems with a good performance ratio at each step (such as has been the case with the DC-3 aircraft).

Perhaps the most telling example of the contrast between short-life and long-life products is seen in the contrast between what has come to be called the modern "world car" and Henry Ford's "everyman's car," the Model T. The former is designed for quick and cheap manufacture, and it relies upon nonrepairable parts (including electronic "black boxes"). The Model T was designed so that its relatively simple components could be repaired by any local blacksmith. Today, however, fewer and fewer car owners (and even mechanics) feel competent enough to work on their cars. Many of us recall maintaining and repairing our Volkswagens of the 1960s, but we find the complexity of a 1980s VW daunting. A VW service manager once expressed to me exactly that kind of feeling. This makes neither economic nor psychological sense. People need to feel empowered if the sustainable society is to come about. We need to be able to rely upon locals for service.

All in all, product-life extension is a cornerstone of the sustainable society. It makes the best use of resources and puts into perspective short- and long-term profit. It also offers the prospect of meaningful, often family-based work because it is labor intensive and constructive in a way that many other forms of enterprise are not. And it promises to put people to work, a basic need. Thus, it offers itself as a force for stabilizing and justifying both the physical and social ecologies. Many roadblocks now prevent the implementation of this course, such as tax disincentives and psychocultural biases that favor rapid depreciation and turnover. But once we recognize these issues, we can deal with them. Specifically, we need to change taxation policies that provide depreciation allowances and thus reward new production. We need to reverse the biases that currently discourage reusability, manual labor, and self-reliance and encourage fashion, disposability, and conspicuous consumption.

Internalizing the externalities. Certainly one of the keys in making the transition to a sustainable society is the matter of "internalizing the externalities." Externalities are factors outside the priced costs of production and thus outside enterprise's accounting. If private for-profit enterprises are to have a role in this transition, we must bring factors such as pollution, depletion, and impact on the social environment into the costs of doing business. Where this is done fairly and homogeneously, it should help increase the profitability of competent enterprises. Done less fairly, it may threaten the profitability of enterprises receiving discriminatory treatment. If not done at all, the physical and social environments are dependent upon the goodwill of business. The tragedy of the commons is the probable result.

Constitutional lawyer Arthur Miller (1982) believes that one way to compel private for-profit enterprises to act responsibly is to change the constitutional status of corporations. The current ambiguous constitutional status of corporations, he argues, gives them too many privileges and not enough responsibilities. A change in constitutional status would provide a firm basis for requiring that corporations deal with the physical and social environment in a responsible manner. Miller's analysis dovetails with others that stress the role of social responsibility in private for-profit enterprises as a force in innovating, developing, and implementing technological tactics for making the transition to a sustainable society. This kind of social engineering is a key to creating and implementing the needed breakthroughs in physical engineering.

At the core of this problem of social engineering is what we may call "corporate self-reliance," in which the private sector assumes full responsibility for the social and environmental consequences of its actions in host communities. An economically sound system of production should sustain and nurture host communities as much as it conserves the physical environment. The concept of corporate self-reliance proposes that we conceptualize, develop, maintain, and evaluate private enterprises in terms of their *total* costs and benefits—social as well as physical—to the planet's ecosystems. To do this, enterprises must act as citizens, reflecting Arthur Miller's idea that corporations must be seen as a special kind of citizen.

In the social sphere, corporate self-reliance by the private sector allows it to assume the roles of worker, family member, and citizen, developing the personnel needed for a sustainable society. These people will feel a sense of responsibility to the environment, an attitude that is the essence of adulthood. Socialization to adulthood means acquiring the skills and attitudes necessary to assume full responsibility in the work place, the home, and the community. When the primary social roles of worker, family member, and citizen are out of kilter, the efficiency and productivity of all three settings (work, home, community) declines. When they are in harmony, all three function better.

This focus on the social context of private for-profit enterprise is necessary and appropriate. Those who work on global models (such as the Club of Rome) have reached an empirical and theoretical consensus on the proposition that the major variables in future worldwide scenarios are sociopolitical rather than technological. Technology certainly has an important role in bringing about the sustainable society. On that front, the work of the Intermediate Technology Group (inspired by the work of E.F. Schumacher) and the New Alchemy Institute could certainly be invaluable. But technology it not the critical issue. Political will and social organization are needed to put the tools of technology to their full use. The Club of Rome has come to focus increasingly on the sociocultural aspects of the world problematique for this very reason. The issue is, as always, human quality (Peccei, 1979).

The primacy of social rather than technological issues is consistent with corporate self-reliance and the implications such self-reliance has for community. Technological and social challenges differ in the degree to which they lend themselves to centralized, consolidated solutions. Technological innovations lend themselves to single-site development, testing, and dissemination, as is evident by the success of various agricultural research laboratories. Efforts must be made to ensure that such technological innovations are sufficiently consistent with local conditions. However, these innovations can be centrally developed without necessarily violating basic human needs and values, without sacrificing essential human quality.

The same cannot be said of the social innovations required for the transition to the kind of society that combines sustainability and human quality. Here centralized development, testing, and implementation are not nearly enough. Social innovation is much more closely tied to decentralized local research and development. Broad ideas and even society-wide "rules of the game" may come from central social laboratories. But the full development of these ideas into patterns of behavior and belief must occur in response to needs, traditions, and ecological realities at the community level. A prime example of this is the agricultural and retail "free market" serving as a regulator of a society's economic life. As a source of social creativity, the "free" and community-based society stands in refreshing contrast to the spiritually stultifying climate of highly centralized societies, such as the former communist countries. The complexity of the task—an ecologically sane approach to society—demands flexibility. We must adopt this approach if we are to create a sustainable society that is spiritually based.

Cultural diversity is as important as biological diversity in enhancing evolutionary resilience and human progress. Freedom is the cornerstone of this crucial social edifice. Without it, negative influences inherent in the unsustainable society will prevail. A sustainable society is a free society; an unsustainable society must be an exploiting master enslaved to its appetite ("Slaveship Earth"). And in such a society, private enterprise likewise tends to be exploitive.

The idea of the private sector's assuming full responsibility for social consequences stands in contrast to contemporary thinking that casts only government ("the welfare state") in this leadership role and asks of business only that it do no demonstrable social harm. The concept of corporate self-reliance is a major departure from the modern laissez-faire approach that has viewed both corporate responsibility and labor/management relations primarily in narrowly monetary terms. In broadening the mission of corporate responsibility and labor/management relations to make them more consistent with the demands of a sustainable society, we must negotiate the fine line between corporate paternalism and corporate social neglect. Perhaps the image of corporate "maternalism" is apt, recalling our discussion about the feminine voice in chapter 7. A nurturing and reconciling force is what we need, not a harsh, divisive one.

Paternalism connotes authoritarian and judgmental regulation as the price one pays for concern and regard. Maternalism, on the other hand, connotes supportive discipline, meeting needs because they exist, and generally engendering allegiance and responsiveness through nurturing. Corporate self-reliance is the feminine voice in business, derived from the characteristically feminine approach to moral development and conflict resolution. The following analyses seek to show that this self-reliance is ultimately in the best interests of the individual, the family, the community, *and* private enterprise.

Strategies for corporate self-reliance[1]

Example 1: From Strike Town to International Model

One prerequisite of corporate self-reliance is the transformation of the traditionally adversarial relationship between labor and management into one of cooperation and mutual trust. This is part of what we need to establish guild socialism. An enterprise works best when participants share the same goals, seek solutions to the same problems, and agree to weather hard times together. But how do we attain such a state given the traditional lack of trust between labor and management and their historically validated differences of class interest?

One idea is the labor/management committee, a new form of organization that has emerged in diverse communities in the United States over the last two decades. The specific purposes of such committees may vary from community to community, but in general their underlying goals are to improve the labor climate by enhancing productivity, reducing the likelihood of strikes, and maintaining the stability of the local work force. In this they resemble Japanese planning committees and the wage/price boards envisioned by Walt Rostow.

Jamestown, New York, is the site of one of the best known labor/management committees, the Jamestown Labor Management Committee (JALMC). The JALMC was established in 1972 by corporate management, union leaders, and local government as an antidote to the gradual disintegration of the community's labor climate. At that time, the economic life of the area was in disarray. In the 1960s, thirty-eight strikes occurred in Jamestown (population 40,000), costing a total of 1,401 strike days; many businesses were relocating or ceasing operations.

The committee was made up of local government officials and labor and management leaders from local factories. Working with consultants, the JALMC gradually transformed the community of Jamestown. They set up committees within companies to improve the quality of work life. These committees were composed of managers and workers, who each pooled their individual expertise to solve complex issues.

The success of the JALMC is a matter of public record. Only twenty-six strikes occurred in the 1970s for a total of 490 strike days. New industry has come to the area, creating jobs and opportunities. Older companies once in danger of going under have streamlined their operations and enhanced productivity, often because of their workers' technical expertise.

Labor/management committees are just one strategy for developing self-reliance at the corporate, community, and individual levels. The idea is not radical, in that the relative status of labor and management remains the same. What is new, however, is the cooperation, trust, and active participation of all involved. These themes weave their way through three other strategies for self-reliance.

Example 2: What's Small Potatoes to Sperry Rand is Bread and Butter to Herkimer, New York

When a plant is shut down permanently, there is little a labor/ management committee can do. The issue is not the quality of work life but loss of jobs and the revenue they generate for the local community. Plant shutdowns in the United States increased in the last decade. A plant is not always closed because it is not profitable, however. Frequently, it is owned by a large conglomerate whose national headquarters are far away from the local plant. As the conglomerate grows, it may liquidate small plants that make modest profits, writing them off as tax losses. Such an event may be a mere business decision to the corporation, but to the employees and the local community, it may signal disaster, particularly in the case of towns and rural areas highly dependent upon the plant. And the community's economic well-being is the principal factor that determines the character of its social environment.

One constructive response to the threat of a plant shutdown is worker ownership. A case in point is the Library Bureau, a furniture factory in Herkimer, New York, which was once a subsidiary of Sperry Rand. In 1976 Sperry Rand decided to close the plant. The plant was making a considerable profit, but it was low by company standards, and the corporation was no longer interested in the furniture business. And so, in a dramatic example of community mobilization, the work force and the local community combined resources to buy the plant from Sperry Rand. Six months after the announcement of the shutdown, ownership of the Library Bureau passed to its employees and members of the community. As a result, the community has survived, avoiding a crisis in mental as well as in economic health. More than that, it has triumphed and became more self-reliant.

What is the role of the private for-profit sector in such community efforts? As the holder of title to such an enterprise, this sector must facilitate, not oppose, community/employee purchase. As a member of such a community, it must join in the effort to maintain community integrity. Of course, it would be naive to assume that employee ownership is always in the best interests of the workers, as Don Goldstein's article (1983) in *The Nation* (1983) points out. In his analysis of employee ownership of the Weirton, West Virginia, steel plant, Goldstein shows that when remote and profit-hungry conglomerates are involved, the costs to workers may be so high that they outweigh the benefits. As always, nothing is simple, and the possibility of getting ripped off always exists.

Example 3: Getting Business in the Family Way

A third strategy for corporate self-reliance requires that the private sector recognize that corporate policies and practices have immediate and enduring consequence for the family and community lives of employees. This strategy involves instituting specific "employer-based family supports"—a long-term investment in workers and the host community.

The interrelatedness of work, family, and community is the subject of a growing body of research. Work can provide support for families that goes beyond economic well-being. Through innovative practices and policies, the private sector can enhance the social and psychological well-being of employees and their families.

Existing employer-based family supports fall into three categories. *Innovative scheduling* offers options such as flexible hours ("flex- time"), job sharing, and increased availability of part-time employment. *Corporate benefits* include maternity and paternal leave, flexible or "cafeteria" benefit packages, and employee assistance programs aimed at reducing drug and alcohol abuse. *Corporate sensitivity to the needs of working parents* means special assistance to two-career families, work site child care, or other forms of family support.

However, it is true that the needs of family and community can cause productivity problems for companies. In her study of a manufacturing plant, Ann Crouter (1980) found that working mothers of children under the age of six were the most likely to admit that problems at home affected their performance at work. They admitted to being absent from work to care for a sick child, being preoccupied at work when worried about unsatisfactory child care, and turning down job transfers because new hours would have been inflexible. There are reasons for believing that home-based child care most meets the needs of a sustainable society, especially with today's emphasis on the family household as an economically productive enterprise. However—at least during the transition to a sustainable society—most parents will still require formal child care services.

Company-sponsored, high-quality child care would relieve many mothers and fathers of considerable pressure and thus enable them to be more efficient and committed at work. In such a case no one loses. The company gains an effective, loyal employee; the parent receives social and economic support for his or her child rearing responsibilities; and the child receives quality care and supervision, a service many now go without. Companies that have implemented some form of child care (including Stride-Rite Shoes and Corning Glass) are enthusiastic about it.

Example 4: Making the Whole Greater than the Sum of Its Parts

For these strategies to succeed, workers must be able to participate in day-to-day decision making and problem solving. In the United States, such "participative" work usually involves setting up semiautonomous work teams that work together to perform a fairly large, complex task from beginning to end. Often individuals are rewarded for the number of skills they acquire, the goal being that all team members eventually will be able to perform all the tasks involved in the job.

In the plant where Ann Crouter conducted her research, teams managed their own inventory, monitored safety and quality control, handled performance problems, and hired new members. They were responsible for investigating production problems, scheduling, meeting deadlines, and many other activities. This stands in dramatic contrast to traditional jobs with their stultifying routine, hierarchical supervision, and lack of challenge.

A company that introduces participative work is usually motivated by the desire to enhance productivity or decrease alienation among workers. There are positive benefits for the individual as well. Studies have shown that self-direction at work can actually make an individual's intellectual functioning more flexible. Employees gain skills that are also useful off the job, including communication, problem solving, public speaking, listening, and decision making. It is not surprising that people in participative jobs are more satisfied than their peers in traditional jobs. They are more effective with others and better able to function autonomously in a complex environment. Such qualities make individuals more receptive to the life styles necessary for global sustainability and to what Duane Elgin calls "voluntary simplicity"—a conscious decision to live in a sustainable manner.

There is much to recommend self-reliant work groups. By taking on such tasks as inventory or quality control, which were once be performed by specialists, the group gradually becomes a self-reliant collective which is able to cope when a team member is absent, to plan ahead, and to perfect the work process.

The company also has much to gain from self-reliant workers. It gains a skilled, stable work force with high morale and improved productivity. As competence within the company increases, the organization has less need for outside experts and becomes more self-reliant. If the organization is better able to compete in the market, its chances for survival increase.

Finally, the community benefits from participative work and its effects. It is stabilized if local employers are able to reduce or eliminate lay-offs and cutbacks. Job security strengthens families, and breadwinners are able to transfer their new skills to their lives at home. Many employees in the plant Crouter studied said that participative work had helped them learn to listen to their children better, organize family life more democratically, and be more open with their spouses. This has important implications not only for child development but for marriages and family stability. The community also benefits when employees take their newly developed abilities in group work and join volunteer organizations. Community participation is all the more important today when high rates of female employment have resulted in a decrease in the number of individuals working as volunteers, which have traditionally been women.

Without corporate self-reliance, such promising concepts as labor-management committees, worker ownership, and employer-based family supports are unlikely to succeed. Such innovations cannot simply be imposed upon a work force or a community from on high. Employees often do not use work site child care if they are not involved in planning it, for example. Likewise, the Head Start program is most successful when parents actively participate as partners with the teachers.

Clearly, corporations have much to gain from restructuring the work process so that workers have a voice in decision making and problem solving.

Many of the strategies outlined above are relevant to all societies, but in some ways they seem most relevant to the already modernized societies. When we turn to the rest of the world, we can see that there are more areas in which private for-profit enterprise can play a role. These include agribusiness cooperatives, labor-intensive small businesses, and private investment for development.

Agribusiness cooperatives. In most of the Third World, the private for-profit enterprises most important for the transition to a sustainable society are agricultural. Agriculture is necessary because it reduces food shortages and the pressures for urbanization. Around the world, small farms in which the farmer has a personal stake are the most efficient food producers. The startling increase of production and real personal income among Chinese peasants in the wake of the new Responsibility System testifies eloquently to this. It seems clear that small farms (one to five acres) are the strategy of choice, particularly if they receive technical assistance, capital, and other support from corporate agribusiness. The "corporate core" provides access to technology, while the small landholder provides the motivational anchor. This model can be adapted to many different settings, so long as the goals are related closely to meeting basic needs. David Hopcroft (1977), for example, has contrasted the commercial and economic wisdom of ranching animals that are indigenous to the African plains with the ecological and commercial folly of using cattle foreign to the area. Certainly one of the items of highest priority in Third World countries is the creation and maintenance of agricultural enterprises with high long-term profitability and low environmental costs. A partnership between small landholders and agribusiness can achieve those goals (and also provide an agrarian social order conducive to strong functional families).

Small business. Small, labor-intensive businesses make relatively small demands on capital and are thus the natural choice for developing societies. Such enterprises can exist without the dangers of centralized direction, respond to local conditions, and provide a good labor-to-capital ratio that can help stabilize the social scene. Like small farmers, small businesses can profit from the technical assistance and capital reserves of larger corporate entities. They are amenable to low-energy, low-capital appropriate technology, as has been determined by

E.F. Schumacher and his colleagues. Efforts to stimulate such enterprises (e.g., by the Women's World Bank) are the core of the sustainable approach to economic development.

The job-creation potential of small businesses even in a modern industrialized society has come under scrutiny in recent years. The Brookings Institution reported that businesses with fewer than 100 employees accounted for 51% of the new jobs created in the United States between 1976 and 1980. A 1980 Massachusetts Institute of Technology study reported a 70% figure for the 1969–1976 period. Small businesses seem to be more adept at creating jobs in times of national prosperity than in times of recession, when their lack of financial reserves often makes them vulnerable. A study of the years 1978 to 1980 reported that small businesses created only 37% of the new jobs. However, data for the 1981–1982 recession indicate that small businesses were more successful in retaining jobs, in part because they tend to operate outside the manufacturing and mining domains, where economic slowdown translates most directly and quickly into unemployment.

Private investment funds for development. As von Oppen (1982) has argued, developing societies face several investment problems. For one thing, they need capital for projects that are ineligible for governmental aid and unable to attract conventional private investment because they do not promise short-term payoffs. Von Oppen proposes private investment as a solution.

Such funds would permit individuals from industrialized societies to aid in promoting Third World development, without significant risk. With governments underwriting interest rates, the short-term profit to the private investor would be competitive with conventional investments. Simple marshaling of capital will not result in sustainable development. But it can play a pivotal role if the developing countries themselves have set a course that leads to sustainability through agricultural and business enterprises of the sort outlined earlier.

Prospects for the future

"If the only tool you have is a hammer, you tend to treat every problem as if it were a nail." This aphorism, attributed to Mark Twain and later expounded by psychologist Abraham Maslow, is apt to our discussion. It highlights the fact that our tools shape the way we identify and define our issues and problems. For our purposes, we might reverse the aphorism to read: "If you define your problem as a nail, the only tool you will look for is a hammer." We need to expand our traditional concept of private enterprise and begin to see it as a tool for advancing the transition to a sustainable society. We must, for example, distinguish between private enterprise based upon individuals from private enterprise based upon collectives (guild socialism). The trick is to broaden our conception of the issues and thereby see the relevance of *all* our tools. These issues appear to us now as unresolved problems and as questions for further study.

The popular and professional press has made much of Japanese management. It is easy to exaggerate and overgeneralize the benefits of the Japanese approach, but a more objective perspective reveals it to be a sound model for developing management strategies geared to the needs of the sustainable society. Certainly the keystone of this approach is a view of output that goes beyond short-term and narrowly defined worker productivity. Taking the long view, productivity is stimulated principally by reinforcing competent performance, encouraging worker-to-company and company-to-worker commitment, and linking together the fate and prospects of worker and company. If we add "sustainable environmental impact," we have an appropriate set of standards. Just as the energy utilities are coming to see conservation as a major target for "productive investment," so too must other industries see that long-term investment in human capital is an idea whose time has come. Business must assume responsibility for the impact its enterprises have on the community and on society.

The goal of sustainability puts short-term sacrifice in a different light than does the cannibalization of the planet for the middle-run benefit of socioeconomic exploitation. Leaders must understand that while you can't take it with you, you *can* take future generations down with you. Unless we can harness the profit motive on behalf of future generations, the only choice for them may be self-destructive capitalism or stultifying collectivism. Our great-grandchildren deserve better. Goals do matter in evaluating the costs of alternative means. If ends don't justify themselves, they can hardly justify the means used to achieve them.

One of the biggest unresolved issues facing the private for-profit sector is how to assume full economic and social responsibility for waste. As Giarini has shown, waste is the eventual result of all "productive" economic activity. The utilization value of products is the period of their accessibility and usefulness for meeting human needs. One implication of corporate self-reliance is that the private sector must develop "markets" for its waste. In fact, one criterion for judging the sustain-ability of a society is its ability to prolong the utilization value of its raw materials. Thus, for example, when "waste" heat from one plant can be used by another, both enterprises have taken a significant step towards sustainability. Similarly, when an expended product is recycled (either through its first producer or through some alternative) the community experiences a net gain in sustainability. The same concepts apply to hu-man beings, where durability and productivity stand against waste of human capital—i.e., the lives of individuals, families, and communi-ties. Thus, in evaluating the worth of enterprises—in terms of tax and credit incentives—a careful analysis of waste, material *and* social, is im-perative. If small is beautiful, so too are those things which are durable, frugal, and efficient in the broadest sense. Private enterprise, when it operates with a real concern for people and the planet, can be beautiful too.

All told, the private for-profit sector can do much to quicken the transition to a sustainable society. As it is presently constituted, its ac-tivities can be consistent with short-term and long-term profitability. Even more can be done if fiscal and regulatory rewards and punish-ments are altered so that they create a climate of incentives. The private for-profit sector can accomplish even more if it focuses its internal op-erations and community relations on improving the well-being of soci-ety. Done properly, such efforts will engender and sustain a sense of corporate self-reliance. And we all will profit from business *not* being done as usual.

NOTES

1. This section is based in part upon a 1982 Mitchell Prize–winning essay written by my colleague Ann Crouter and me entitled "Corporate Self-Reliance."

NINE

The Politics of Posterity

March 1981. Tokyo, Japan. Japan is the success story of the 1970s and the 1980s. So say the weekly news magazines, arbiters of popular myth and opinion. "These Amazing Japanese: How Do They Do It?" asks one story. How indeed? Japan shows me two worlds: one, an ancient culture that is alien to me, the other, a modern culture coming to terms with America. Many Japanese are enthralled with America—McDonald's is already here in Tokyo, and a Japanese Disneyland is in the works. How does one reconcile the old with the new? How does one accept the modern and still embrace the traditional?

An alluring metaphor presents itself as I wander through the Meiji Shrine in Tokyo, a parklike estate dedicated to the restoration of the Meiji Dynasty to the Imperial Throne in the nineteenth century. At its heart is a Shinto temple, where I mix with the other tourists (mostly Japanese) and devotees. A wedding party passes—priests in traditional garb, the others wearing the modern Japanese uniform, dark suits or tasteful print dresses. Shinto tradition permits only the priests and the wedding party into the temple for the ceremony. Continuing my self-directed tour, I am charmed to watch a "christening" (to use the Christian term; my Unitarian-Universalist friends would call it a "dedication"). Most families are represented by an ancient relative, usually a grandmother, who offers up the child with obvious pride.

It is a beautiful ceremony, and I linger a few minutes after it ends. Later I observe the wedding party, now established in a handsome reception room. In what seems a triumphant blend of old and new, the party is watching a videotaped replay of the wedding ceremony in living color on a Sony television. Who says you can't have your cake and eat it too when it comes to culture and technology? Is this the path to a sustainable society? Is this appropriate technology for a modern industrial society that wants to respect its roots and honor its families? I am tempted to answer "yes."

But then later I am caught in a two-hour traffic jam between the hotel and the airport.

Appropriate technology refers to physical and social devices that seek to serve a sustainable society, one that is designed to endure permanently, that meets basic human needs, and that is just. Appropriate technology embodies ecological intelligence on a social, physical, and moral level. It blends smart economics and humane social welfare systems. It nurtures and sustains the wealth of families.

Inappropriate technology violates one or more of the assumptions of a sustainable society. The most glaring violations are those that voraciously exploit the planet's resources with an eye for short-term profit and a blind spot when it comes to justice. In general, the energy-intensive industries are inappropriate in this sense. They transform enormous quantities of precious material into ephemeral products which lapse into waste with alacrity. They are not built to last. And the community faces the task of coping with that wastes, often in perpetuity. What a legacy for our grandchildren—all so *we* might have disposable bottles, razors, and phones.

But such physically inappropriate technologies are not the whole story. Also included are social institutions that methodically work against a life style that meets human needs. Modern society is increasingly suspect in that respect. Much of the work it offers is not satisfying or violates human circadian rhythms. Just as inappropriate is the introduction of techniques that undermine the supportive social arrangements families rely on. Much of the modernization experienced by rural agrarian societies disrupts the economic and social resources of rural mothers and leaves them isolated and vulnerable.

Finally, where techniques inhibit the establishment of justice by reinforcing inequities, they are rightly called inappropriate. We see this when a government subsidizes energy- and capital-intensive agricultural models that displace family farms. These "modern" techniques prevent small farmers from competing with big farmers, who have access to financial reserves for equipment and fertilizer. The result can be that small farmers are driven out of business, even though small farms are more appropriate in the long run, because they provide more genuine work, cohere around families, and lend themselves to recycling, reuse, and conservation. The same can be said (as was shown in chapter 8) about other small businesses, in contrast to large economic organizations.

What does appropriate technology look like? Of course, it varies depending on the situation, but in general a society fully committed to appropriate technology would have the following characteristics: decentralization; labor intensiveness; environmental soundness; and a self-reinforcing character. Each contributes to the effective stability of social welfare systems and the wealth of families. Let us look at each of these characteristics in more detail.

Decentralization: Tasks would be accomplished first by the household, followed in order by the neighborhood, the community, the region, the country, and finally by the international community. This would place the functions of both economic and social welfare systems as close as possible to the day-to-day life of families, where they belong.

Labor intensiveness: Work would provide dignified employment rather than simple short-term monetary return on capital investment. People need good work. Sound and stable employment is the cornerstone of social welfare systems. Where unemployment is out of control, social welfare systems are swimming against the tide (or is it spitting in the wind?).

Environmental soundness: Economic endeavors would maximize conservation, recycling, and prolonged multiple use, and they would deemphasize extraction and the transformation of materials and "products" into waste (particularly nonbiodegradable waste). If the material aspects of day-to-day life were in order, it would be easier to right our social arrangements.

Self-reinforcing character: Tasks would be organized around incentives and penalties that together would reward ecologically intelligent behavior and cultivation of human quality. Human relationships form interlocking social systems, so we must structure our institutions to support sustainability.

Each of these elements demands further elaboration, for together they comprise the sustainable society. Without them the prospects for families and their social welfare systems are grim.

Decentralization

"Small is beautiful." Schumacher's classic dictum rings true in general. Some tasks do require large-scale operations, but most do not. Further, when the full costs of operation are taken into account, smaller is usually more sustainable than bigger. Thus, smaller economic units are the policy of choice, unless proven otherwise. Whether it be food, health, housing, or manufacturing, large-scale bureaucratic and technocratic approaches have just about run their course in most areas. This is true of public-sector social welfare systems as well, most of which are lumbering giants, unwieldy and inefficient at best.

Household operations can be incredibly effective in meeting multiple needs. Besides providing food, the fish pond or vegetable plot offers children an opportunity to learn responsibility, gives parents and their offspring a natural context for interaction, and provides children and the elderly with dignified roles that make economic and psychological sense. The same recycling scheme that reduces the volume of garbage also permits a parent to care for a child at home without facing a severe economic penalty for doing so. Restoring *real* productive functions to families will go a long way toward reducing demands upon formal social welfare systems.

The technology for achieving this is at hand. *The Integral Urban Household* (Farallones Institute, San Francisco) shows how food and energy can result from an ingenious network of integrated systems, all of which emphasize renewable energy sources and materials, smart technology, and recycling. Reading it, one is struck by how well the family's economic and social needs can mesh. An amazing degree of household self-sufficiency is possible with only a few hours of labor per week per family member for a family of two adults and two children (the appropriate family size in a sustainable society).

Such an approach is an appropriate alternative to pie-in-the-sky policies that seek "full employment" as defined in conventional economic terms. The most practical solution to the employment crisis includes, but is not limited to, *withdrawing* people from the monetarized labor force. It favors genuinely productive work outside the monetarized economy (with, perhaps, part-time forays into the labor force for cash to supplement the family's nonmonetarized "income"). This is not a dream. It is the practical real-world alternative, as the coming decades will demonstrate with ever-increasing and irrefutable clarity. How do we translate this idea into practice? One way is to implement tax policies that encourage it; a second is to use existing public university extension systems to transmit the technology and the will to use it.

Of course, not all tasks are appropriate to the household, and so then we look to the neighborhood. Many definitions of neighborhoods exist, but one with special appeal bases itself on the walking range of a young child (perhaps holding a grandparent's hand). That makes sense. A neighborhood is the web of social and physical arrangements that surround one's household. And it manifests itself in what Kromkowski calls "pride in the neighborhood, care of homes, security for children, and respect for each other." Certainly a prime indicator of quality of life is how well social environments achieve these four goals (Bronfenbrenner, Moenr, and Garbarino, 1985; Garbarino and Associates, 1992).

Stated this way, the significance of neighborhoods as support systems for families is clear. Ecologically sane enterprises that are appropriately located in the neighborhood reinforce each other and contribute to family well-being as well. They thus reduce demands upon formal social welfare systems at the community level. Being able to walk to work, shopping centers, and recreational areas is an ecological virtue that harmonizes with family life. It also increases feedback and nurturance, essential elements of social support. Repeated incidental contact with people leads to eventual associations and ultimately to friendships. The more that neighborhoods become economically functional, the more socially cohesive they will be.

Using a car to accomplish daily tasks that could be done without one is a misdemeanor against the Earth and posterity. Social policies that encourage driving and discourage walking are crimes against the planet. This may seem rhetorically excessive, but it isn't. It's only as dramatic as the issues themselves. This is, after all, a struggle for the future.

A sustainable society includes economic and social cooperatives at the neighborhood level. Here families collaborate to meet productive and service needs that cannot be met at the household level. In doing so, they learn and demonstrate important social skills. These settings are also places where families can provide nurturance and feedback to members. Neighborhood-based enterprises such as these need practical support from families. Tax policies, zoning ordinances, and public works allocations can all nurture neighborhood economic activities. Some of these activities include child care, clothing exchanges, shared use of tools such as chain saws, wood splitters, ladders, and perhaps recreational equipment. This kind of sharing is frequent in some communities, and it would become even more so in a sustainable society.

One way to increase sustainability is to limit the use of automobiles. Fewer automobiles and limited use of those that exist will increase the quality of a pedestrian and bicycle-friendly environment—the neighborhood. Of course, in the short run, emphasizing human powered transportation will expose the social and economic deficiencies of many neighborhoods, highlighting the fact that they lack shops, work sites, recreational areas, and meeting places. Such exposure will demonstrate the need for social reorganization and political action, such as instituting policies that strongly discourage (even penalize) families from owning two or more cars, heavily tax gasoline, restrict automobile access, and reward communities that offer services at walkable distances. For a start, all public services should seek to become accessible on foot or by mass transit or by a combination of the two.

Community-level organization is necessary for transportation systems, formal education, industrial enterprise, and the like. And some social welfare systems (e.g., pension plans) also must operate beyond the neighborhood. But when households and neighborhoods become more sustainable, the need for more "essential" community- level activities decreases. When recycling and conservation reduce waste to an absolute minimum, refuse collection becomes a much smaller matter, for example. In modern societies, activity at the community level is likely to lessen. In nonmodernized societies, community activity will probably increase to provide such services as electrical power and sanitation without overshooting the mark as modern societies have done.

A community's economy determines its social life. Before industrialization and mass transportation, most communities had an agricultural base. Now, there is a greater variation. Some communities are based on an industrial plant, while others exist to provide a pleasant environment for commuting workers. Others are clustered around offices housing white-collar services. Most have lost any semblance of economic autonomy.

In a sustainable society, few communities will be wholly self sufficient. Most will trade for what they cannot acquire through local resources. This implies that appropriate technology will involve a regional component. Regional variations in climate predict differences in the need for a "heating industry," for example. Passive solar heating could furnish virtually all the household heat needed in Los Angeles—but only 60% in New York, 57% in Boston, 52% in Seattle, and 42% in Madison, Wisconsin. Hydroelectric power can supply all the needs of the Pacific Northwest but little or none of the Midwest. Appropriate technology is appropriate in its geographic scale. And it generates dignified employment.

Labor intensiveness

Appropriate technology meets the requirements of the sustainable society by minimizing the use of physical resources and maximizing the use of human resources, while exploiting neither. One of the basic human needs that a sustainable society must meet is the need for dignified employment. Simply providing work is not enough. Premodern societies are labor intensive, but that labor is too often drudgery that breaks spirits and bodies.

Appropriate technology promises to pare away as much destructive labor as possible while leaving or creating as much dignified work as is needed. The plow developed by the Schumacher-inspired Intermediate Technology Group is a good example. It relieves the backbreaking burden of working an oxen-powered plow, but it is not a conventional tractor. In their clever arrangement, a small engine pulls a plow across a field using a wire, while two farmers use their skill and strength to guide it. The result is better plowing with a less expensive tool and provision of meaningful work. And of course, the existence of permanent, ecologically sensible jobs at a relatively low capital cost per work site minimizes the demands upon formal social welfare systems.

In the film, *The Other Way* (1976), Schumacher recalls the time he visited an Indian industrial park. In a nearby village he met a potter who worked a hand-powered wheel. At the industrial park he met a trainee learning how to use an expensive modern machine. When he asked the trainee if he would be able to work in his home village using such a machine, the man replied, "No. I could never have the money to buy such a machine. No. I must go to the city to look for a job."

Schumacher's story is relevant to conventional economic development projects, be they in Chicago or the Third World. On a visit to Sao Paulo, I encountered a Brazilian economist/technocrat who described his visit to a government-financed industrial park in a desperately impoverished part of the country. He tells me of a Brazilian trainee who cannot afford the machinery he needs to perform his job, a story which perfectly mirrors Schumacher's. That industrial park in Brazil, like the one in India that Schumacher visited, was inappropriate in terms of the resources needed to create it, and it didn't meet the needs of the inhabitants of the area. Poor neighborhoods in the United States face many of the same issues these Third World communities do. Infant morality rates are often comparable, and the prospects for entering the middle class are equally unlikely. And I have heard plans for economic development in these neighborhoods that are as unrealistic as the development Schumacher observed in India.

The rudimentary technology used by the village potter is not advanced enough to generate the kind of income one would need to live comfortably in a modern society. The trainee's technology, on the other hand, requires a large capital investment. Both need a middle way, a technology more powerful than the potter's simple wheel but not as grandiose and expensive as the trainee's. That middle way is appropriate technology, and modernizing societies often achieve it by blending traditional techniques with modern mechanisms.

The Chinese have an expression that conveys this idea: "China walks on two legs: one traditional, one modern." (An observer witnessing the transformation of China into a modern economy might say that the country was limping a bit.) *Good Work*, the topic and title of Schumacher's final book, examines this concept of two-leggedness. The idea is that we make use of our highest technological insights to meet our most profound human needs as lovers of labor. It appreciates and uses the magic of modern technologies, but it husbands and cherishes their output rather than squandering them cavalierly. How do we encourage a labor-intensive, appropriate technology? First, local, state, and national governments must formulate economic development policies that insist on it. These policies must require an accounting of "cost per work site" for all enterprises. The appropriate enterprises can receive public support and encouragement, while capital-intensive jobs can be discouraged through taxation, regulation, and public opprobrium.

Environmental soundness

Appropriate technology must minimize its impact on the physical environment, just as it must enhance the social environment by providing dignified work. This concept has already been clearly articulated; much has been written about renewability, conservation, recycling, and reuse. Yet, the application of these concepts must proceed with intelligence, a conscious effort to seek the lowest level of environmental disruption possible, and a systematic plan to strengthen and support families.

A 1982 report by the National Audubon Society warned that the kind of devices we would need to begin using renewable energy are not without dangers. Passive solar collectors could prove dangerous to birds and insects, as could the pathogens used to grow large quantities of vegetable matter. This suggests that our best hope is to reduce energy consumption and maintain a relatively small population.

There is no such thing as a free lunch, even if we *can* put the bill on our grandchildren's tab. We must remember Garret Hardin's first law of ecology: "You can never do only one thing." The less we have to do to make global ends meet, the less we'll have to cope with unintended and unanticipated consequences.

Potential problems not withstanding, solar power, organic farming, the use of wood and natural fibers make up the material centerpiece of appropriate technology and the sustainable society. They necessarily imply that a sustainable society will blend with the natural rhythms and appearance of the Earth. We must reverse our estrangement from nature, a move which will require us to make some important changes in our social and political orientation.

Many of our motives are sound, or at least benign. Particularly in their private lives, few people deliberately seek out socially and personally destructive paths. But modern technology's alluring promise that we can have our cake and eat it too (and not gain weight!) is dangerously seductive. Researchers in the late 1940s and early 1950s found the reason people most often bought television sets was "to bring the family together." The irony, of course, was that once brought together *physically* by the television set, families were then separated *emotionally* by the experience of watching it.

Hardin's first law of ecology thus applies to the social as well as the physical environment. Perhaps the Amish recognize this in their efforts to remain aloof from the equipment of the modern life style. Perhaps we should respect their outlook more, lest we be compromised by our gadgets. Like the Amish, we would do well to be cautious—even paranoid—about adopting modern technologies. We should consider the likely spiritual impact these technologies have on social life in general and on family life in particular. Choosing what we *should* do from all that we *can* do is the modern challenge, particularly for the affluent. But even for the poor, the quality of day-to-day life can fluctuate depending upon the decisions they make and how those decisions impact the environment. One of our biggest challenges is to end the connection between low income and developmental harm. We know from international research that this is possible in the domains of infant mortality, and we realize what it means for the well-being of children and families. We can see it in other areas as well.

Perhaps we can use appropriate technology as a fulcrum to move us onto the path toward sustainability, a kind of *homo sapiens ex machina*. Theology that sees the natural world as an obstacle to the assertion of human power is dangerous. One hopes that appropriate technology at the household and neighborhood levels will aid in the resocialization necessary to achieve an ethic, even a theology, based upon *harmonizing* human beings and other parts of the natural environment. We will not get very far until we as a society embrace an attitude of nonviolence toward the nonhuman environment—until we speak to the trees and listen to the birds.

One is struck by the parallels between the economic system and the social welfare systems. Both suffer from a bigger-is-better attitude; both are losing touch with basic human realities; and both stand in an unsustainable relationship with the human community. Reductions in one can help facilitate reduction in the other.

A self-reinforcing system

Appropriate technology is as much social as it is mechanical and electronic. For a decentralized, sustainable society to function, there must be a network of policies and practices that reward behavior that is ecologically sensible and discourage behavior that is not. First, rewards for appropriate technology in the household must be consistent and powerful. Second, community-level enterprises (particularly businesses) must reward behavior that contributes to collective sustainability rather than to individual interests. We are so far from meeting these goals today that is frightening and profoundly discouraging.

The benefits of appropriate household technology must be consistent enough and powerful enough to motivate people and their societies to live environmentally friendly life styles. This means that they must make decisions about taxation, subsidies, zoning, and the like with an eye to supporting household sustainability. Immediate, clear feedback has a powerful effect upon behavior, as has been demonstrated in studies in which people monitor how much energy they use. In such cases electrical use declines. This same principle has been applied to a wide range of human behaviors with comparable results. Whether it is lowering blood pressure, wiggling ears, reducing a child's temper tantrums, or cutting down on calories or salt, clear and immediate feedback goes a long way towards establishing self-control.

One of the obstacles to sustainability is the fact that so many of the consequences of our life style are invisible to us. Our garbage disappears each week. Our food appears. Turn on the tap and there's water; a flip of the switch brings electricity. This modern magic dulls our ecological sensibilities; it makes us ethically flabby. To move along the path to a sustainable society we must sharpen our consciousness and rely on feedback systems that tell us, "Pay attention!" The benefits of household sustainability must be real and demonstrable, compelling and encouraging people to do what needs to be done.

The need for this kind of thinking presents social engineering with a tremendous challenge. Hardin's classic tragedy of the commons tells us that the collective good suffers when people serve their self-interest by exploiting a common resource at little or no short-term cost to themselves. The challenge is to harness self- interest in the service of the collective good. This means nurturing traditional value systems and social arrangements that already accomplish this and creating new social arrangements where they don't already exist or have been destroyed by the process of modernization.

We should nurture material frugality wherever we find it. Where conspicuous consumption is valued we must discourage and penalize it. "Fashion" is an enemy of sustainability; "making do" is its friend. We need a web of values that emphasizes nonmaterial avenues for expressing creativity, individuality, and mastery. Necessary material expression must be confined to areas consistent with steady-state environmental economics. We should applaud and reward clever ways of recycling, as well as brilliant ideas for substituting renewable for nonrenewable resources. But we must outlaw fashionable waste in whatever form it takes. We can't afford it.

Some practical utopian thinking

Let us now examine the important features of day-to-day life in the sustainable society, with special reference to the role of social welfare systems in family development. To do this we must engage in utopian thinking, since the sustainable society *is* the modern utopia. Like utopias of old, it is a visionary solution to the essential problems of the age in which and for which it is created.

Day-to-day life in the sustainable society will differ from culture to culture, especially between modernized and modernizing societies. In already modernized societies, the shape of day-to-day life will be determined by the current physical and social arrangements, albeit scaled down and redirected. There is little likelihood that either the state or the multinational corporations will wither away. To the contrary, strong social control is needed to create and maintain policies that demand and reward ecologically responsible behavior by individuals, institutions, businesses. Freedom will be absolute in the realm of ideas and expression but minimal in the domains of environmentally threatening behavior. The community will be organized so that it can speak and act in the interest of future generations (the only meaning of "the future" that makes real sense to us).

In unmodernized societies, day-to-day life will reflect a compromise between people's aspirations for material affluence and the availability of resources. No one knows for sure what that will mean. But it seems to suggest that everyone will be able to own bicycles, have access to schools and trains, use telecommunications, and afford decent food and housing. The family will be crucial.

The prospect for creating this new world depends on four domains: population; transportation and housing; food and energy; and health and social welfare services.

Population

The ability to maintain a stable population that is well within the society's carrying capacity is essential for long-term sustainability; it provides a cushion for cyclic ups and downs. To achieve a stable population, countries will have to establish a comprehensive and pervasive family planning program and carefully monitor immigration. At minimum, accomplishing this will require incentives for keeping family size at the replacement level, penalties for exceeding that level, and complete access to contraception. It will mean that family size will be limited to two children.

The "natural" workings of the marketplace in the form of financial costs and benefits of child rearing can help accomplish this task, and it has in most modernized societies. The high cost of rearing children tends to reduce family size. Surveys indicate that Americans will not forego parenthood because of cost, but they will reduce the number of children they bear. Is this enough? It may be. But then again, it may not.

It may be necessary to back up individual choice with institutional management. Population specialist Kingsley Davis has suggested a childbearing license—a birthright that individuals could use, give, trade, or sell as they so desire. The net effect would be an upper limit on population. However, the implications of this approach for civil liberties and bureaucratic processes are disturbing. One suspects it will not happen except in times of crisis. Even in China, the One Child Policy relies on a mixture of rewards and inducements with informal social pressure. The threat of penalties is real but mostly latent.

The key will be a growing recognition that population control is fundamental to social welfare and the wealth of families. One can envision greater public willingness to adopt subsidies and tax policies that reward small families and punish large ones. The traditional and contemporary bias against the only child should be dispelled by more research and by better distribution of existing research that denies the negative stereotype of the only child.

In any case, a sustainable society will have a low ratio of children to adults. The number of children will be geared to replacement, and adults will live longer, further decreasing the ratio of children to adults. The community will view each child as a resource to cultivate, as it will need to enhance efficiency and allow a "no-growth" population to adequately support its elderly. Although this *should* lead to an institutional climate that nurtures and rewards responsible families, it will not do so automatically. The ratio of children to adults declined in the 1970s and 1980s and society didn't demonstrate any appreciable inclination to value its children. But as the dependency ratio grows more lopsided because of the greater ratio of elderly to adult workers, the importance of nurturing children to become effective adults will likewise grow. Efforts to educate the political leadership to this fact will become increasingly important.

Transportation and housing

For modernized societies, we can envision an increased orientation to the neighborhood, more "complete" communities, and transportation services compatible with such residential patterns. When people carry out their daily errands on foot or by bicycle, we can assign the automobile to its proper marginal role. This will require that we encourage people to redefine their conceptions of walkable distances, which has shrunk dramatically. One can see people driving distances as short as a quarter mile, a distance that people only a few decades ago would have walked. "Forget the fitness club! Walk more!" is the message. The effect of such a move will ripple positively through the family.

In *Helping Ourselves*, Bruce Stokes notes that "walking and cycling substitute food energy, a renewable resource, for petroleum, a non-renewable resource, as well as providing exercise and a sense of independence that no car driver experiences" (p. 45). Exactly. What is more, walking can be a potent force for mental as well as physical health (adopting for a moment what is really an artificial dichotomy between mind and body). Walking and cycling can also bring family members closer, since both encourage social interaction. Walking, in particular, can strengthen the ties of families who establish a tradition of taking an after-dinner walk.

Another benefit of this kind of exercise is that it helps children lose weight; indeed, obesity among children is a growing problem. The answer to this is not sending overweight youngsters to treatment programs but creating a more healthy, active social environment in the first place. In a recent study, Steven Gortmaker and William Dietz reported that between 1960 and 1980, the number of obese six- to eleven-year-olds nearly doubled, from 15% to 27%. Among teenagers, the numbers increased from 15% to 22%. More recent research confirms this and points out that the general level of physical fitness has similarly declined. A sustainable society will promote a more healthy way of life for all of us, particularly our children, and it will allow a pace of life better suited to the needs and capacities of children and the elderly.

The automobile-oriented real estate development of the post–World War II era has stood squarely against the transition to a sustainable society. It encouraged suburban "bedroom" communities, which lack the infrastructure of a genuine community or neighborhood. These communities have also been developed without regard for household energy conservation or food production. Houses aren't built to collect passive solar heat. Neighborhoods aren't designed and landscaped in ways that conserve energy: sometimes they don't even have sidewalks! These neighborhoods are built on the assumption that energy will be cheap and that transportation needs will be met by the automobile. The existence of the neighborhood depends upon commuters, who import economic life by exporting themselves to distant jobs. More than being merely anachronistic, such areas may be harbingers of environmental and social ruin.

In a sustainable society, housing must be laid out in a manner that keeps neighborhood and community functions in mind, so that walking, cycling, and energy-efficient mass transit will be logical forms of transportation. It's unreasonable to expect people to walk when there's no place to go, to cycle when they must travel on heavily-trafficked roads, or to take the bus when it doesn't follow a useful schedule. Some residences need to be converted into shops and stores, transforming housing tracts into small communities. And most if not all residences need to become food and energy producers, individually or cooperatively. Zoning changes can spur colonization of commercial urban centers so that they include private residences. Geographic specialization will decline; heterogeneity will increase.

This will prove especially important in dealing with the emerging urban "underclass." As Nicholas Lemann (1986) has demonstrated, heterogeneous urban neighborhoods inhibit the developmentally destructive habits that wreak havoc on people living in ghettos. Homogeneity has been the trend in recent decades in many cities. In the homogeneous model, the need for social welfare systems far exceeds their capacities. In a heterogeneous neighborhood, demand is reduced to manageable levels. This alone should tell us that the transition to a sustainable society is not a dream but a hard-nosed analysis upon which to build social policy.

Production and use of food and energy

In the sustainable society, food and energy production will be as decentralized as possible in order to increase self-reliance and decrease wasteful and unnecessary shipment of commodities. The role of middlemen will decrease. This means continuing the trend towards household gardening in the modernized societies and maintaining and enhancing household food production elsewhere. Here again we need to recognize that we are all dependent on each other and to use that knowledge to move to self-sufficiency (in part to avoid draining off resources from other communities and societies). With this kind of thinking, we can follow Buckminster Fuller's classic maxim to "think globally; act locally."

Household and community gardens can successfully produce fruits and vegetables, and in some cases even grain. Recall the World War II Victory Gardens. The same is true of energy production. Decentralized solar energy facilities can meet most energy needs in most places, most of the time. Wood and agricultural wastes are natural sources of energy, particularly in nonindustrialized societies. Food, labor, and energy are intertwined. A great deal of energy is required to grow, transport, and prepare for serving processed vegetables, in contrast to locally grown, fresh vegetables. And, of course, growing food at home strengthens family ties, because it offers shared activities and productive labor for children and the elderly.

Household food and energy production increase the ability of family members to work with one another. They enhance the economic integrity of the family by making the time parents spend as homemakers more valuable and by providing positive economic roles for children, who are mainly a cost to a family that relies on purchased commodities. This kind of activity is particularly useful for poor families that cannot make it in the cash economy. We need innovative demonstration projects to show families how to take control of their own food and energy production.

The many family functions that arise from household food and energy production find a parallel in neighborhood gardening. It too provides many social, physical, and economic payoffs. Neighborhood gardening brings households together in ways that can support other collective enterprises such as energy conservation, crime control, and political action. In the nonindustrialized societies and impoverished sectors of modernized societies, gardens can supply nutritious food and thus improve a child's health. All these functions accrue further benefits in increasing the supply of—but decreasing the demand for—formal social welfare systems. In a sustainable society, all systems and policies are complementary.

In sum, food and energy production by households and neighborhoods in modernized societies can reduce their need for capital- and energy-intensive agribusiness and its allied enterprises, such as processing, transporting, and distributing goods. In nonindustrialized societies, it gives individuals the opportunity to provide for their own food and energy in a dignified manner. The net result is a better social environment for families and an increase in their real wealth.

Health and social welfare services

A sustainable society will be a healthy society, in several senses. Its life style promotes physical and mental well-being. Family planning, residential activity, and food/energy production imply a day-to-day pattern that is demonstrably more healthy than either conventional affluence or impoverishment. In modernized societies, exercise from walking and cycling, healthier food from gardens, physical labor, cooler houses, and smaller families *all* will reduce harmful physiological and psychological stress. In nonindustrialized societies, sanitation, better nutrition, access to technical information and energy, and family planning will have equally important benefits. In a sense, working for the transition to a sustainable society at this point in our history is an effort to ensure that each society has the best of whatever world it is a part.

The sustainable society will also have informal social support that augments and works in tandem with professional services. Because of their cost and their limited effectiveness, health and welfare services are not entirely useful as cash commodities. What most people need in times of stress or dysfunction is the highly motivated attention of a member of their enduring social network. Professional services are critical for some people some of the time, of course. A "home health visitor" can serve both social and medical needs. This is an appropriate professional role, and a way to bind together neighborhoods and demonstrate concretely the community's commitment to families.

But in a sustainable society, professionalized services, rather than seeking to displace the informal social support systems of friends, kin, neighbors, fellow church members, and coworkers, enhance and collaborate with them. In the sustainable society, such services blend together. Housing, transportation, food, and energy enterprises overlap. Relationships and institutions designed to meet one set of needs enhance enterprises designed to meet others. Formal and informal social welfare systems work hand in hand, resulting in a better psychological prognosis for the individual and a better sociological prognosis for the collective. Home health visitors can help to forge these links.

Utopian writers have already told us much about life in a sustainable society. Each real sustainable society mixes two visions: one traditional and agrarian, one modern the other industrial. Few societies approximate a pure form of either; in most, one or the other predominates. In the traditional agrarian society, people live in low-tech rural villages and work at labor-intensive subsistence agriculture. It combines the

best of nineteenth-century state-of-the-art farm life with carefully selected twentieth-century benefits, such as electricity, telephones, and
preventive medicine.

In their movement to a sustainable society, most of the modernized
world will take a somewhat different path. Some societies will return to
the land, but most of them will still be urban, with people living in
high-tech communities linked together by electronics. The power of
modern technology will be turned to household energy and food production (the "integral urban household"). Microprocessors and sophisticated information processing systems will manage these complex operations efficiently. In short, it will be an ecologically smart cousin of
our current life style with a heavy dose of "voluntary simplicity." Austin
Tappan Wright's *Islandia* (1942) presents the low-tech, tradi-
tional/agrarian path, while Ernest Callenbach's *Ecotopia* (1975) presents a high-tech, modern/urban model. These works are simply and
unabashedly utopian, but they are not fantasies or fairy tales in the
same sense that Cornucopian writings are. Herman Kahn's vision is impossible because it violates or denies the physics, chemistry, and biology of the planet. It is a fantasy. Wright and Callenbach propose social
transformation set within ecological realities. This makes them utopias.
As such, they serve the very practical function of showing us where to
go.

How do we get there from here? The *transition* to a sustainable society, the attainment of a utopian vision, can happen on many levels, at
once or at different times. There are signs that components of the sustainable society are being envisioned, created, and field tested now and
then, here and there, across the world and across the twentieth century.

Lester Brown's *Building a Sustainable Society* identifies some of these
components, such as stabilizing populations in some countries. In
Helping Ourselves: Local Solutions to Global Problems, Bruce Stokes cites
examples of progress in the areas of housing, energy, food, and family
planning, among others. Duane Elgin offers a detailed picture of the
significant number of North Americans who are creating and participating in a life style of voluntary simplicity, in which families carry out
the day-to-day activities that would be universal in a sustainable society. By reducing personal consumption and waste, these pioneers model the needed transition and make a real, though as yet numerically
small, contribution to living lightly upon the Earth. Amidst all the bad
news about global trends, there are some bright signs.

The Institute for Appropriate Technology and the New Alchemy Institute offer many social and physical technologies that we will need. The nations of Southeast Asia have drawn up a comprehensive plan to save endangered species by protecting their ecosystems. Innovative planners are field-testing clever ways to meet basic transportation needs without creating wasteful new systems. One example of this is a program that allows individuals to catch rides with mail handlers who drive rural routes. The microelectronic revolution *can* also offer low-power, smart services consistent with the needs of sustainability.

The core issue is one of hope versus despair. Faced with staggering political, military, demographic, and technological obstacles, despair seems the most likely response. On the other hand, hope is the only reasonable strategy. Anyone who, like me, is a parent, whose children will be young adults in the year 2000 and who hopes to be a grandparent in the twenty-first century, has no other choice but to work for the transition to a sustainable society. Do we want to see our grandchildren or their children live in that "worthless state of existence" envisioned by *The Limits to Growth*? What we need is not idle hope but active, intelligent hope. And that means politics, the politics of posterity.

August 1981. Upper Canada Village, Ontario, Canada. I have come to this restored nineteenth-century village to see a technologically simpler way of life in demonstration. Like Williamsburg in Virginia and Old Sturbridge Village in Massachusetts, Upper Canada Village uses architectural, agricultural, and manufacturing concepts and operations long since obliterated by energy- and capital-intensive technology. Of course, life was physically hard when Upper Canada Village (a composite of several villages, really) was in operation a hundred years ago. Now, it's part nostalgia and part speculation. In any case, it's a pleasant experience, until a bit of personal past and present intrudes.

In the brick mansion that serves as the Village's museum and centerpiece, I overhear a vaguely familiar, soft Southern voice engaging the official Village hostess. "Why don't you have places where people can stay here in return for working on restoration?" The hostess replies with something vague but pleasant. "Why don't you have a worker's collective to run this place? And, what about the real political history of Village life, of workers and ownership?"

The hostess smiles, says something, and extricates herself, looking for someone who will ask easier questions. I move closer, remembering the voice and now the face. She is a ghost from my college years. We were political sci-

*ence majors and active in the International Relations Club; we even traveled
to Montreal together to attend a Model United Nations (representing Taiwan when it still officially represented China). Back then she was a sweet,
pretty but very idiosyncratic Southern belle, and I was the up-and-coming
campus radical. It was the 1960s, after all. She was a clear pool of her unusual self, and I was busy starting the campus peace group, organizing the
first political demonstrations on campus, and becoming the second independent since Kirk Douglas to be elected president of the student government.*

*She tells me she has spent the years since graduation in Europe working
with leftist political committees and study groups. She's back in North America to pursue her political vision. "And you?" she asks.*

*I tell her about testifying before legislative bodies and consulting with gov-
ernment agencies on child welfare issues—child abuse and child care in particular. And I mention the Club of Rome, for some reason wanting to justify
myself politically to this ghost who used to seem so soft but who now has a
hard-cutting edge.*

*"So," she says, "you've copped out politically. Isn't the Club of Rome a
rightist kind of group for someone like you? But then, maybe you've
changed."*

*That ends the conversation quite effectively. In a moment she's gone, not
really interested in meeting my family. After she moves on I find myself remembering a joke I used to tell in college with political gusto and the confidence of youth:*

> *Question: What's the definition of a liberal?*
> *Answer: A radical with a wife and two kids.*

Then my son and pregnant wife return.

Is the concept of a sustainable society a political cop-out, a smoke
screen for the "real" issues of economic and social justice? Or is it *the*
political issue—and all the issues of conventional politics simply diver-
sions? It seems to me the latter. This question brings to mind another
joke: "This is the pilot speaking. I have some good news and some bad
news. The bad news its that we are lost. The good news is that we are
making good time." Any political path that does not seek sustainability
is a dead end, however speedily it is traveled.

Just what are the politics of Spaceship Earth? Defining the sustainable society partly in terms of justice begins to answer the question, of
course. But the politics of justice are many splendored, and they can
support several ideologies. The politics of environmental permanence
are even more variable. A right-wing scenario might have most of the

world's people in subservient subsistence (low resource drain), with a small elite living in energy- and capital-intensive materialist affluence. The result, Slaveship Earth, might be physically sustainable despite its moral untenability. A left-wing scenario might have everyone go down in environmental disaster as they struggle for social justice rather than permit enterprising elites to enjoy a privileged position at the expense of the masses.

And what about the politics of the actual transition? Are conventional right/left dichotomies relevant? One is tempted to say "No, but . . ." In today's world one sees examples of ecological soundness and madness from both ends of the political spectrum. Left-wing, state-owned enterprises have devastated the physical environment in order to modernize in the name of populist justice (such as China and most of Eastern Europe under communism). Right- wing, capitalist governments sponsor important reforestation projects (such as Korea). Effective and ineffective population control policies exist in both right- and left-wing politics. Multinational corporations run amok trying to generate profits while externalizing as many costs as possible; state-sponsored enterprises behave just as badly.

Concerning "pollution as the cost of doing business," it seems Eastern European societies have been some of the grossest offenders. As a *New York Times* article (December 12, 1982) put it:

> In a system in which meeting or exceeding the official production plan takes priority over everything else, and which discourages an independent, vocal environmental lobby, there is little incentive for managers and Communist Party officials to install costly pollution control equipment that cuts down efficiency. (p. 9)

The specific examples are legion: Polish rivers so contaminated that their waters are unfit even for industrial use; East German industrial towns with levels of lead in the air several times higher than authorized maximums; an area in Bohemia in which whole forests are dying because of acid rain; Siberian cities so polluted that some children are born with deformities. These problems have equalled and often exceeded those of capitalist societies. Perhaps the single most damning indictment concerns the former Soviet Union's commitment to nuclear power. Reports indicate that it plans to increase the proportion of its nuclear-powered energy from 10% to 25%. The chronically slipshod character of Soviet manufacturing, safety, and environmental efforts raises the specter of increased pollution and multiple atomic accidents. The Chernobyl disaster of 1986 is thus not all that surprising, and more such accidents are likely. Will the fall of communism improve the prognosis? Perhaps, but there are no guarantees.

Two political threats loom before us today. The first is right-wing to-talitarian control of day-to-day life, which forces subsistence living on the masses so that elites may live in affluence. I call this scenario the "Soylent Green Solution," after the film version of Harry Harrison's novel *Make Room, Make Room.* Some envision such a scenario for Mexico, where bust has followed the oil boom of the 1970s. In this case, societies could become steady state in the crudest sense of limiting environmental impact, but they would lack the moral stature of true sustainability. And they might be internally unstable, as citizens resist oppression, and externally disruptive, as citizens emigrate to the greener pastures of other countries and thus complicate lifeboat ethics for richer societies.

The second political threat comes from left-wing efforts to establish Western levels of consumption on a massive scale under the banner of populist justice. The introduction of energy- and capital-intensive life styles to the world's population is a serious threat, because it represents a very narrow and shortsighted (however well-intentioned) concept of justice. The intrinsic appeal of giving everyone access to the good things in life becomes a tragic flaw when it is linked to gross materialism of the modern sort. The seeming justice of the proposition that everyone should be able to live like the "best" in unsustainable material terms morally invalidates the proposition's claim.

Played out on an international scale, these visions have domestic parallel in the United States. Although it's a caricature of sorts, it seems the Republicans play the role of the corporate elite, while the Democrats seek a more populist route. Neither sets forth a program for making the transition to a sustainable society. The former generally favors scaled-back formal social welfare systems; the latter typically seeks to expand those systems. Both fail to offer an approach that will reduce demand by creating a less stressed and less disrupted global ecology. Indeed, most of the conventional political debate is only a dispute over the means to achieve the same false ends.

Can we have both justice and ecological balance? The answer is "yes," but only if we reject gross materialism and work to have a *relatively* small population. If human societies and communities exist on a small scale, with a small population and minimal impact upon environmental systems, then (and only then) can we have *both* justice and ecological sanity. This is the life envisioned in *Islandia* and *Ecotopia* and in the early writings of Karl Marx. This is the human side of paradise, the steady-state society in which human dramas, triumphs, and tragedies may play themselves out without consuming the Earth at the same time.

Are we psychologically equipped for the kind of politics characteristic of a sustainable society? Many say no. Psychologist B.F. Skinner, whose 1948 utopian novel *Walden Two* presents a blueprint for one kind of sustainable society, doubts that we have the necessary political will. He argues that the "free" world has lost sight of the social control we need to encourage responsible behavior and that impoverished societies have lost sight of the mechanics needed for economic progress.

The political doubters are legion. The self-serving greed of profit-oriented corporations is well known and well documented. It exists in both capitalist and communist societies. How does this motive get channeled into sustainable paths? The political payoffs for short-term "solutions" to social problems are so great that they can preempt the meeting of long-term needs. From this perspective, it seems suicidal to entrust society's fate to conventional economic and political institutions. This is the premise of the worldwide movement of the Green Party, which seeks an authentic politics for posterity. While the frustrations of dealing with conventional political institutions have led the Greens to introduce some wacky ideas, their basic orientation is sound.

Futurists promise that space exploration and other high-tech projects will create new criteria and resources for sustainability. Beyond this fantasy world is a narrow hedonism that discounts the importance of looking beyond tomorrow, arguing that "now is enough."

April 1987. Chicago, Illinois. The shoreline of Lake Michigan at Chicago is the scene of a philosophical and ecological struggle. Narrow economic interests are always on the lookout for a way to dispose of parks and make a fast buck. This year the specific agenda for environmentalists is to resist efforts to build a new football stadium on Lake Shore Drive. Environmentalists have also gone on the offensive to urge the closing of the lakeside airport (Meigs Field) and convert it into park land. The battle pits the "do-gooders" against the "slobs," to put it bluntly. The latter wage a campaign of litter and graffiti; the former try to clean things up. As I walk along the shore it looks to me like the slobs are winning.

Two mallard ducks are paddling close to shore. Three teenage boys approach, rocks in hand. One lets loose and misses the ducks, but not by much. I can't stand it and make bold to intervene: "Hey, guys, don't throw rocks at the ducks. Don't hurt them. Isn't there enough pain in the world?" They hesitate; then one responds, "Do they belong to you?" What a fantastic question. How profoundly discouraging that someone should ask it. Of course, these kids are merely expressing precisely the same attitude as their elders in high places and low. They would exploit and degrade the whole planet with the same cavalier selfishness these boys show in stoning the ducks.

Yes, they belong to me, and I to them.

What stands against this armada of forces allied in ecological darkness? Are there constructive spiritual forces strong enough to overcome the dark side of materialism? Perhaps our Hare Krishna friends are right in asserting that we must countermand the bad karma our way of living generates by transcending materialism and seeking a path of pure spirituality. Perhaps there can be a politics that respects the spirit and the land. On the grossest level, political action is afoot to unite disparate groups in a campaign to thwart the self-interested efforts of individuals and groups who seek transitory financial gain through environmental madness.

In the United States, environmentalists are building political bridges to other political organizations. Environmentalists for Full Employment, for example, is seeking to overcome the purported conflict of interest between organized labor and environmental protection. Its 1982 report, *Fear at Work: Job Blackmail, Labor, and the Environment*, reveals that the capital-intensive structure of modern industrialization *reduces* employment, in contrast to labor-intensive forms of appropriate technology. This is the basis for a natural alliance.

Another potentially promising sign comes from opinion polls. A 1982 national survey conducted by Research and Forecasts, Inc. of New York reports that 49% of the American public believes we must accept a slower rate of economic growth in order to protect the environment, and only 24% believe we must relax environmental standards to achieve economic growth. About 55% support pollution standards even if it slows down energy production. However, 60% want to see their local communities continue to grow economically, and 80% say "a strong national economy" is among their top priorities.

More broadly, in congressional elections the "green vote" has helped to elect candidates who are pro-environment. The League of Conservation Voters claims that in 1982, forty-six of sixty-three candidates it backed were elected, while the Sierra Club claimed a success rate of over 80% for the 158 candidates it endorsed. The 1982 "green vote" was a promising sign at a time when national leadership presented an image of willful and callous hostility to the concept of a sustainable society. Looking back on the 1980s from the perspective of the 1990s, we can see this "green vote" as a kind of holding action, an effort to hold onto a point of view while mainstream politics were undergoing a right-wing binge.

Is the glass half full or half empty? Should we find encouragement in the fact that about half the people have a vague (perhaps unreliable) commitment to environmental protection and a glimmer of understanding about some of the costs of conventional economic growth? Or should we be discouraged that after all that has been said and done, the general public is still of a mind to have its cake and eat it too? In 1965, only 17% of the public identified pollution as one of the three highest national priorities. In 1970 (following Earth Day), 53% did so. In 1980, the figure was 24%. So it goes.

As public opinion ebbs and flows we need to return environmental concerns to the front burner. To some extent this means seizing the opportunities environmental crises present us—namely, to enlighten the public about the need to create a sustainable society. And it means that we need a massive, ongoing program of public education aimed at improving popular understanding of what it will take to live in a sustainable society.

While some people delight in voraciously gobbling up the Earth for short-term private gain, others hug trees and find political channels to express their respect for the world. The forces for life achieve small triumphs amidst the forces of death and chaos.

Because children are special targets for the forces of environmental madness, family is the most promising focal point for the forces of light. Protecting children can become an important focal point for a political coalition working to bring about a sustainable society. Freedman and Wier have reported on this struggle in their article "Polluting the Most Vulnerable" (1983). They begin with a damning assessment of how efforts to dismantle environmental laws "have drawn little notice" and proceed to note that:

> In particular, signs of the growing health crisis for children, who are substantially more sensitive than adults to the toxic effects of many pollutants, have been all but ignored by reporters and regulators alike. (P. 600)

They proceed to chronicle the grisly story of what *The Nation* calls "Reagan's War on Children"—increased efforts to reverse protection of children and expedite industry's search for profits to their detriment (child health being expendable because it is a financial externality). Despite President Bush's claim that he seeks a "kinder and gentler America," he has merely extended the corporate-oriented priorities of the 1980s into the 1990s. The overall record is dismal, brightened only by the occasional successes of political coalitions fighting rearguard actions to slow the forces of greed and madness. The political agenda, however, places the need of commercial profit-making first and the interests of children last. A political climate of "anything goes" in the search for profits means virtually unrestricted introduction of toxic substances into the environments of children, with no testing required even on young *animals*. How much insight does it take to say, "This is wrong!"

Only by shifting our attention to children and their families will we have a consistent focal point for the politics of a sustainable society. As anthropologist Margaret Mead saw it, family provides the individual with a concrete historical perspective. Her words are worth recalling here:

> As in our bodies we share our humanity, so also through the family we have a common heritage . . . the task of each family is also the task of humanity. This is to cherish the living, remember those who have gone before, and prepare for those who are not yet born. (Mead, 1965, p. 11)

We must help people and societies project that vision of connection forward and outward from ourselves and from our children to form a politics of posterity. If we can firmly place "family" in the "community of nature," we will have the spiritual resources we need for a politics capable of making the transition to a sustainable society.

This is most evident in what Duane Elgin calls voluntary simplicity. His survey of those who are moving "toward a way of life that is outwardly simple, inwardly rich" provides concrete examples of the politics of posterity and of a covenant with nature—e.g., the Green Peace Movement and the New World Alliance. Elgin observes that:

> A majority of those pioneering a life of conscious simplicity are not strongly identified with any traditional political dogma. What seems to bind this group together is not political ideology but an appreciation for the dignity and preciousness of all life. (p. 69)

But would such a life be fun? Many people wonder whether all this political action, sensibleness, conservation, and avoidance of conspicuous consumption would be boring. Certainly this concern could be a disingenuous ploy. But it might be genuine. A student of mine once expressed this to a class in a particularly forceful manner. "I don't want to hear any more of this!" she said after a reading assignment and class discussion of the ideas of revisionist economist Georgescu-Roegen. "It's paralyzing to think that we can't enjoy anything without feeling guilty that we're wasting *something*. I hate it!" The reaction is not unlike the backlash against cancer warnings: "To hell with it. Living gives you cancer. I'll damn well enjoy myself rather than be careful all the time."

Would life in a sustainable society be fun? It might not, if it is lived within a totalitarian political context and a Puritanical cultural climate. (Of course, if we wait too long that might be the only technically feasible approach—or at least it might seem so in the face of widespread environmental crisis.) But we can be confident that a sustainable society would permit a flourishing of fun. By existing in harmony with the physical environment, we could free human experience for what poet Lawrence Ferlinghetti called "a rebirth of wonder." We could afford to concentrate intensely on relationships, on spiritual development, on playing, on *being*.

With the demands upon formal social welfare systems at manageable levels, we could afford to concentrate upon human "actualization." That *would* be fun. Many of those whom Duane Elgin describes as having chosen the path of voluntary simplicity report just such a rebirth of wonder. One says:

> My life is suffused with joy, and that transforms even the ordinary day-to-day unpleasantries that come along. (p. 60)

Another person says:

> The most satisfying thing is that you can see life right in front of your nose—feel it all around you—running through you and continuing on. (p. 81)

Elgin himself puts it this way:

> The overriding objective of the industrial era has been to maximize one's personal pleasures while minimizing one's personal discomforts. Life

has been lived as a constant process of "pushing" (trying to push away from discomforts) and "grabbing" (trying to acquire or to hold on to that which gives pleasures). With the loss of inner balance that accompanies a largely habitual "pushing" and "grabbing" approach to life, a deeper pain ensues. . . . By choosing balance we can more easily negotiate a skillful path through the world. (p. 84)

This message runs through both *Islandia* and *Ecotopia*. In *Ecotopia*, characters often speak about their freedom to indulge themselves emotionally because of the social stability of their steady-state society. They dig deeply into the essentials of life—love, work, and play—because the material ephemera of life are arranged and do not distract them.

Islandia conveys this message best of all, however. The essential passages of human experience are direct, simple, universal, and unchanging: mating, childbearing, child rearing, puberty, adulthood, old age, dying. *Islandia* envisions a society in which technology is *selected* to permit a life style in which the fundamental human concerns are the principal agenda, an agenda unencumbered by false issues of materialism and conspicuous consumption. Family is central, backward and forward in time, with the generations ahead and behind in the hearts and minds of those currently occupying the planet. And it is an emotionally and spiritually rich life. An Islandian speaks for this life when he says to his American friend:

We are put in a world of nature, of wind and sun, rain, clouds, growing trees and plants, of other animals and of other human beings. We are out of tune if we alter our natural environment too much. At least so we think here, though you foreigners often don't think that it matters or don't think at all. In this natural world we have natural desires—hunger, love, exertion of our powers in our minds and in our muscles. If the natural satisfaction of those desires is in any way checked we are out of tune. But we have simplified our problems greatly. We have a mode of life that gives us satisfaction of hunger and as full an opportunity as we wish to exert our minds and our muscles. You foreigners have built up for yourselves an environment that makes the satisfaction of those desires less easy, for its complexity makes the desires complex, and its diversity makes the desires of the mind confused and obscure. . . . it is so hard for you—harder for you than for us. (p. 395)

What next?

So what are we to do? An agenda for making the transition to a sustainable society might include the following items:

1. *Support "green" politics.* The green movement, based as it is upon a realization of the world problematique, can become a worldwide force for ecological sanity and life-giving reform. The transition to a sustainable society is fundamentally a political enterprise. Existing groups such as Sierra Club, National Wildlife Federation, Audubon Society, and Global 2000 Coalition are crucial, particularly in coalition with progressive and *genuinely* conservative political actors. Those who want to find a way to participate should consider subscribing to *New Options Newsletter* (P.O. Box 19324, Washington, D.C. 20036; phone: 202–822-0929) and reading *Green Politics* (Capra and Spretnak, 1984).

2. *Support policies and institutions that maintain family functions.* Family is the heart of the matter. Faced as we are with unsettling trends in family formation and dissolution, it becomes all the more important that the community invest in family life. One way of doing this is to insist that communities set a high standard for child care and help parents meet those standards. Communities should share joint custody of children with parents. We must resist the current trend toward the "feminization of poverty." We can encourage household energy and food initiatives as a matter of basic social policy. Second, we can support efforts to improve family life education, including mediation services for estranged spouses. Third, we can require "registration and inspection" of young children so that the community can monitor child development and not lose track of the children for which it is responsible. Fourth, we can involve men move fully in child rearing, particularly in the intimate details of infancy. This will help "tame" men and prepare them for the nurturing roles needed in a sustainable society. With these experiences they will be better prepared to speak in and listen to the feminine voice. In the family, as in social life in general, each of us should know the nitty-gritty details of life—from changing diapers to taking out the garbage. Thus will we be empowered to see things clearly and be protected from the imaginary world

that the mass media so often presents to us. Our families offer the best grounding in what really matters.

3. *Insist upon responsible procreation.* Knowing as we do that population growth is one of the engines that drives the world problematique, can anyone who gives birth irresponsibly make a moral claim on the world? The exact meaning of responsible procreation is open to some debate, of course. But the presumption must always be that to have more than two children requires some special justification, for it makes special demands upon the world. At this point in history, how can any husband and wife justify anything more than adding to the population two children to replace them? For some that seems like strong, perhaps distasteful medicine. But we need to take it. Concentrate on quality rather than quantity. That's the message.

4. *Support programs that encourage household and neighborhood projects to grow food and conserve energy.* Almost every family could grow some of its own food and conserve energy; every neighborhood could also accomplish significant things in this regard. It takes leadership. The symbolic and practical significance of the act is not to be taken lightly. The technology for doing it becomes more clever and ecologically sensible all the time. Among several useful guides are *Gardening for all Seasons*, produced by the New Alchemy Institute, and *The Integral Urban Household*, by the Farallones Institute. Locally grown food (rather than food transported over long distances) is cousin to homegrown food. Here too we must look to social policy for support in the form of zoning, tax, and subsidy laws.

5. *Support programs that plant trees and cherish the natural environment.* Each of us can strengthen the natural ecosystems and our own spiritual union with the chain of being that links our fate to the fate of the Earth. Planting trees is one very practical way to demonstrate this union in a caring way, and it helps children discover their place in the world. In one year, one big sugar maple tree can remove the lead emissions from 1,000 gallons of gasoline burned in automobiles. Planting trees to commemorate family occasions further strengthens the connection between family and Earth. And even if it feels foolish at first, hugging a tree is one way to express the fellowship of being. Another is to join our Native American Indian friends in offering "special greetings and thanks" for the natural wonders of day-to-day life. This spiritual dimension is im-

portant. Putting it into political practice through support of environmental action groups is the next step.

6. *Vote for local governments that seek to restructure community life to promote mass transit, walking, and cycling and to discourage driving.* Individuals can look for ways to drive less often. Most of us could walk and cycle more than we do. Keep track of the miles you drive and examine the record periodically. Look for ways to keep the automobile in its proper place—the garage. Take a family walk around the neighborhood rather than a ride around town. Walk or cycle to work. Walking and cycling are good for the spirit and the body; driving is wrong for both. Every gallon of gas used is lost forever. Avoid trivial uses of the Earth's nonrenewable resources. Don't rob our children's children so you can escape the pleasure of strolling on foot rather than rolling under gas power. Use these personal experiences and insights as the basis for local politics. Every community makes decisions in these domains every week. Are they part of the problem or the solution?

7. *Endorse the campaign to reject fashion.* Fashion is an enemy. Consumerism is a disease. We are bombarded daily by the message that buying new things is a matter of cultural and economic patriotism. But we have a higher loyalty. Virtually everyone in a modernized society has more material possessions than he or she needs, and everyone buys replacements and additions on the basis of fashion. Individuals can resist fashion. Governments can penalize it (e.g., by levying special taxes on new products when old ones exist). As a start, each of us can forego at least one significant purchase per week as an act of defiance against fashion and consumerism. We can put half the money "saved" into meeting the *real* basic needs of a truly impoverished, Third World family through Oxfam, UNICEF, Save the Children, or Foster Parents Plan International; we can put the other half into political campaigns to advance the transition to sustainability.

8. *Base decisions on true costs.* Remember that the true costs of any purchase is *not* the dollars that change hands, but the effect of the transaction on our global ecosystems. Anything made of nonbiodegradable plastic costs more than something made of wood, no matter how many dollars change hands. Anything crafted by human hands costs less to the world than something made on energy- and capital-intensive machinery. The same object made locally usually costs the world less than it would if transported over long

distances. Each of us can do something to contain the cost of our presence on the Earth. We all make choices every day as we select or reject plastics, processed/packaged "convenience" foods, and petro-energy. We can translate this insight into community life by insisting that local governments use true cost, not price in decision making. Think of it the next time you see a worker using a gasoline-powered leafblower instead of a rake, a snowblower instead of a shovel, "disposable" plastic plates instead of reusable, washable plates.

9. *Insist upon economic indicators that reflect true wealth.* Measures such as GNP simply reflect cash transactions. We must reject any such system of accounting in favor of efforts to measure wealth in terms of the utilization value of goods. What is more, simple averages (such as per-capita income) are besides the point if they obscure polarized discrepancies between haves and have-nots. Social accounting comes before economic accounting: infant mortality, literacy, life expectancy, child maltreatment—these are the crucial measures for families. Gear accounting to the issue of supply and demand for formal social welfare systems.

10. *Build professional roles in ways that harness and enhance the human ecology of families and neighborhoods.* Social support systems work through social networks of kith and kin. They are the primary structures that sustain families. As such, they are informal social welfare systems. Professionals should seek to build up and collaborate with these networks. The techniques for doing so are understood (Garbarino, Stocking, and Associates, 1980; Whittaker, Garbarino and Associates, 1983). We must go beyond the mechanics of collaboration between formal and informal social welfare systems, however. We must strive to harness the synergy that comes from a way of life that is ecologically responsible. In such a way of life, the economic/physical/biological dimensions of life are in harmony with the social and psychic.

This is the overriding message: the future of social welfare systems and the wealth of families depends upon moving toward a sustainable society. The alternative is physical, social, and moral disaster. In the decades following the year 2000, when we are all caught up in the struggle to make global ends meet, our children and their children will ask us what we were doing in the 1980s and 1990s, when the world problematique was becoming dramatically evident. What will we answer?

Bibliography

Adams, Henry Brooks. *The Education of Henry Adams*. New York: Modern Library, 1914.

Aldiss, Brian. *Galaxies Like Grains of Sand*, New York: Dell, 1974.

Auel, Jean. *The Clan of the Cave Bear*. New York: Crown, 1980.

Becker, Gary. *A Treatise on the Family*. Cambridge, Mass.: Harvard University Press, 1981.

Bell, Daniel and Irving Kristol. *The Crisis in Economic Theory*. New York: Basic Books, 1981.

Bernard, Jessie. "The Good Provider Role." *American Psychologist* 36 (1981): 1–13.

Blumberg, Rae. "A Paradigm for Prediction of the Position of Women." In *Sex Roles & Policy* 2 (1976): 1–15.

Boulding, Elise. *Women: The Fifth World*. New York: Foreign Policy, 1980.

Boulding, Kenneth. *Evolutionary Economics*. Newberry Park, Calif.: Sage Press, 1981.

Bronfenbrenner, Urie, P. Moen, and J. Garbarino. "Families and Communities." In *Review of Child Development Research*, edited by R. Parke. Chicago: The University of Chicago Press, 1984.

Bronowksi, Jacob. *The Ascent of Man*. Boston: Little Brown, 1974.

Brown, Lester. *Building A Sustainable Society*. New York: Norton, 1980.

Callenbach, Ernest. *Ecotopia*. Berkeley, Calif.: Banyan Tree Press, 1979.

Campbell, Angus. *The Sense of Well–Being in America*. New York: Russell Sage Foundation, 1981.

Campbell, Donald. "On the Conflicts Between Biological and Social

Evolution and Between Psychology and Moral Tradition." *American Psychologist* 30 (1975): 1103–1126.

Caplan, Gerald. *Support Systems and Community Mental Health*. New York: Behavioral Publications, 1974.

Carson, Rachel. *Silent Spring*. New York: Houghton–Mifflin, 1962.

Cherlin, Andrew. *Marriage, Divorce, Remarriage: Changing Patterns in the Post War United States*. Cambridge, Mass.: Harvard University Press, 1981.

Christopher, Robert. "The Changing Face of Japan." *New York Times Magazine*, 27 March 1983.

Crouter, Ann. *Participative Work and Personal Life*. Ithaca, N.Y.: Cornell University Press, 1982.

Crouter, Ann and James Garbarino. "Corporate Self Reliance and the Sustainable Society." *Technological Forecasting and Social Change* 22 (1982): 139–151.

Daly, Herman. *Economics, Ecology, Ethics*. New York: W.H. Freeman, 1980.

———. *Steady State Economics*. Washington, D.C.: Island Press, 1980.

Davis, Nancy. "Children and Single Women in Early Twentieth Century America." *Family Issues* 3 (1982): 431–458.

Dodson–Gray, Elizabeth. *Green Paradise Lost*. Wellesley, Mass.: Roundtable Publications, 1980.

———. *Patriarchy as a Conceptual Trap*. Wellesley, Mass.: Roundtable Publications, 1982.

Ehrlich, Paul. *The Population Bomb*. New York: Ballantine, 1967.

Elder, Glen. *Children of the Great Depression*. Chicago: The University of Chicago Press, 1974.

Elgin, Duane. *Voluntary Simplicity*. New York: Morrow, 1979.

Elkind, David. "Strategic Interactions." In *Handbook of Adolescent Psychology*, edited by J. Adelson. New Brunswick, N.J.: Transaction, 1980.

Elshtain, Jean Bethke. "Feminism and Family." *American Educator* 11 (1983): 20–34.

Erdman, Paul. *The Crash of '79*. New York: McGraw–Hill, 1976.

Eron, Leonard. "Prescription for Reduction of Aggression," *American Psychologist* 35 (1981): 244–252.

Etzioni, Amitai. *An Immodest Agenda*. New York: McGraw–Hill, 1983.

Ewen, Stuart. *Captains of Consciousness*. New York: McGraw–Hill, 1983.

Farallones Institute. *The Integral Urban House.* Pasadena, Calif.: Sierra Press, 1979.

Ferguson, Charles. *The Male Machine.* New York: Norton, 1976.

Finkellhor, David. *Child Sexual Abuse.* New York: Free Press, 1984.

Forrester, Jay. *Urban Dynamics.* Cambridge, Mass.: Harvard University Press, 1969.

Freedman, T. and P. Weir. "Polluting the Most Vulnerable," *The Nation*, 12 January 1983.

Friedan, Betty. *The Feminine Mystique.* New York: Norton, 1968.

Fromm, Erich. *To Have or To Be?* New York: Bantam, 1955.

Garbarino, James and Associates, *Children and Families in the Social Context.* New York: Aldine, 1982.

Garbarino, James and Stocking and Associates. *Protecting Children from Abuse and Neglect.* San Francisco: Jossey-Bass, 1980.

Georgescu-Roegen, Nicholas. "The Entropy Law and the Economic Problem." In *Economics, Ecology, Ethics*, edited by Herman Daly. New York: W.H. Freeman, 1970.

Giarini, Orio. *A Dialogue on the Wealth of Nations.* New York: Pergamon, 1981.

———. *Dialogue on Wealth and Welfare.* New York: Pergamon, 1981.

Gilligan, Carol. *In a Different Voice.* Cambridge, Mass.: 1982.

Goldstein, Don. "Saving Jobs But At What Price?" *The Nation*, 10 December 1983.

Gordon, Suzanne. "The New Corporate Feminism." *Nation*, 1983.

Grant, James. *State of the World's Children.* New York: Oxford University Press, 1986.

Grant, Lindsey and John Tanton. "Immigration and the American Conscience." *The Environment Fund.* Washington, D.C.: The Environment Fund, 1981.

Greer, Colin. "Six Views of the American Family." *New York Times*, 15 October 1976.

Hardin, Garrett. "The Tragedy of the Commons." In *Economics, Ecology, Ethics*, edited by Herman Daly. New York: W.H. Freeman, 1980.

Harrison, Harry. *Make Room, Make Room.* New York: Ace Books, 1962.

Hawrylshyn, Bohdan. *Condemned to Co–Exist: Road Maps to the Future.* New York: Pergamon, 1980.

Hazzard, Shirley. *The Transit of Venus.* New York: Viking Penguin, 1980.

Heilbroner, Robert. *Business Civilization in Decline*. New York: Norton, 1978.

Hewlett, Sylvia. *The Cruel Dilemma of Development*. New York: Basic Books, 1980.

Hirsch, Fred. *Social Limits to Growth*. Cambridge, Mass.: Harvard University Press, 1981.

Hollander, Cynthia. "Thanks for the Recession." *Newsweek*, 25 July 1983.

Hopcroft, David. "Commercial Applications of Indigenous African Animals." In *Quest for a Sustainable Society*, edited by J. Coomer. New York: Pergamon, 1979.

Houseknecht, Sharon. "Voluntary Childlessness." *Family Issues* 3 (1982): 459–472.

Huxley, Aldous. *Brave New World*. New York: Harper Collins, 1948.

Jacobs, Jane. *Cities and the Wealth of Nations*. New York: Random House, 1984.

Kahn, Herman. *The Coming Boom*. New York: Simon and Schuster, 1982.

———. *Global 2000 Revisited*. New York: Simon and Schuster, 1983.

Kromkowski, J. *Neighborhood Deterioration and Juvenile Crime*. South Bend, Ind.: University of Notre Dame Press, 1976.

Krutch, Joseph Wood. *The Modern Temper*. Orlando, Fla.: Harcourt Brace, 1956.

Lamb, R. "The Economic Pie Isn't Growing, But More Americans Need Shoes." *New York Times*, 10 November 1982.

Lawrence, D.H. *Lady Chatterly's Lover*. New York: The New American Library–Dutton, 1928.

Lehmann, Nicholas. "The Underclass." *Atlantic* 254 (1986): 1–25.

Leiss, William. *The Limits to Satisfaction*. Toronto: The University of Toronto Press, 1980.

Lesh, D. "Summary of the Limits to Growth." Washington, D.C.: U.S. Association for the Club of Rome, 1978.

Lovins, Amory and Hunter Lovins. "Electrical Utilities: Key to Capitalizing the Energy Trovertion." *Technological Forecasting and Social Change* 22 (1982): 120–138.

Maslow, Abraham. *On Becoming Human*. Princeton, N.J.: Van Nostrand, 1951.

Mead, Margaret and K. Heyman. *Family*. New York: MacMillan, 1965.

Meadows, Dennis. *The Limits to Growth*. New York: The New American Library, 1972.

Meadows, Dennis, John Richardson, and Gerhart Bruckmann. *Groping in the Dark*. New York: Wiley, 1982.

Mesarovic, Mihajlo and Edward Pestel. *Mankind At the Turning Point*. New York: Pergamon, 1974.

Miller, Arthur. "Constitutionalizing the Constitution." *Technological Forecasting and Social Change* 22 (1982): 152–167.

Mills, C. Wright. *The Sociological Imagination*. New York: Oxford University Press, 1963.

New Alchemy Institute. *Gardening For All Seasons*, 1983.

Orwell, George. *1984*. Orlando, Fla.: Harcourt Brace, 1948.

Peccei, Aurelio. *The Human Quality*. New York: Pergamon, 1976.

Potter, David. *People of Plenty*. Chicago: The University of Chicago Press, 1958.

Reich, Robert. *The Next American Frontier*. New York: Random House, 1983.

Reiss, Ira. *Family Systems in America*. New York: Holt, Reinhart and Winston, 1980.

Rosenblatt, Roger. "The Male Response to Rape." *Time*, 18 April 1983.

Rossi, Alice. "Transition to Parenthood." *Journal of Marriage and the Family* 30 (1968): 26–39.

Rostow, Walter. *Stages of Economic Growth*. New York: Cambridge University Press, 1964, 1972.

Sahlins, M. *Culture and Practical Reason*. Chicago: The University of Chicago Press, 1982.

Sanger, Marshall. *Autobiography of Margaret Sager*. Irvine, Calif.: Reprints Service, 1938.

Savard, R. *World Military and Social Expenditures*. Washington, D.C.: World Priorities, 1982.

Schell, Jonathan. *The Fate of the Earth*. New York: Knopf, 1982.

Schumacher, E.F.. *Good Work*. New York: Harper and Row, 1985.

———. *Small is Beautiful*. New York: Harper Collins, 1974.

Scitovsky, Tibor. *The Joyless Economy*. New York: Oxford University Press, 1981.

Seuss, Dr. *The Lorax*. New York: Random House, 1971.

Shannon, Gary and E. Cromely. "Settlement and Density Patterns." In *Habitats for Children*, edited by J. Wohlwill and W. Van Vilet. Hillside N.J.: J.L. Erlbaum, 1985.

Simon, Julius. *The Ultimate Resource*. Princeton, N.J.: Princeton University Press, 1983.

Skinner, B.F. *Beyond Freedom and Dignity*. New York: Knopf, 1970.

———. *Verbal Behavior*. New York: Knopf, 1952.

———. *Walden Two*. New York: MacMillan, 1948.

Smil, Victor. *China and the Environment*. New York: Basic Books, 1983.

Smith, Gerald. "The Teleological View of Wealth: A Historical Perspective." In *Economics, Ecology, Ethics*, edited by Herman Daly. New York: W.H. Freeman, 1980.

Spretnak, Charlene and Fritjof Capra. *Green Politics*. Santa Fe, N.M.: Bear and Company, 1984.

Stahel, Walter. "The Product Life Factor." *Technological Forecasting and Social Change* 22 (1982): 152–167.

Steinbeck, John. *The Grapes of Wrath*. New York: Viking Penguin, 1939.

Stinnett, Nick, B. Chersen, and J. DeFrain. *Building Family Strength*. Ann Arbor, Mich.: Books on Demand, 1979.

Stokes, Bruce. *Helping Ourselves*. New York: Norton, 1981.

Thurlow, Lester. *Dangerous Currents*. New York: Random House, 1983.

Tinker, Irene. *Persistent Inequalities: Women and World Development*. New York: Oxford University Press, 1979.

Toffler, Alvin. *The Third Wave*. New York: Bantam, 1982.

Trivers, Robert. "Parent–Offspring Conflict." *American Zoologist* 14 (1974): 249–264.

Turner, Frederick Jackson. *The Frontier in American History*. Melbourne, Fla.: Krieger Press, 1976.

Van Den Berghe, Pierce. *Human Family Systems: An Evolutionary View*. Prospect Heights, Ill.: Waveland Press, 1979.

Von Oppen, M. "Toward Private Investment Funds For Development Aid." *Technological Forecasting and Social Change* 22 (1982): 186–201.

Veblen, Thorsten. *Theory of the Leisure Class*. New York: Kelley, 1912.

Wattenberg, Benjamin. *The Birth Dearth*. New York: Pharos Books, 1987.

Whittaker, J. and James Garbarino and Associates. *Social Support Systems in the Human Services*. New York: Aldine, 1984.

Winn, Marie. *Children Without Childhood*. New York: Viking, 1983.

———. *The Plug-In Drug*. New York: Viking Penguin, 1985.

Wright, Austin Tappan. *Islandia*. Salem, N.H.: Ayer Company Publishers, 1942.

Wynne, E. *Growing Up Suburban*. Ann Arbor, Mich.: Books on Demand, 1977.

Index